THE TRUST REVOLUTION

While conventional wisdom dictates that people's trust – in the government, in corporations, in each other – is at a historic low, the rise of the internet is offering new ways to rehabilitate and strengthen trust. Uber is probably the best example of a new company that, on the surface, allows individuals with smartphones to get rides with strangers, but at a deeper level is in the business of trust. In *The Trust Revolution*, Todd Henderson and Salen Churi trace the history of innovation and trust, linking companies such as Uber with medieval guilds, early corporations, self-regulatory organizations, and New-Deal era administrative agencies. This book should be read by anyone who wants to understand how trust—and its means of creation—has the potential not only to expand opportunities for human cooperation, but also to reduce the size and scope of government and corporate control over our lives.

M. Todd Henderson is the Michael J. Marks Professor of Law at the University of Chicago Law School. He has written dozens of articles and books on corporate law and regulation. He serves as an advisor to several start-up companies and a venture capital fund. Henderson has worked as an engineer, a law clerk, an appellate lawyer, and a management consultant.

Salen Churi is a founder and partner at Trust Ventures, a venture capital fund that invests in and supports startups operating in heavily-regulated industries. Previously, he was a professor at the University of Chicago Law School. Prior to teaching, he worked as a corporate attorney at Kirkland & Ellis and Sidley Austin.

The Trust Revolution

HOW THE DIGITIZATION OF TRUST WILL REVOLUTIONIZE BUSINESS AND GOVERNMENT

M. TODD HENDERSON

University of Chicago School of Law

SALEN CHURI

Trust Ventures

CAMBRIDGE UNIVERSITY PRESS

CAMBRIDGE
UNIVERSITY PRESS

University Printing House, Cambridge CB2 8BS, United Kingdom

One Liberty Plaza, 20th Floor, New York, NY 10006, USA

477 Williamstown Road, Port Melbourne, VIC 3207, Australia

314–321, 3rd Floor, Plot 3, Splendor Forum, Jasola District Centre, New Delhi – 110025, India

79 Anson Road, #06–04/06, Singapore 079906

Cambridge University Press is part of the University of Cambridge.

It furthers the University's mission by disseminating knowledge in the pursuit of education, learning, and research at the highest international levels of excellence.

www.cambridge.org
Information on this title: www.cambridge.org/9781108494236
DOI: 10.1017/9781108664011

© M. Todd Henderson and Salen Churi 2019

First published 2019
Reprinted 2019

Printed in the United Kingdom by TJ International Ltd., Padstow, Cornwall

A catalogue record for this publication is available from the British Library.

ISBN 978-1-108-49423-6 Hardback
ISBN 978-1-108-71419-8 Paperback

Although he is not going to agree with all the arguments in this book, we dedicate it to our teacher, colleague, and friend Richard Epstein, from whom we've learned more than anyone else.

[T]he strength of the Pack is the Wolf,
and the strength of the Wolf is the Pack.

– Rudyard Kipling, *The Jungle Book*

Contents

Figures

Preface

This is a book about trust, how it has improved the human condition, and how it evolved alongside technological and societal changes.

The idea came to us several years ago when discussing Uber's[1] clashes with local regulators and incumbent taxi cab companies. It seemed obvious why cab companies fought to preserve the status quo system where government-granted medallions (basically taxi licenses) guaranteed medallion-holders complete insulation from competition. It was less obvious why government would work so hard to thwart a service that so many in the public obviously like.

In trying to unwrap this mystery, we started with a simple question: what does Uber sell? It seems obvious: it sells rides, just like taxis. But that isn't really the case. Uber doesn't own any cars or employ any drivers. It is not really in the taxi business. Instead, it sells a passenger the information she needs to trust a stranger to give her a ride. Specifically, it provides information on all nearby people willing to offer a ride and all nearby people seeking a ride, then efficiently matches passengers and drivers. Perhaps most importantly, it aggregates information on driver and passenger quality on a five-star rating system, which creates incentives for good behavior on both sides of the transaction. This simple system is very similar to the one provided by local taxi commissions, namely regulatory bodies that auctioned off medallions at sky-high prices in exchange for the privilege of painting a car yellow and allowing it to carry riders. We stumbled on a strange insight: Uber's real competition isn't the taxi

---

[1] Throughout this book, "Uber" is used to mean ridesharing companies, including Lyft, Via, Sidecar, Getaround, and others. We take no position on the relative merits of these companies. When we seem to be singing the praises of a particular company, we are not actually doing that. Companies are human institutions, which means they make mistakes and can occasionally act in terrible ways. When we appear to be advocating Uber, eBay, or the like, we are merely using them as placeholders for the social technology of trust that their kind represents. That some ridesharing companies have made some missteps and public-relations flops recently is not surprising, given the radical conceit behind such companies and their list of enemies in the trust provision business. These companies took on government without permission, which takes chutzpah; however, this might have some negative implications for these companies as well. In addition, because such companies pose a threat to many who are strongly vested in the status quo, it would not surprise us if a lot of news stories are exaggerated for political advantage.

companies, it's the taxi commission. Through our prism, the taxi commission and Uber provide competing visions of how best to supply the trust necessary for you to get into a stranger's car.

This book is about how technology companies such as Uber are revolutionizing the supply of trust – that is, coming up with better ways to deliver it – and how this will transform our society. We examine the providers of trust on a level playing field, from business (where brand serves to create trust in a product), to the interpersonal realm (where tribal identifiers allow you to rely on a counterparty), to government (where regulation lets you feel safe drinking a glass of milk). These providers work together in an overall trust stack. They coexist, compete, and evolve over time. In many areas of life, technology will reshape centralized trust mechanisms, such as government, and provide new opportunities for more distributed trust mechanisms, leveraging better information in ways that will dramatically alter the political landscape of the United States and the world.

Not everyone will be in favor of changing the way trust is supplied. Politicians will lose some power and leverage over citizens. Now-obsolete bureaucrats, such as taxi regulators, stand to lose their jobs. Interest groups and incumbent firms that have organized themselves to exploit the current system will be made worse off. Like toll takers in booths, however, these jobs are not likely to be missed and society will be better off. We will get what we need to prosper, and at lower cost.

Pardon our optimism, but we think these technologies can accelerate our progress toward a better tomorrow. Rather than being forced to follow centralized, static regulations provided by government, or relying on the information crudely signaled by brand, humans will shop for dynamic, voluntary "microregulations" provided by technology platforms. This term signals not just a change in the amount of regulation or the source of regulation, but a different type of trust that is inherently more modest and narrowly tailored to particular transactions and preferences than the blunt tools that preceded it. We define microregulators as technologies and tools that enable people to cooperate in more efficient ways. Microregulators, as we will show, are just the latest evolution in a long line of trust technologies.

If society were a computer, the level of trust would be its processing power. Where trust is plentiful, it's easy to get things done. But trust, unlike processing power, doesn't increase according to predictable rules.[2] Instead, old trust mechanisms tend only to shrink in importance as new ones grow to replace them. Sometimes this is peaceful, but often great shifts in trust are accompanied by turbulence. Uber's clashes with local regulators can be seen as the opening salvo in a much larger dislocation, where some functions of the nation-state will be supplied by centralized digital platforms.

---

[2] The prediction that has largely come true is that processing speeds have doubled every eighteen months, a rule known as Moore's Law.

We do not claim that microregulators will supplant the nation-state altogether. The social contract isn't dead. (At least not yet!) Instead, we envision many more voluntary social contracts between individuals and microregulators such as Uber, Amazon, or eBay. Rather than having one group of full-time employee experts (such as Chicago city council or US Congress) pass judgment and find the wisdom for all the residents of a given place, those residents will be able to buy such judgment and wisdom in a marketplace. As we enter the information age and more issues lose their local flavor, we will be free to untether ourselves from location in many important ways. Regulation will increasingly be made to order and will transcend national boundaries or the reach of national governments. World government of a sort may be possible, but in ways unimaginable to the utopian visionaries who brought us the United Nations or World Bank. The world government we imagine is all of us.

City councils regulate lots of things. They regulate rides and food and sexual mores. And they regulate them for every person within their territory. If you don't like them, tough luck. Consider Khulood, a model in Saudi Arabia who was punished by government for posting photos on Instagram wearing a t-shirt and skirt.[3] For those with preferences outside what is considered acceptable by the regulator, the best solution is often to leave, if that solution is available at all – for most of history, it hasn't been. And while it is noble to stay and push for change, this can be dangerous and change often comes slowly, if at all. Sometimes, pushes for political change backfire. The revolutions in Iran, Cuba, and, more recently, Venezuela and the Arab world have all resulted in material degradation of those societies. Even short of revolution, repressive governments understand our natural (and often irrational) attachment to a particular geography, and therefore can extract wealth from us equal to the total costs of moving our lives.

Microregulators work differently. They regulate one or a narrow range of things based on a global perspective. While Uber uses some localization to solve location-specific problems (e.g. special tollways in different cities), it builds and improves its data globally. And because one opts in to a microregulator, there's true competition. If you don't like Uber, you'll try Lyft or Via. You can vote out a microregulator in real time by deleting its app. Decamping with your family from Chicago to Indiana or from the United States to India is much more difficult. The amount of bad behavior that regulators can get away with scales accordingly.

Microregulators specialize in regulating the one activity they know well. Uber doesn't regulate your food or sexual mores, so you're free to mix and match the combination of microregulators that suits your preferences. You might trust Uber (instead of the cab commission) with your rides, Airbnb (instead of the range of regulators of hotels) with your lodging, Bitcoin to exchange value (instead of the Federal Reserve or the Securities Exchange Commission [SEC]), and so on. Unlike

---

[3] Kelly McLaughlin, "Social media star sparks furious calls for her arrest in Saudi Arabia after filming herself walking around in a T-shirt and short skirt," *Mail Online*, July 17, 2017, available at: www.dailymail.co.uk/news/article-4704052/Model-sparks-calls-arrest-Saudi-Arabia.html

microregulators, which allow you to vote with your feet, there's no opting out of traditional regulatory systems. Microregulators are a more flexible solution for a more demanding contemporary customer. Amazon consumers have a hard time with the Department of Motor Vehicles (DMV).

Microregulation doesn't work for everything. We all have to agree on some things, and some of these things are inherently tied to place. In transportation, you can't have multiple systems of stoplights or you'll have chaos. Economists call these situations natural monopolies. They are situations in which competition doesn't make sense. There is no reasonable alternative (yet) for much of what government does to improve our lives. This is true too of microregulators: they don't belong everywhere. However, as technology improves, they have the potential to better regulate more and more services in areas currently controlled by government.

Our grand vision is of a more robust basket of trust providers than you have today, many of which you'll have chosen voluntarily and which you'll be able to kick out and replace at your leisure. When you had your first disappointing experience with a brand or found yourself frustrated when a candidate you supported took a disappointing stance once in office, you experienced a failing of our current crop of trust providers. We think that smaller, ground-up trust providers can solve this problem by making very narrow, very clear promises based on ever-improving information.

The world we imagine is one of decentralized planning. The New Deal innovation was designed to harness the knowledge and skills of experts to make one-size-fits-all decisions from a marble perch in Washington. This new form of government – that is, various forms of centralized planning – was deployed in its most benign form by US expert agencies, especially when compared with analogues in Russia and elsewhere. The virtues of the US approach, found in administrative agencies, have always been tarnished by the familiar problems of capture by interest groups, the inability to satisfy local preferences, and a host of other concerns. Centralized planning has a bad name.

In contrast, the platforms we describe in this book decentralize regulatory planning. They organize disparate and deep information, but without the need for bureaucrats and experts in a marble building in Washington or the state capital. The platforms thus resist the problems of politics corrupting the regulatory process. They do this by structuring digital marketplace methodologies into previously unconnected systems. If traditional regulations are trust products, the contemporary consumer demands a more customized and varied offering. As with everything else in the market, microregulators will come to satisfy this impulse.

There are reasons beyond convenience that point to the idea that technology will reshape the nature of regulation and the state, because the state is poorly placed to control it. The state is slow moving and is limited primarily to physical force – all law is premised on the threat of physical violence. This is a blunt instrument having trouble adapting to the twenty-first century.

Government will have a harder time preventing new technological shifts. These technologies are genies who cannot be stuffed back into their bottles. Technologies such as gene editing (also known as "clustered regularly interspaced short palindromic repeats" or CRISPR), Bitcoin, and additive manufacturing (3D printing) are much harder to restrict and control than the operation of a factory. This is because they have the characteristics of software: unlimited parallelism and the ability to quickly transfer information. If a factory isn't compliant with a Food and Drug Administration (FDA) regulation, you can march a sheriff in and shut it down. But what should government do with a child born with edited genes? You can send DNA on a piece of paper.[4] Therefore, gene editing can be done much more surreptitiously than typical medical evasion of law. Similarly, think of weapons manufacturing. It's easy to regulate a factory that manufactures guns, but what about plans that can be distributed online and printed in a 3D printer anywhere?

The faster things can move and proliferate, the harder they are to regulate – software is harder to regulate than hardware. Today, everything is in the cloud, that is to say, everywhere and nowhere at the same time. The centralized mechanism for production has become decentralized and, as a result, is harder for centralized regulators to control.

The vital types of power in the coming century are digital, transmittable, and not easily controllable. CRISPR gives biological factors the characteristics of software; 3D printing gives physical objects the characteristics of software. This will naturally decentralize power, because these things aren't expensive or geographically guardable. In the past, elites could gate things to keep people out. They could lock them up, regulate them, tax them, confiscate them. The recourse was force. But force can't break software (short of catapulting us back into the Stone Age). This is true of software for information, Bitcoin for money, CRISPR for biology, and 3D printing for construction.

Another way of looking at this is that we can no longer trust regulators to keep up with the pace of change. Their answer to new technology is typically: "Stop until we can figure out what's going on." To make things worse, their incentives and capabilities don't run to actually figuring it out or, if they do, to optimizing regulation to social needs. Too often, regulators err on the side of avoiding politically damaging outcomes or favoring entrenched incumbents over challengers threatening to upend the status quo. Like the old red flag laws in the United Kingdom – where the introduction of a new automobile onto the road required a person to wave a giant red banner in front of the car as it drove – these impede the progress that society demands. We deserve better. Twentieth-century global citizens deserve to feel the full benefit of technology as it develops, not when regulators are able to get up to speed and decide "it's time" or decide what is safe or good for us.

---

[4] See University of California, Santa Barbara, "Shipping of Plasmids on Filter Paper," October 3, 2011, available at: www.surrey.ac.uk/biomed/blackbournlabmethods/plasmidsonfilterpaper.pdf

A new breed of trust provider is called for. The future, if not the present, will put stress onto corporate brands and government beyond what they can bear. We need algorithmic trust mechanisms that are opt-in, nimble, and microtargeted to particular cutting-edge problems. We need prototype-able microregulations that can keep up in an era of exponential change. The FDA will scoff at this, regarding it as irresponsible, unethical, and scary. It will try to ban it. But the reality is that another more opportunistic country will develop it first, and if you're on your deathbed, you won't care much for the FDA's warning letter when you can download a potential cure. Traditional regulators are now vulnerable to being outmaneuvered by supply and demand in a world where both grow exponentially more empowered by technology. There are real risks in a technology such as gene editing. But there are also tremendous possible gains, such as eradicating disease, extending life, or improving memory and cognitive function. The old ways in which we answered these questions are unlikely to look like the new ways.

New pressure will be put on the state itself, as people become more globally mobile and economic empires are built in the cloud where they cannot be seized, rather than in factories, which can be nationalized. There are many potential responses for states. They can adopt lighter-weight regulatory structures that allow consumers to choose their own basket of microregulators while controlling externalities. They can adopt a sandbox approach to allow innovation to adapt slowly and can attempt to craft safety rules in tandem with technology. Or they can adopt a more aggressive approach that aims to harness technology to tightly control dissent and enshrine centralized control. China's social credit system and digital firewall, coupled with its focus on investing in frontier technology (following the story of the first gene-edited children), is instructive here. We cannot predict the future, but the challenges ahead of us are ill-adapted to our old trust systems and we are confident that dramatic change is ahead.

While we remain optimistic about what technology promises for our future, this book is descriptive, not prescriptive. You don't have to buy into a grand vision to find this book valuable. A more modest takeaway from this project is to establish trust as a lingua franca for discussion of issues that are often thought of as discretely political but actually needn't be. We'd like to offer trust as a mental model for thinking about societal evolution and progress, and a novel way to analyze technology and history. We see this project as a natural evolution of the "public-choice economics" thinking we are trained in, accounting for behavioral economics and a world of rapidly proliferating technologies. We mention behavioral economics, an area of study that takes account of our evolved responses (and the irrational carryovers from our prehistoric ancestors) because we believe digital platforms are enabling us to trust in the most intuitive and inherently human way. This is a book about the social technology of trust, how it has evolved alongside us, and how it has come full circle. This book is about technology, but also about humanity.

Acknowledgments

Countless colleagues, friends, and students contributed to the ideas in this book. We'd leave someone out if we tried to name them all and, even if we tried to list them, we'd undoubtedly wear out your patience. So, instead of trying to thank everyone before the band starts to play us off the stage, we thought we'd just get started. The people who helped us know who they are and know how grateful we are for their help. If our ideas are unpersuasive or wrong, that is our fault; but if we are onto something, the credit is not all ours. Everyone from Adam Smith to Milton Friedman and from Richard Epstein to Saul Levmore contributed to us and to this book. Thank you all.

Introduction

Riding with Strangers

Think about your first ride in a stranger's car. If your parents were like ours, we suspect you heard from them not to get into that panel van, even to see puppies or get candy. As you got older, you probably heard you shouldn't hitchhike either – it is too risky. Or, thinking of it another way, you can't trust a stranger to give you a ride from point A to point B. This is good advice and, if you followed it, it has kept you out of a lot of potential mischief. Trust cannot be assumed; it must be earned or created.

But then, at some point, perhaps, as it was for us, you took a ride with a stranger in a yellow cab on a visit to Manhattan. You entrusted your luggage to the driver and fell asleep while whisked from LaGuardia to Midtown. Why did you trust the driver not to steal from you, long haul you, overcharge you, or worse? The short answer: regulation. (This is hard for us to admit, since before we started this project we were inclined to think most regulation was not worth the cost. But, as you will see, we've come around to a new way of looking at the world – a way that we think acknowledges the important role played by government, without believing that this role is as essential going forward.)

You trusted the cab driver because of government regulation, in the form of a taxi commission, licensing requirements, insurance mandates, and so on, all expressed in the form of a generic package – the yellow color, the "taxi" sign on top, and the license under glass and in view from the back seat. Government gave you the trust you needed to get from point A to point B, enabled through rules and regulations, and this made your life better. You could get rides from strangers, as well as friends. You had more options, and options make you better off. It is options that create the opportunities for wealth and human flourishing.

Today, there is another option – a competitor for the government in the provision of the trust necessary to ride with strangers: Uber. "Uber," as we think of it, doesn't drive you anywhere – instead, Uber built the platform that supplies the trust necessary for a stranger to drive you safely from A to B. In this sense, Uber isn't an alternative to *taxis* but to *taxi commissions*. Both Uber and the taxi commission are in the business of providing trust to consumers through regulation, among other things. Interestingly, as we show later, Uber in fact provides *more* regulation than the taxi commission. Thus, if we were able to calculate the amount of regulation in the domain of riding with strangers, it has probably gone up since Uber's emergence. Social welfare has gone up too. We have more choices; we have better service (from new competitors in the marketplace and the incentives they've created for incumbents); and the net results – more rides, lower prices, more opportunities for work, more efficient deployment of costly resources, fewer drunk-driving deaths, and so on – are impressive. Humans want to trust because it enables us to cooperate. Uber, like the taxi commission, provides that trust.

If you doubt the point about these services providing *more* regulation and *more* trust, consider one startup offering services in Chicago, and soon in other big cities. It is called GoNanny. The service is Uber for kids. GoNanny shuttles little overachievers to their soccer games or piano lessons, providing important driving options for busy parents. While older city kids might take public transportation, no sane parent would send their middle-schooler in a taxi or on the train these days. Most parents probably don't trust Uber enough either. Hence the creation of GoNanny to fill the trust void for this particular group of customers. GoNanny's website trumpets the safety of its approach: "Our GoNannies are rigorously vetted through our screening system GoNannySafe. This 22-point screening system, which surpasses that of top childcare and child transportation services, enables GoNanny to maintain its top priority: your child's safety." The provision of additional trust in the form of a private company increases opportunities for cooperation and thus enhances human wellbeing.

Both the government (here, the taxi commission) and Uber (and GoNanny) are "social technologies" – human-invented tools to create trust among suppliers and demanders of rides. Both are a way of resolving a coordination or collective-action problem. We all benefit from trust creation, but we cannot build sufficient trust on our own. How many of us have ridden with the same cab driver twice? How many of us have ever chosen one cab company over another based on our experience? We cannot create the trust we need alone. We have to work together. We have to team up to collectively develop ways of building trust. In the case of government, the mechanism of collective action is a political body designed to reflect individual preferences for trust, along with preferences about the service and features. In the case of Uber, the mechanism of collective action is an internet-based platform that enables individuals to aggregate their assessments of drivers and riders.

THE MARKET FOR TRUST

In the pages that follow, we expand on this idea of trust as a social technology or product that is supplied by competitors in what we call the "market for trust." Markets are the familiar way in which scarce goods and services are allocated. Markets match the demand for something and its supply. In the case of cucumbers or computers, the idea of a market is straightforward. People want delicious vegetables and tools to access the internet and do word processing; farmers and companies such as Apple oblige them by meeting these demands.

Trust is not something we typically think of as being demanded or supplied in this way, but the logic of the market is the same. As we discuss later, trust makes people better off in demonstrable ways, and trust is not something that can be self-produced. Accordingly, third parties – whether they be the government, eBay, or Uber – attempt to satisfy this demand by supplying the mechanisms or tools that enable trust to be achieved.

There are no explicit prices for trust, as there are for other things sold in markets. But the parties that supply trust charge for this service indirectly, whether it is in the form of taxes (for government suppliers) or fees (as in the case of eBay, Uber, and the like). Competition in this market is therefore less intense. Customers of primary products, such as trinkets or rides, do not see a list price for "trust," but rather shop for the underlying thing. As such, producers of trust have to bundle other aspects of their product with the trust component. When the government is a first mover in the trust business, displacing it can be difficult, given the government's monopoly on violence and coercion, as we consider later.

More generally, this discussion points to something unusual about the market for trust. In the market for trust, the government is both a regulator of the market and a supplier in the market. This is not the case in most other markets.[1] Governments don't produce cucumbers or computers. The government regulates cucumber producers and computer companies; however, in doing so, it does not run the risk of favoring itself. (It does run the risk of favoring those who favor it, of course, but that is always true of government action.) But, the government is, as we discuss later, the biggest supplier of trust today, as well as the regulator of other trust providers. To ensure an efficient market for the provision of trust, the government must not favor itself in the provision of trust without good reason. The government can, in effect, compel individuals to "purchase" trust from it through taxes and therefore it may naturally (but wrongly) favor itself at the expense of more efficient providers of trust.

The government monopoly on trust is beginning to crack. We are observing new suppliers of trust that have demonstrated they are more efficient at delivering the trust necessary to make transactions happen that, up to this point, have required government action. New suppliers – we hesitate to call them institutions because that concept may be increasingly passé – have begun to build platforms for trust that will continue to eat away at traditional institutions, and ultimately replace them.

---

[1] There are some markets where this is true. For instance, Todd Henderson and Anup Malani wrote about the "market for altruism," in which businesses, non-profits, and the government compete to offer individuals opportunities to help other people. See M. Todd Henderson & Anup Malani, "Corporate Philanthropy and the Market for Altruism," 109 Colum. L. Rev. 571 (2009).

THE THIRD AMERICAN REVOLUTION

The implications of our thesis go far beyond buying and selling trinkets on eBay or whether you take a taxi or an Uber to the airport. They extend to our oldest and most contentious debates about the role of government in our lives and how to build a better society.

During the 2016 presidential campaign, like all others in memory, a central question was the optimal level of regulation. Hillary Clinton, the candidate of the Democratic Party, defended various regulations promulgated by the Obama administration, including Dodd–Frank and the Affordable Care Act (better known as Obamacare), while now-President Donald Trump, the Republican candidate, has set out to cut two regulations for every new regulation issued. These positions more or less stake out the sides in a century-old political debate raging in the United States. Those on one side see the bulk of regulations issued since the New Deal as government overreach, while those on the other see them as necessary to create a better society. Politics is primarily about whether we have too much or too little regulation. (Does anyone think we have just the right amount?)

We offer an alternative view of history and politics that casts the New Deal and subsequent debates over the amount of regulation in a new light. By focusing on and rethinking the idea of trust, we ask not *whether* the amount of regulation is too high or too low, but rather *who* is the most efficient provider of the trust (and the regulations that enable it) that citizens demand. In short, we argue that individuals facing a complex world demand the trust created by regulation, and that providing this trust – creating institutions that enable it – is what has made society so well off. But, in many cases where more regulation is demanded, microregulators are a better provider of it than traditional suppliers such as government or corporations.

Trust is what makes us human and fabulously wealthy compared with our ancestors. The crucial question is: Which entity or institution can most cost-effectively create sufficient trust to enable cooperation and voluntary transactions in this world? Those who claim the growth of government was wrong miss the point, just like those who call for it (and only it) to do more.

What worked at one point in our history does not necessarily work at other points. After the Industrial Revolution enabled massive growth in wealth and an increasingly globalized society, new mechanisms of trust were necessary to enable cooperation across the nation and throughout the world. At the time, with the technology then available, government grew to fill that void. We don't have to take a strong position on whether that was a good or a bad thing – what is clear is that, with current technology, government is probably not the optimal trust supplier in many of the areas it operates in. We can rethink what our government does to provide trust without attacking it for what it has done to get us to this point.

Tracing this view of trust, and a market for it, backwards, we can think of much of the infrastructure of civilization as about creating mechanisms to provide trust. Humans want to cooperate because it benefits them, and cooperation requires trust. We humans have invented and built ever more intricate and effective ways of supplying trust to meet growing demand.

The human inventions of language, religion, law, brand, and now internet platforms, such as Uber, eBay, and Amazon, are mostly about creating trust that enables us to work together in ways that create wealth and improve social welfare. Our primate ancestors did not trust beyond their narrow family groups, and this probably explains why they still swing from trees, as we trot around the globe in jets sipping Champagne watching movies streamed on our phones. We can do business with billions of people. They could work together with only their closest kin.

Projecting the idea of a market for trust forward, we argue that a new era of humanity may be upon us. We see a world in which information technology has brought us to a potential inflection point in the history of human governance and cooperation. The American Revolution (1776) supplanted the idea of monarchy as the means of obtaining the best society and put the individual at the center of the social project. This was a triumph of decentralization, where disperse citizens governed based on local information. This was the "Revolution of the Individual."

The New Deal (1937) in turn replaced this model with an expert-based approach to regulation to enable sufficient trust to make the modern world tick. Upton Sinclair, Ida Tarbell, and others exposed the high costs of the pre-New Deal system of trust. Then along came the New Dealers. They believed the world had grown too complex for it to be regulated by citizen legislators, so we needed a new branch of government that would develop expertise designed to protect consumers and citizens. While the New Deal governance model also did other things – including redistributing wealth from rich to poor, from young to old – a central feature of it was the creation of an elaborate trust-enabling mechanism in Washington, DC. The SEC, the Federal Communications Commission (FCC), the Federal Trade Commission (FTC), the FDA, and so on were, in part, created over the ensuing decades to bring order and trust to buyers and sellers, whether of securities, radio spectrum, or pharmaceuticals. In this model, federal regulators controlled a disperse body politic using centralized information. This was the "Revolution of the Expert."

We are seeing a new phase in the relationship between the government and society emerge: a third American governance revolution, namely a third trust revolution – the "Revolution of the Digital Tribe." In this new phase, citizen-consumers using digital platforms (as one example) can act collectively to create a more effective and efficient form of regulation. With digital platforms tapping into the wisdom of crowds or bringing technological advancements in verification, we can have the best of both worlds: a *centralized* platform that harnesses *disperse* information.

Just as our foraging ancestors organized into tribes to increase trust, these platforms are creating many "digital tribes"[2] of decentralized consumers, harnessing the power of technology to build trust around a common interest. The rise of the digital tribe is making centralized trust providers such as government obsolete for many functions and is unleashing tremendous potential for human progress.

In this telling, the United States was built on individuals, with cooperation happening through voluntary transactions; this then evolved into cooperation through centralized, expert-based rules. Now, we are finally entering a period of individualized cooperation as part of a digital tribe. The digital tribe promises the best of both worlds: it is based on individuals and voluntary choices, and it harnesses more information than historically available to any one individual or bureaucrat.

Our goal in the pages that follow is to have you think about trust as more central to social order than you might have imagined, to see it as something capable of being provided by diverse institutions in a market for trust, and to believe that this digital trust revolution is worth protecting from the forces aiming to preserve the status quo.

PLAN OF THE BOOK

In Chapter 1, we document the apparent collapse in trust in our society. Polls of US citizens overwhelmingly show what we all feel – trust in US institutions, ranging from government to the media, are at historic lows. The cynicism of the modern United States is not easy to exaggerate and, based on these data, one might have little faith that the future could be bright.

Thankfully, in Chapter 2, we demonstrate that the obituary for trust is premature. In fact, there has never been more human trust than there is today. Our complex, hyper-globalized world would be impossible without enormous amounts of trust baked into the system. We conclude this chapter by discounting polling as looking for trust in all the wrong places. Instead of asking whether people trust the police or the *New York Times*, we should be asking how it is that eBay processes 10,000 transactions per second between strangers all over the world without a government anywhere in sight.

Chapter 3 makes the case for trust, linking it to the level of human flourishing or wellbeing in a society. The difference between wealthy, happy countries and poor, unhappy ones can largely be traced to the level of trust in the society. This is because trust enables human cooperation to happen at a lower cost than it would otherwise, and collective action is what enables human achievement. To put this in economics parlance, higher trust means lower transaction costs, which increases efficiency. After establishing why humans *demand* that trust be created, in Chapter 4, we identify the entities and institutions that meet that demand by *supplying* trust to

---

[2] We wish to connote a positive voluntary association by the use of this term, rather than divisive tribalism. In fact, we think a key selling point of our idea is the ability of the digital tribe to displace the tribes we currently use to create cooperation.

citizens. There are three types of trust: personal trust, which is provided by other individuals acting alone; government trust, which is provided by various institutions characterized by a monopoly on legal violence; and business trust, which is provided by profit-seeking businesses that are also selling other things.

Chapter 5 then traces the history of how trust has been provided by these three methods. Starting in the cave and moving forward to today, we show how the provision of trust has evolved based on the social conditions, technology, and geopolitics of the four periods of human history: the hunter-gather period, the agricultural period, the industrial period, and the information period. The history of trust is a history of change in innovation and a virtuous cycle in which more trust begets gains in human welfare, which then begets a need for more trust. Humans invented law, language, printing, the guild, the modern regulatory state, corporate brands, and now internet platforms all as means of enabling greater trust to exist.

In Chapter 6, we describe the way in which trust is demanded and supplied as a market and explore the ways in which the market for trust is different from other markets. All of these differences exist because government is a participant in this market. Unlike other markets, where government is a bystander and regulator, the government is the biggest provider of the social technology of trust today. Accordingly, the market acts differently from other markets. Government doesn't charge prices for the trust it provides; instead, it compels the purchase of trust from it in the form of taxes. Government also generally writes rules that apply equally to everyone, thus making the tailoring of regulations to individuals difficult; other trust providers are free from this restriction, enabling them to match regulation to individual preferences much more easily. Finally, because government is both a trust provider and a regulator of other trust providers, it may be tempted to shackle upstart trust providers that threaten its role.

In Chapters 7 and 8, we apply this concept of trust to two historical examples of innovations and developments of new trust technologies. The first (Chapter 7) is the development of the private regulation of stockbrokers in the late 1700s, a practice that continues to this day. The New York Stock Exchange (and now the Financial Industry Regulation Authority [FINRA]) came into existence to provide trust, after New York legislature banned New York courts from being in the trust-provision business. The history of the self-regulation of Wall Street leaves many lessons for the future of the private provision of trust.

The second example (Chapter 8) is the history of the regulation of taxi cab and other ridesharing services. Taxi regulation goes back a century and, for most of this time, it was an essential mechanism for ensuring a vibrant ridesharing market in most places. In fact, as this chapter explores, there were attempts in the 1980s to deregulate taxi markets in a variety of jurisdictions, but they all failed. Given the technology at the time, there was no efficient way of effectively creating trust between drivers and passengers. The development of the internet, the smartphone, and various reputation technologies, such as five-star rating systems, then opened up the possibility of alternative providers of trust in this market.

Chapter 9 considers the implications of the ridesharing example for the provision of trust more generally. This chapter examines the way in which Uber (and its ilk) disrupted the regulation of the ridesharing market, namely by not only offering additional trust (or regulation), but also supplying trust as a replacement for existing government providers. This example provides a strategy roadmap for others to challenge government monopolies on trust, and foreshadows the future of trust provision.

Finally, Chapter 10 briefly looks at some places in which the government is currently the primary trust provider but where new technologies may offer a more efficient solution. Although very preliminary and incomplete, our hope is that this treatment will be a call to action for entrepreneurs and policy wonks to help move human cooperation to the next level.

PART I

In this part, we set out the problem of trust and an analytical framework for analyzing how it is supplied. While it appears that societal trust is falling, we argue that there are some instances in which trust increasingly resides in our society. Measured in the amount of human cooperation among strangers, levels of trust have never been higher. We trust countless people in our daily lives from all around the planet in ways that would shock our ancestors or our primate cousins. This trust has enabled us to become fabulously well off compared with all previous generations.

This trust did not arise naturally, but rather was created by various social technologies invented by humans. We explore a variety of these – from language to law – in a genealogy of trust in Chapter 4. The punch line of this inquiry is that trust is a product that individual humans demand to enable them to cooperate with each other, and thus repeat the benefits of specialization. Over time, various institutions and tools have been developed to deliver this trust, competing with each other in a market for trust. Sometimes, this trust has been supplied through businesses, such as in the merchant cartels of medieval Europe and the brands of post–World War II USA, and very often through government. The key insight in this part is that trust is not the exclusive province of any of these domains, and society should want it delivered in the most efficient means possible.

1

The Collapse of Trust

Trust appears to be falling, if not collapsing. Data from the 2014 General Social Survey, the National Opinion Research Center's poll of US attitudes, found that only 30 percent of respondents agreed that people could generally be trusted, down from 46 percent in 1972. In his 2000 book *Bowling Alone*, Robert Putnam documents and laments the fall of civil engagement by US citizens and claims that a consequence of this will be the erosion of trust in our social fabric.[1] Based on polling data, Putnam's prediction seems to be coming true.

Digging deeper, the state of trust appears even worse. Levels of interpersonal trust look high when compared with trust in public institutions. US citizens' trust in the government and in the media are declining rapidly and systematically.[2] According to Gallup, US citizens' trust in institutions is at an historic low.[3] For instance, confidence in Congress has fallen from nearly 50 percent to less than 10 percent since the 1970s.[4] When the question is asked about "government" in general, the collapse of trust is also evident. According to the Pew Research Center, the percentage of people who trust in government to act in the public interest most of the time is at its lowest point since World War II. These data are shown in Figure 1.

This decay is consistent across almost all of the various institutions or areas studied by Gallup, from the media to banks and from churches to the police.[5] People in Flint don't trust the water; people in Ferguson and countless other cities across the United States don't trust the police; the police don't trust the people; and hardly anyone trusts our representatives, be they in Washington, DC, state capitals, or city hall.

The decline in trust was evident in (and no doubt stoked by) the 2016 US presidential election. Campaign themes on both sides of the political aisle described a "rigged system," whereby elites were getting ahead at the expense of the average US citizen. If the system is "rigged," by the media, bureaucrats, or

---

[1] Robert D. Putnam, *Bowling Alone: The Collapse and Revival of American Community* (2000).
[2] See www.edelman.com/trust2017/
[3] See www.gallup.com/poll/1597/confidence-institutions.aspx
[4] Ibid.
[5] Only the military is viewed as more trustworthy today than in the 1970s. This is likely because of the collapse in trust in the military during the draft and the Vietnam War.

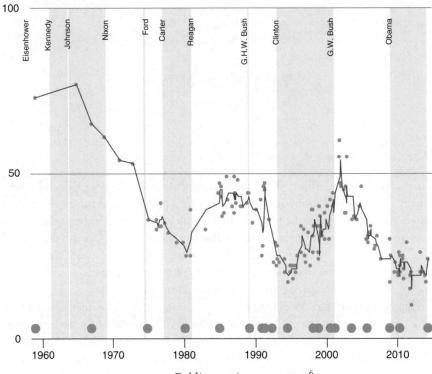

FIGURE 1: Public trust in government[6]

the wealthy, it can't be trusted. Bernie Sanders on the Democratic side and
Donald Trump on the Republican side both spoke passionately about the down
and out and the left behind, and why they rightfully had lost trust in elite
institutions.

Trump's unexpected victory has not halted the erosion of trust. According to the
2017 Edelman Trust Barometer, Democrats' trust in four institutions – government,
media, business, and non-governmental organizations (NGOs) – has dropped by an
average of six percentage points following President Trump's victory. Trust in
government is down over ten percentage points. Importantly, the decline in trust
for Democrats is not offset by increased trust among Republicans – their trust in
government is unchanged. With a majority of neither side trusting government, the
ability of government to address pressing social, fiscal, and geopolitical problems is
in doubt.

6   The percentage of people reporting that they trust the government most of the time. See Pew Research
    Center, "Public Trust in Government: 1958–2014," November 13, 2014, available at: www.people-
    press.org/2014/11/13/public-trust-in-government/

Ironically, the rhetoric and themes of the Bernie and the Trump supporters were consistent with years of elite thinking in an academic field called "public-choice economics." Scholars, such as Nobel Laureates James Buchanan and Kenneth Arrow, argued that there is a large and inevitable gap between the public interest and the policies adopted by government institutions.[7] The simple reason is that voters and politicians do not become angels when participating in policymaking, but rather attend to their own parochial concerns, at least in part. While we'd like to believe that going to Washington, DC, or the state house turns our representatives into public-minded do-gooders, there is little evidence to suggest this describes reality. You don't have to think *House of Cards* is a documentary to suspect that, when politicians vote, they do so because of the influence of cronies and special interests, with an eye toward the only goal that matters – reelection.

The characteristics and behaviors of voters exacerbate the problem. Many voters are apathetic, as voting is costly and no individual is likely to be the deciding vote. Accordingly, the average voter does not invest very much in trying to understand the merits of policy questions. As Bryan Caplan wisely observes in his book *The Myth of the Rational Voter*, voters are not likely to be the marginal voter that determines the policy enactments of their representatives, but they do capture all of the value or bear all of the cost of affiliating with one team or the other.[8] An individual voter does not determine whether the minimum wage rises or government mandates contraceptive coverage, but he or she can feel good about being for or against the candidate who is for or against these things. These psychic gains or losses drive voting, as they swamp any possible gains or losses from actually determining the law or policy of government.

Voters cast their ballots for a team or a tribe – Democrat or Republican – just as they cheer for the Chicago Cubs or St. Louis Cardinals. Politics, like sports, is distillable to a bumper sticker. Figure 2 is illustrative. The bumper sticker celebrating the Cubs World Series championship sits right next to a Clinton–Kaine 2016 bumper sticker, as well as a "Cats for Obama" sticker. Politics is as much about identity and signaling as it is about issues. The driver in this picture is a Cubs fan and a "LIBERAL." She is telling everyone to like her or find fellowship with her for these reasons. Mythology and branding about the parties and our ideological preconceptions drive policy, not discrete and informed opinions. As the economist Robin Hanson put it, politics is not about policy. It's largely about signaling the virtues of being on one team or another.

Our team allegiances are not necessarily rational or based on facts about the world. At a faculty lunch a few years ago, one of us asked around a dozen colleagues if they shared the same political beliefs as their parents. All but one did. When

[7] See, for example, James M. Buchanan & Gordon Tullock, *The Calculus of Consent: Logical Foundations of Constitutional Democracy* (1962), and Kenneth J. Arrow, *Social Choice and Individual Values* (1951).
[8] See Bryan Caplan, *The Myth of the Rational Voter: Why Democracies Choose Bad Policies* (2007).

FIGURE 2: A bumper seen in the Hyde Park neighborhood of Chicago[9]

pressed, there was a wide range of political beliefs, as well as experiences at home –
some had parents who talked a lot about politics, while others said it never came up.
And yet the best predictor of the politics of a faculty member at the University of
Chicago Law School was what their mom and dad thought. (We probably inherit
our sports allegiances from our parents too!) Whether this is genetic, environmental,
a mix of the two, or something else entirely, the point is simple: our politics are about
more than what impact we think our vote will have.

These preferences are also not particularly sensitive to performance. How many
people do you know who have switched from being one flavor to another?
Accordingly, there is much that politicians can get away with without suffering at
the hands of the electorate. If you are a Democrat, imagine how badly the country
would have to be run by Democrats for you to vote for a Republican. Or, if you are
a Cubs fan, think how badly they would have to play for you to root for the Cardinals.
This helps explain why congressional approval ratings are in the near-single digits,
but reelection rates in the US House are routinely over 90 percent.

Another factor confounds politics. Elections are about hundreds of issues and
therefore voters may tolerate a lot of inefficiencies because the few issues they care

9   Photo by M. Todd Henderson.

about are supported by their brand. This means that particular issues, say taxi regulation, do not motivate voters or move elections, even though citizens might benefit dramatically as a whole from reform. If a Republican ran for mayor of Chicago on a plank of reforming taxi regulation, she would not win. This is true even though we now have demonstrable evidence that hundreds of thousands of Chicagoans have been made much better off because of the reform to taxi regulation delivered by ridesharing companies such as Uber and Lyft. After all, it is very unlikely that anyone ever voted in an election based on government policy regarding taxis, except, of course, taxi drivers and taxi regulators, both of which are in favor of the status quo (before ride sharing).

Finally, political choices are, as the economist Thomas Sowell observed, inferior to other choices because they are based on promises, not reality. In his book *Basic Economics*, Sowell writes:

> [T]he public usually buys finished products in the marketplace, but can choose only among competing promises in the political arena. In the marketplace, the strawberries or the car that you are considering buying are right before your eyes when you make your decision, while the policies that a candidate promises to follow must be accepted more or less on faith – and the eventual consequences of those policies still more so. Speculation is just one aspect of a market economy but it is the essence of elections.[10]

Think again about taxi regulation. Even if people voted based on the issue – which we are certain rarely, if ever, happens – politicians would merely promise action to get votes. It is true that sometimes voters hold politicians to account for reneging on particular promises. But whatever discipline this brings to promise-making is swamped by that provided in competitive markets, where goods and services, not promises, are bought and sold.

The point here is simple – politics is not idealism, as much as we would all like it to be. The economist James Buchanan put it this way when characterizing the field he helped pioneer called public-choice economics – the field is simply "politics without romance." Consumers of government are forced to buy policies that are frequently bundled in counterintuitive ways and without any guarantee that the elected candidate will follow through. Once we strip away the romance, when we see politicians as flawed humans most interested in reelection or other selfish ends instead of the public interest, then it is easy to see the system as "rigged," as the Trump and Bernie fans do.

This problem gets worse as the government gets bigger and more involved in additional aspects of our lives. Big, powerful governments are more complex, less transparent, and less easy to understand than smaller, less powerful ones. This means the opportunity for unobserved deviations from the public interest are greater for larger governments than for smaller ones. An extreme example is a dictatorship, in

[10] Thomas Sowell, *Basic Economics: A Citizen's Guide to the Economy*, 445 (2015).

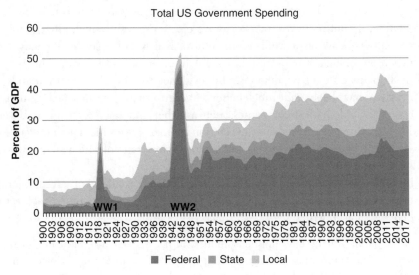

FIGURE 3: Growth in government[11]

which all policies, large or small, are determined by an individual or party. This problem is more acute at the federal level than at the state or local level, all else being equal. The more things a government controls, the more issues voters have to think about and monitor. This means that bigger government will be less responsive, all else being equal.

This is the cycle of public choice: government grows in part because voters cannot effectively check it, and the bigger the government gets, the more difficult it is for voters to do so. The result is a one-way ratchet. Government gets bigger and bigger, regardless of the party in power or the reason it is given power. The role of government in our lives did not decrease because of the Republican wave election of 1994, despite the explicit promise – in the Contract with America – that they would reduce it. Figure 3 shows the growth in government relative to the size of the economy that results from these dynamics. This figure understates the growth of government in a sense, because there is no obvious reason why government should necessarily get bigger as the economy grows. Nevertheless, the trend in this chart is unmistakable.

Larger governments leaning toward concentrated or special interests, including the politicians and government itself, has undoubtedly led to the erosion of trust in government since the 1970s. But government has not been alone in this regard.

Toward the end of the 2016 presidential campaign, the phenomenon of "fake news" or "alternative facts" arose. Having only accelerated since then, this phenomenon has decreased the public's faith in the veracity of the information it consumes from established and long-respected sources. Nearly 60 percent of people now report

[11] Data from St. Louis Fed: www.usgovernmentspending.com

that they trust their peers for information as much as traditional media outlets. Wally, the friend of a friend of a friend on Facebook, is the new Walter Cronkite. There is no single news source whose integrity is unanimously respected.

The internet has dramatically improved human welfare, but one of its side effects is the ability of specious information to propagate. There are plenty of wacky conspiracy theories at every turn, from 9/11 Truthers to those who think global warming is a giant conspiracy to get federal research dollars for climate scientists. While most of these are dismissible out of hand, pieces of false information have prominently impacted today's public life. The rumors about Hillary Clinton's subordinates running a child-sex ring out of a Virginia pizza shop made their way around the world before the truth had even put on its shoes, as the saying goes. And, as of the time of writing, there is serious debate taking place about whether "fake news" (some of it funded by Russian hackers operating with government imprimatur) helped Donald Trump win the presidency. But, even if one doubts this example, the problem is still recognizable. The anti-vaccination views held by parents in wealthy neighborhoods of West Los Angeles, Portland (Oregon), and Brooklyn (New York) have been spread by rumor and false evidence because no single person can be trusted to rebut them definitively. As truth becomes democratized, fiction has a chance, especially when believing it serves other important functions – such as signaling one's virtues or belonging to a particular group. As such, "scientific consensus" and "conventional wisdom" mean much less today than in the past. You may believe that this is, on net, a good thing or a bad thing – for now, our only point is that it is a true thing.

The end result is a deep cynicism that has seeped into our everyday lives. President Obama entered office on a promise of hope (as President Clinton, the boy from Hope, did before him), and nearly three in four Americans stood behind the nation's first black president. President Trump entered office amidst large protest across urban centers and a bitterly divided America, and the erosion of trust is a topic of serious public debate.[12]

We should be clear – we are not claiming that the United States of yesteryear was a paradise of trust and confidence and good will toward all. Our history is full of violence, political turmoil, and plenty of ill feeling toward our fellow man. But, the erosion in public trust of institutions, from a baseline of the post–World War II era, is plain in the data. And, we all feel it too. One need not dwell in the depths of internet comments or in the cesspool of Twitter to have a sense that there is a dearth of trust in the United States today.

---

[12] For a recent example in the news, see Salena Zito, "Americans don't trust anymore, and that's a big problem," *Washington Examiner*, February 5, 2017, available at: www.washingtonexaminer.com /grappling-with-the-trust-gap/article/2613926

2

Hiding in Plain Sight

In Chapter 1, we presented abundant data that show that public trust is eroding. But this is demonstrably false – trust among humans has never been higher than it is today. We are just measuring it incorrectly. Those who say that trust has collapsed are looking for trust in the wrong places. That we do not trust the government or the media as much as our parents or their parents did does not mean that the overall level of social trust has fallen. Trust may exist in other places not captured by the survey data.

After all, the government is not the sole provider of trust. It never has been in human history and (hopefully) never will be. The same is true for the news media, as important as it is. No one institution can or should have a monopoly on trust, and we should expect old forms of trust delivery to fade away as new circumstances in the world make them less valuable.

Humans have an amazing ability to invent things, casting off old ways of doing things in favor of new technologies and approaches. We don't ride around in horse-drawn carriages anymore or plow our fields with horse-drawn plows because those things, as well as they once worked, are not efficient anymore. Today, a Tesla gets us from point A to point B much better and faster, and a GPS-guided mechanical tractor plows a field much better than horseflesh. If we measured our wellbeing by counting horses instead of looking at the cost per output, we would be missing the point. Likewise, if people today trust government less than in the past, this doesn't mean that social trust has fallen. It just means trust in government is lower. Overall trust might be higher, lower, or the same amount as before, and simply provided by other mechanisms.

Polls don't capture the amount of public trust because trust is being provided in new ways; it is hiding in plain sight. Trust is now increasingly provided by a diffuse network of individual trust assessments (e.g. five-star ratings of everything from coffee shops to lawnmowers), instead of by centralized sources such as governments. In the future, perhaps this type of interpersonal trust will be provided by sensors in our bodies measuring dopamine levels or other metrics of wellbeing. Can you trust that the experience at that bar, restaurant, or park will be a good one? You won't have to rely on the opinions of only those people who took the time to rate it on Yelp or the stale information of reviews in the past. Just check the wellbeing heat map that tells you how all people feel about it right now. Trust may be disintermediated completely, so that you don't have to rely on intermediaries, who might shade the truth about what people are really experiencing. Reviewers may have strange preferences; rivals may slander competitors. With a fully decentralized metric of happiness, we may be able to fine tune our trust to get better assessments of what is good and bad.

But we don't need to look to the future to make this point: this type of trust is already all around us. Our parents would never have eaten at a total stranger's house – they would have eaten at home, at a friend's house, or at a restaurant that embedded some mix of trust from brand, reputation, and government (including a mix of health department certification through inspection and the possibility of filing a lawsuit in the event of food poisoning). But today, a host of "Eat With Strangers" apps are enabling people to expand their options and dine safely in the homes of complete strangers. Apps such as Feastly and EatWith provide a platform that connects cooks and diners. These apps create the trust necessary to make these transactions happen – to eat food cooked by a total stranger beyond the reach of any government inspectors – just as Airbnb has expanded our ability to sleep in strangers' homes and Uber and GoNanny have allowed us to ride with strangers.

The decentralization and democratization of trust that we are now seeing is a phenomenon with far-reaching implications. It has the potential to disrupt our society in many ways, but also to unlock a better future for humanity. After all, trust being provided online through a five-star rating system, blockchain technology, or a dopamine heat map is probably far more efficient than building a massive government bureaucracy to provide trust. Bureaucracies can grow out of control or even turn against the citizens they serve, all in the name of progress. This has always been the hidden cost of providing trust. Trust is expensive to supply, especially when considering both the direct and the indirect costs. We will say more about this later, but consider the costs of creating trust among citizens regarding crime and violence. The police are expensive – just ask taxpayers on the hook for police pensions in Chicago! – and, more troubling, they can turn the awful power of the state against innocents, whether by pressuring false confessions or shooting them dead, even when they pose no risk.

Consider a recent tragic example, which is unfortunately just one of the way too many times that individuals have been killed by the government for relatively minor violations of law, if any. On July 17, 2014, the New York Police Department approached Eric Garner in Staten Island, New York, accusing him of selling cigarettes without the legally required tax stamps. When Garner demurred, he was put in an illegal choke hold that the coroner concluded caused his death. Garner's death over taxes is an example of how a seemingly simple and benign law can become a death sentence.

As we will explain in detail later, many core government functions are fundamentally about providing trust. If this trust can be provided through less costly means, then society can operate more efficiently – better and at lower costs – freeing up resources (government and otherwise) for other things. Importantly, this is true whether you believe in big government or not. As you read the pages that follow, imagine not that government gets smaller, but rather that monies saved by providing trust in other ways are spent on other things, such as educating children, investing in scientific research, or building housing for the disadvantaged. By doing so, you will be able to abstract away from political debates about the size of government and focus on the "what" of government.

In the near past, trust was the province of government and other large institutions. Trust was expensive – it required bureaucracies and massive government buildings to convey reliability. Trust was also an excuse for governments to engage in other activities that, while they purported to be about core government functions, were really about politicians punishing their enemies and rewarding their friends. Trust was transparent, but the mechanism that provided it was not.

In today's economy, trust is increasingly created out of sight and out of mind. We trust not because the government stands behind a deal or because it takes place in a building made of heavy stone resembling an ancient temple (and therefore has the appearance of trustworthiness), but because of countless contributions of trust from individuals who came before us. We rely not on an alphabet agency to bless a transaction or on government inspectors to give us their seal of approval, but on Yelp or eBay or Amazon or Uber or Airbnb or EatWith, which aggregate disperse experiences of strangers just like us. Today, trust is not transparent, but the mechanism that provides it is.

In our modern society, many billions of transactions happen every day that would have been unimaginable to people just a few years ago, not to mention to our cave-dwelling ancestors. With the click of a mouse, we transmit money through fiber-optic cables around the world, trusting that the recipient in Boston or Bangalore will send us what we paid for. Economists who study these interactions use as their baseline the assumption that such exchanges cannot happen – in a world without law or reputation, no one would trust that they would be treated fairly by someone they couldn't see and didn't know on the other side of the world. In this account, we have laws precisely to enable these transactions to take place.

But it's not just moving money: eBay, for example, resolves the inevitable disputes between buyers and sellers, creating a parallel dispute-resolution system to the government-supplied court system. Why does eBay do this? It isn't charity or with an eye on the public good. It does it for selfish reasons: to build trust among users in order to lower the transaction costs of transacting on eBay. If the government-supplied court system was as efficient at creating this trust – if you could sue a fraudster in Bangkok who took your money and never sent your Tom Brady jersey, and could get your money back with as little cost as using the eBay system – eBay wouldn't have built its system. And the eBay platform – a combination of its reputation-based interface and its offline dispute-resolution system – works amazingly well. On a recent Cyber Monday, eBay seamlessly processed 10,000 transactions *per second*! That's a lot of trust. And eBay achieved this with nary an old-fashioned trust delivery supplier, such as the government, to be seen. The trust was provided by eBay users – by all of us.

Not surprisingly, 2016 was the sixteenth consecutive year that technology was named the most widely trusted industry (with 74 percent of people trusting in tech).[1] We believe this reflects a shift in the way trust is disseminated. The old institutions that supplied the trust that people need for society to function have begun to break down. This is more than just a momentary contraction in an uncertain economic and divided political time. And it is far from lamentable. In fact, we celebrate it. The change in trust delivery that we are witnessing is not unprecedented. The history of humanity is a history of changes in the way that we create the trust necessary to collaborate. We will explore this history later, but first we turn to the importance of trust in human society.

---

[1] See "2016 Edelman Trust Barometer finds global trust inequality is growing," *Edelman*, January 17, 2016, available at: www.edelman.com/news-awards/2016-edelman-trust-barometer-release

3

Trust and Human Flourishing

Trust is essential to human flourishing. It enables us to work together, to engage in voluntary trades, and to specialize in ways that dramatically increase our productivity and wellbeing. "Trust" can mean many things, but we define it as the information and reliability that enables two or more parties to coordinate, to cooperate, or to do business while having confidence in fair dealing. We trust that our parents will not harm us, that strangers will not attack us, that a hamburger at Shake Shack will not be poisonous, and that the shipment of steel will arrive as scheduled. The big question is: "Why?"

Modern life would be impossible without trust. Being able to rely on others to live up to their promises has enabled humans to become specialists, and this has generated enormous wealth. Adam Smith first explained the tremendous gains possible when people can rely on others to do things that they used to have to do for themselves – Smith noted that productivity increases nearly 5,000 times owing to specialization in the manufacture of pins.[1] One person working alone might be able to make one pin in a day; a team of people could make 4,800 pins per day, *per person*. Cooperation or collective action enables greater human achievement.

But this surely underestimates the gains possible in modern economies. Cooperation now happens on a global scale, which would have been unimaginable to Smith, who wrote at a time when Paul Revere had to spread word of the British invasion by shouting from horseback. Today, the president tweets and instantly engages his 25 million followers on Twitter. In business, multinational corporations coordinate work across hundreds of thousands of workers to a common task, despite differences of language, government, time, and values. This is a long way from managing an assembly line of pin makers. Human cooperation has never been greater and we are not going back.

Adam Smith was not the first person to realize the value of cooperation and specialization. He had insight, but he was not an innovator. Humans have known the value of trust for millennia, in part because of its obvious benefits. All our endeavors involve collective action, whether that be putting a person on the moon or putting food on the table. Individualism is essential to human progress, but

[1] Adam Smith, *The Wealth of Nations* (1776).

collective action is what enables individual achievement and fulfillment. As the poet Rudyard Kipling wrote, "[T]he strength of the Pack is the Wolf, and the strength of the Wolf is the Pack." Even great geniuses known for individual achievement, such as Van Gogh, Beethoven, or Shakespeare, would have achieved nothing had they not been able to trust their baker to provide them with their daily bread.

Fortunately, trust seems to be written into our DNA. From birth, we instinctively rely on our parents, who sustain us physically through our most vulnerable years. But being able to rely just on mom and dad wouldn't get us very far – we'd probably never leave the house if they were the only ones we could trust. To expand our horizons, we have to learn to trust all sorts of people and organizations for a broad range of things: our cultural and religious institutions to provide good values; the government to keep us safe from invading armies; and brands such as Apple and Whole Foods to supply us with quality products. Along the way, our ability to trust enables us to do everything from close our eyes and sleep soundly at night to engage in complex business deals. Social scientists call this "ultra-sociality" and characterize it as one of the aspects that makes us distinctly human.[2] As Adam Smith said, "no man ever saw a dog make fair and deliberate exchange of a bone with another dog."[3]

If you wander into practically any human community on a Friday evening, you will see dozens of strangers mingling in close proximity in bars and restaurants. Backs will be turned to people whom they have never met and will never see again. This takes enormous trust. Trust ensconced in our genes through thousands of years of history, but also trust enabled by socialization and government regulation. We take this behavior for granted, but humans are the only species that trusts this way and this much. Go instead to the jungle and find our closest ancestors in the animal kingdom, chimpanzees or other great apes, and you will not see them trusting strangers this way. They will trust their kin, more or less, or others brought into a small group, but not apes they've never seen. Gorillas are comfortable with each other because they are all related; the level of trust in human society enables bar-goers to feel the same level of comfort with complete strangers.

Bees and termites work together in large groups, but every bee and every termite is directly related to the others they cooperate with. The queen is the mother of the entire cooperating community. Bees are one tribe. As humans, we trust beyond our genes, and this has given us the Louvre and penicillin and gotten us to the moon and back.

There is strong evidence that levels of trust are correlated with social wellbeing. A leading researcher on the subject, World Bank economist Steve Knack, has shown a link between trust and levels of gross domestic product (GDP). He has argued that trust, as we define it, explains, "basically all the difference between the per capita

[2] Donald T. Campbell, "The two distinct routes beyond kin selection to ultrasociality: Implications for the Humanities and Social Sciences," In: *The Nature of Prosocial Development: Theories and Strategies*, D. Bridgeman (ed.), 11–39 (1983).

[3] Adam Smith, *The Wealth of Nations* (1776).

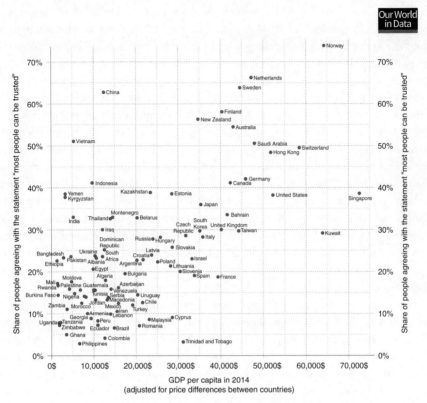

FIGURE 4: Trust and wealth[5]

income of the United States and Somalia."[4] For US citizens, this means "trust" is worth about $20 trillion. US citizens can trust fellow citizens a lot more than Somalis can trust other Somalis, and this permits us not only to engage in significantly more voluntary, wealth-creating transactions, but also to live lives of greater fulfillment and less worry. There is a strong correlation between per-capita GDP and trust, as shown in Figure 4.

Of course, there are parts of the United States that are poor, although not by Somalian standards, and a generality like this can be deceiving. Averages can too, although the average US citizen earns about $61,000 per year, compared with less than $400 for the average Somalian. This is difficult to explain based on human desire or capability. Rather, it is likely driven by the lack of social infrastructure – the human ability to cooperate that enabled us to create so much wealth and opportunity.

4   Tim Harford, "The Economics of Trust," *Forbes*, July 21, 2010, available at: www.forbes.com/2006/09/22/trust-economy-markets-tech_cx_th_06trust_0925harford.html
5   Source: https://ourworldindata.org/trust

FIGURE 5: The back of a US $20 bill. Credit: omersukrugoksu/Getty Images.

Francis Fukuyama reached a similar conclusion about the value of trust in his book on the subject, *Trust*. He concluded that, "a nation's well-being, as well as its ability to compete, is conditioned by a single, pervasive cultural characteristic: the level of trust inherent in the society."[6] Not only does our ability to trust demarcate us from other apes, but differing levels of trust across human communities are perhaps the key variable explaining the level of flourishing in those societies.

The late Nobel Prize-winning economist Kenneth Arrow similarly noted that, "Virtually every commercial transaction has within itself an element of trust, certainly any transaction conducted over a period of time. It can be plausibly argued that much of the economic backwardness in the world can be explained by the lack of mutual confidence." The importance of trust is well established and something we all intuitively understand.

It is also all around us. Sometimes it is unnoticed and taken for granted, as in the example of the bar-goers mentioned earlier. Sometimes it is explicit, as it is on US money, which says, "In God We Trust"[7] (Figure 5).

---

[6] Francis Fukuyama, *Trust*, 7 (1996).
[7] The phrase first appeared on US ,money at the end of the Civil War, when trust in the government needed to be reinvigorated. It appeared on paper money in the 1950s.

FIGURE 6: Sainte-Chapelle, a thirteenth-century church in Paris[8]

Other times, it is subliminal. Government buildings and banks – key providers of trust – are massive, built out of marble, and supported by huge columns. This is not just an aesthetic choice: it is to inspire trust in them and, thus, the trust they enabled throughout human society. They are also incredibly costly to build. Faith in gods may have given us more trust in our fellow man, but this trust was hard earned. Untold effort went into building awe-inspiring churches (see Figure 6) and temples, countless millions were murdered in pogroms and wars inspired by religious differences, and today religious disagreements are still at the center of much global controversy – from religious persecution of all kinds to the Global War on Terror.

But we can make the point less controversially. In our neighborhood, several old bank buildings, made of expensive materials hauled over great distances from rock quarries and built with human toil, sit empty, their grandeur a trust-inducing mechanism of a bygone era. A hundred yards away sits a modern bank branch – just an ATM machine stuck into the side of a building – where modern man can do all its banking with the push of a button. Frankly, forget about the ATM. What used to take a stone temple to do can now be done with a click of a button on your phone.

---

[8]   Photo by M. Todd Henderson.

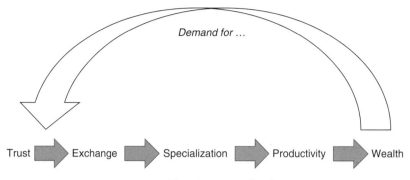

FIGURE 7: The virtuous cycle of trust

TRUST PROVIDERS AND THE VIRTUOUS CYCLE

Trust has been built over time in a virtuous cycle: the more we can trust one another, the more opportunities there are to expand our lives; these achievements or this fulfillment gives rise to demand for more trust, and when this demand is satisfied, the cycle starts anew. Or, to think of it another way: trust permits exchange; exchange permits specialization; specialization increases productivity and requires even more exchange; and so on. The more you specialize, the more you need to exchange, and the more you can exchange, the more you need to specialize (see Figure 7).

Trust is what economists call a "network good," meaning its value increases along with the number of people it connects: the more people you can trust, the more you can accomplish. Small-scale levels of trust enabled our ancestors to move out of the cave and into the village. Once they emerged from the darkness, our ancestors saw the massive gains that could be reaped from creating ever more trust. They built trust-creating institutions, which allowed further wealth generation and specialization. And the cycle renewed. It renews today, albeit less dramatically than in the scene of our cave-dwelling ancestors. In fact, if anything, the speed at which trust institutions are being created and trust levels are increasing today is faster today than at any point in human history.

These social technologies and trust-creating institutions are incredibly varied. They include language, law, religion, corporations, and a variety of other familiar but underappreciated things. In recent times, government has had what seems to be a virtual monopoly on trust provision at a high level. But there have been many different providers of trust. These trust providers, whether they were families, corporations, or self-regulatory organizations, provided new approaches against a backdrop of government-created trust. This is in part because, as trust expanded, the amount demanded exceeded that which could be reasonably supplied by government.

Some of these will be easy to link with trust. Law and trust are natural partners. The United States is not Somalia, in part because our legal system and the institutions that support it enable our stable, trustworthy society. But others will require more imagination and explanation. The corporation, the New York Stock Exchange, and eBay are all trust-delivery innovations of the human mind.

We can categorize trust technologies into three groups or types. Our first goal is to describe the three main types of trust providers: people, government, and business. Each of these types has unique characteristics and different mechanisms of action. Accordingly, they have been expressed differently over the years. In the next chapter, we consider these types of trust creation and then, in Chapter 5, we trace their history and the progress of humanity that they have enabled.

4

A Typology of Trust

In this chapter, we look at the three types of trust: government trust, business trust, and personal trust. Our objective is not to exhaustively describe or characterize them or their applications, but rather to introduce the basic features of how these trust providers work. Trust is unique in that it is something that is extremely valuable, but not something that individuals can create at a large scale by themselves. There is a natural limit on the amount of trust we can create ourselves. As a baseline, we may trust our family and our close friends, and this means the number of people we trust is in the tens or maybe as many as a hundred. There simply isn't time in our days to maintain more friends than this without help. For any interactions beyond this natural limit, we need an intermediary or a technology to expand our trust potential.

Figure 8 illustrates the point simply.
On the X-axis is the cost of engaging in a particular transaction with someone in these categories, including building up the necessary trust (among other things). The Y-axis is the value of being able to transact with them.

Family is in the lower left corner. Trust among family members is relatively low cost, but since family sizes are limited to, at most, a few dozen people, who are often spread around the state or country, being able to rely on them to provide you with all the services you need on a daily basis is unreasonable.

You likely have more friends than family and thus the value of friends is greater in this domain. If you need a ride somewhere or some maple syrup on a Sunday morning, the more friends you have, the more likely you are to be able to get what you need. But friends are costly to create and maintain. While a family might be like a cactus, which you can ignore for long periods of time and it will still survive, friends are more like the infamous ctenanthe plant, which requires finely tuned light, water, and temperature to thrive. Nurturing ten or twenty close friendships is doable, but requires a substantial investment. No one would do it solely to draw on them for rides or favors, especially since our friends cannot be in all of the places in which we need them or have all the things we need to make our lives complete. For that, we mostly turn to strangers.

Strangers have the advantage of being everywhere you go and being willing to, for a price, provide you with nearly everything you need – rides, maple syrup, and so on.

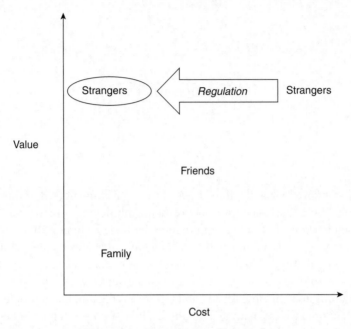

FIGURE 8: A simple trust framework

But trusting strangers is extremely risky, since, unless they are likely to interact with you again, they may have incentives to cheat you, or worse. Strangers are high risk, high reward. It would be great if there were a mechanism that enabled the reward of being able to rely on strangers without all the risk – how can we de-risk strangers? As discussed in the Introduction, when we considered the move from hitchhiking to taxis, regulation is one way to accomplish this.

Beyond ourselves, there are two intermediaries that humans use to create trust. Government is the most obvious, since our daily lives are filled with the sounds of sirens, news about lawsuits and regulation, and the sight of flags and images of the military that protects us. But business trust, even if we don't think of it in the same way, is even more ubiquitous. We all interact – and thus trust – countless businesses every day.

There are thus three main typologies of trust: (1) personal trust, (2) government trust, and (3) business trust. Personal or interpersonal trust is what we all start with, since it is based on kinship or tribe. But, as we will see, it only gets us so far – maybe venturing briefly out of the cave. Government comes next and, over the course of humanity, the rule of law and other aspects of government have been the primary mechanism for creating trust, and therefore a flourishing society. Finally, there is the trust enabled by businesses or corporations, using tools such as guilds or brands.

Our discussion of these trust types starts with government, in part because it is the most dominant category in the contemporary world, but also because personal trust had not, until recently, scaled up along with the modern world and has changed very little historically.

Let's consider government trust first. As Max Weber noted, government operates through a monopoly on legal violence.[1] Government can use this violence and its dominion over individual members of a polity (what we call "sovereignty") to compel socially responsible behavior. Government can tell people what to do and what not to do, using people's freedom as a bargaining chip. This power enables government to create vast amounts of trust in society. We sleep soundly in our beds, eat food prepared by strangers at restaurants, count on things that we ordered being delivered, and on and on, in large part because the government both engages in precautionary regulation – preventing bad things from happening – and promises to punish wrongdoers when bad things do happen. The first type of regulation is commonly called "ex ante" regulation, while the latter is commonly called "ex post" regulation. Ex ante rules are costly to produce, since regulators are required to anticipate conduct and its consequences. They have to be written to cover everyone. They do not admit idiosyncrasies and thus are probably both over inclusive (preventing conduct that is not bad) and under inclusive (not preventing conduct that is bad). On the other hand, ex post regulation – in the form of lawsuits or other punishments – may be insufficient to deter wrongdoing, especially because individuals or companies can only be fined down to zero wealth. This is what lawyers call the "judgment proofness" problem – an individual or firm risking more than their wealth will not be punished adequately, even if all their wealth is taken away.

Because of these trade-offs, government uses a complex mix of ex ante and ex post rules to guide behavior. A simple example is traffic control. Speed limits are classic ex ante rules – covering all drivers and all conditions, and thus proscribing conduct that is sometimes too fast, sometimes too slow, and not tailored to individual drivers. The rules are the same for a road warrior who logs tens of thousands of miles per year, a sixteen-year-old on the way home from the DMV with his or her license, and the winner of the NASCAR championship. The costs of writing tailored rules are simply too high, especially when done by government. Government operates by broad prescription – the rule of law is not always efficient. There is a worry too that passing out exceptions to rules will end up favoring the rich or the powerful – a social disease known as rent seeking – rather than helping those truly deserving of different rules.

Speed limits (rules) are coupled with police patrols, which screen for "reckless driving" (standards), thus giving drivers some certainty while preserving discretion for enforcers of the law to prevent easy evasion. But there is more to the system.

---

[1] This is imprecise. Self-defense, of which there are various types, is a form of legal violence retained by individuals.

Private lawsuits are used to allocate losses when there are crashes, based on ex post determinations about whether drivers were negligent. This system works very well to encourage trust on the road, even when strangers are feet away from each other traveling at high speeds. However, it has large costs as well. These costs include the substantial costs of funding the police but also the negative collateral consequences that sometimes happen during traffic stops. The rampant practice of racial profiling during police stops comes to mind.

As we note later in Figure 10, this system is centralized and top down. To create trust among each other, people elect representatives, and these people, be they councilmen, aldermen, representatives, senators, or the like, then vote on policies. The discussion in Chapter 3 of public choice highlights some of the costs of this system. This is not to say that government has not created a staggering amount of trust. Government institutions, from the police to the property records office, create a critical baseline of trust in our society. Without government, humans would be living in primitive conditions not that dissimilar to our ape ancestors. In fact, the economist Hernando de Soto has characterized the mundane property records office we all take for granted (if we think of it at all) as one of humankind's greatest inventions. The ability to know who owns what enables credit, and credit enables investment and cooperation, which enhances human flourishing. De Soto points out that one of the problems that creates and perpetuates poverty in places such as the slums of Rio or Delhi is the inability of individuals with some property to use it as collateral to borrow money and thus make investments, in human or physical capital. By creating a system of recorded property – a system of trust – this human potential can be unlocked.

Even ardent classical liberals or libertarians recognize the importance of government in establishing the conditions under which voluntary transactions will occur and can be relied on to satisfy the parties' beliefs about the exchange being mutually beneficial. The famed libertarian economist Milton Friedman describes the baseline of government that is essential:

> The organization of economic activity through voluntary exchange presumes that we have provided, *through government*, for the maintenance of law and order to prevent coercion of one individual by another, the enforcement of contracts voluntarily entered into, the definition of the meaning of property rights, the interpretation and enforcement of such rights, and the provision of a monetary framework.[2] (Emphasis added.)

We need government to create the conditions of trust necessary to enable human cooperation to achieve the panoply of things that make our modern world possible.

This doesn't come for free. The system requires vast bureaucracies and the use of violence. In societies of all sizes and complexities – such as the US society of 330 million people with a GDP of nearly $20 trillion per year – it also requires

---

[2]   Milton Friedman, *Capitalism and Freedom* (1962).

delegation of the power of control and violence (including depriving millions of their freedom and thousands of their lives) to agents of the state, tasked with creating the trust we all demand.

This delegation causes lots of problems. Systems of representation create what economists call "agency costs." These are the familiar problems that we see when we ask one person to act in another's interest; for example, when an employee spends time playing on his phone at work rather than doing work for his employer or when a child sent to the store to buy eggs also buys candy. People often act in their own interests when they are supposed to be acing in the interests of others, deviating from what the person hiring them wants or would do if they were doing it themselves.

This is true in government delegation, just as in all other cases of delegated authority. We the people hire agents to write and enforce trust-creating rules on our behalf. But our representatives may shirk their responsibilities or act in their own interests instead of ours. Given these concerns, principals will engage in costly monitoring of agents, agents will act to signal their allegiance in costly ways (called bonding), and inevitably there will be a wedge between principal and agent interests. The sum of these elements – shirking plus selfishness plus monitoring plus bonding plus the inevitable wedge – is the level of agency costs in the system.

One can see this clearly in the recent controversies in various police–citizen interactions across the United States. The police are hired by the people to create safe streets, to arrest criminals, and to otherwise create an environment in which we can trust our fellow citizens. Yet cops, just like anyone else, may shirk their responsibilities. They can also go rogue – google "Jon Burge" (hint: he was a Chicago cop that tortured confessions from about 200 people over twenty years). As a result of these possibilities, politicians, citizens, and NGOs will engage in costly monitoring to police the police. Our colleague Craig Futterman at the University of Chicago Law School (google him too to restore your faith in humanity), the Center for Wrongful Convictions at Northwestern Law School, the Police Accountability Task Force in Chicago, and countless other examples in our city and across the country show the human resources that go into monitoring our trust agents. And, in turn, knowing that we are skeptical that they are always doing what they should be doing, some police will act in ways that are designed to signal to us that they are doing what they are supposed to be doing, rather than in a way that optimally creates trust. These bonding costs might include patrols that are visible to citizens but that are known not to prevent crime, as well as other public relations stunts, such as pulling people over and giving them well wishes or prizes, as is common in some places. The net of all of these various "costs" is the full price of creating trust.

We should be very clear – this is not to say that the police are somehow not worth it. Our current view is that we need the police, just as we need the military, court systems, and a variety of other government services. Our point is not to argue that the police or any of these other institutions are not worth the price we pay, but merely to point out that it would be great if we could receive the same amount of trust at lower cost, namely costing fewer societal resources, fewer lives, and fewer of everything devoted to providing trust.

Importantly, the costs of creating trust grows as the size of the society grows. Thus, growth in a system is accompanied by growth in agency costs. The larger the police force, the more difficult it is to monitor, and the more levels of agency that will be required to do so effectively. We vote for aldermen in Chicago, who then appoint a committee to oversee the police, which in turn outsources its work to a task force, and so on. If there is slack at every step, as we suspect, then the costs of monitoring (just one element of agency costs) increases.

Size also reduces political accountability. At the national level, for example, there are thousands of issues and policy decisions about which citizens may care. Paying attention to them all, collecting information and being up to date, and determining how they all interact to inform one's vote is enormously complex. It is far easier to use a rough proxy, such as Republican or Democrat. But, if tribal proxies are used, there is a lot of opportunity for things to be done in your name that you disagree with, even by members of your own political tribe. One might like President Trump's policies on regulation or taxes but hate his policies on immigration and tariffs. This is agency costs. Yet these costs will be lower the smaller the sphere of governmental control. If we vote for a condo association president instead, we are much more likely to be aligned with all of their policies, since the issues are fewer in number.

When such systems get large enough, bureaucracies arise to play an important role. Although they get a bad name in some circles, bureaucracies are essential. They commonly use bright-line rules and process to constrain agency costs. Think of the rules that bind store clerks from giving you the refund you really deserve. This is the bureaucracy working to reduce agency costs. Individualized attention is costly in time and in potential errors. Empowering the clerk with the power to decide might result in some wins, but it might also result in losses that swamp the wins. The clerk might please a few customers who really do deserve a refund, but then use that power to reward friends who don't deserve it or to steal from the till. As bureaucracies grow, flexibility is reduced, and customer service, broadly defined, suffers. There are inevitable diminishing marginal returns from bureaucracy.

We can therefore see two forces at work. On the plus side, there are likely economies of scale in the provision of trust – larger governments can create more trust and do so across greater space and time than smaller ones. Just as the cost of Walmart or Amazon delivering a product to you is lower on a per-unit basis than a local retailer, because fixed costs can be allocated across a greater asset base, so too can a larger government provide more efficient levels of trust. But, working against this is another economic principle – diminishing marginal utilities. At some point, a dollar invested in buying trust from government will not yield a dollar's worth of additional trust. This may be because of agency costs or the costs of bureaucracy described earlier.

Government provision of trust is limited in other ways. The Constitution and the system of checks and balances it creates proscribes various courses of conduct that might be efficient at providing trust. For instance, governments cannot regulate certain types of speech (prevented by the First Amendment) or search records without a warrant (prevented by the Fourth Amendment), even in cases in which doing so would obviously be in the interest of creating more trust. Moreover, some individuals have a natural aversion to governmental power, given the way it has been abused on occasion throughout history. Governments are also limited by the reach of their sovereignty and by the information they have. Illinois has no jurisdiction in Indiana or in India, and this means that its citizens may have to resort to other means to be able to trust those who they deal with in those places. In the case of Indiana, the governments may reach agreements providing reciprocity or for working together, or the federal government, a sovereign over both of them in many areas, may provide the trust. But this won't all work for India. There could be agreements between our national government and the Indian one, but these would be costly to produce and limited to major issues. Treaties are expensive to produce, to monitor, and to enforce.

So, where can non-governmental trust come from? If people want to cooperate across borders or in ways that are forbidden by limits on government power, how can they do so? Where will that trust be created? It is to one alternative that we now turn.

BUSINESS TRUST

Businesses also provide trust. If you've ever taken a bite of a hamburger at a fast-food joint, sipped a Coke, pumped gasoline into your car, or bought anything online, you have trusted a business. More specifically, you have trusted in individuals you've never met because of the existence of a business standing in between you and them. After all, there is no such thing as McDonalds, the Coca-Cola Company, ExxonMobil, or Amazon. These are just labels we use to describe individuals of all sorts – employees, investors, suppliers, lenders, and so on – cooperating together for a specific objective. Corporations are what lawyers call "legal fictions." We pretend that Amazon is a real thing because it is a convenient way of thinking about the world. After all, every corporation is just a set of agreements by which real people organize their collective efforts to accomplish some goal.

Legal fictions are things that the law treats as true even though we all know that they are not. Thus, while a corporation has no physical existence – it is really just a label that the law creates – it is nonetheless treated as a legally distinct "person" that can act through its employees when they spill oil, manufacture faulty cars, or mislabel food. This is a neat trick that saves everyone, from plaintiffs to CEOs, a lot of hassle in asserting and defending their rights. Only the "corporation" needs to show up in court, whether it is to defend against alleged misconduct of its agents or assert the rights of the real people who constitute it. Of course, the reification of the corporate entity does more than that. Everyone involved with Apple or ExxonMobil, whether they work there, work with it, buy its goods, report on it for the media, scrutinize it as an NGO or regulator, etc., has a much easier time referring to it as an "it" rather than as what it really is – just a bunch of humans cooperating with a specific goal in mind. This is familiar. There is no such thing as the Chicago Bears or the Chicago Cubs or even the Archdiocese of Chicago – these are just groups of hundreds or even thousands of people trying to accomplish something, whether it is entertainment, profit-making, or some loftier goal. But it is easier to wear a Bears jersey or refer to the "it" than to describe the reality.

Humans invented the idea of the corporation in part as a trust-delivery tool. As we will see later, it was the absence or relatively high cost of the government provision of trust that led some English gentlemen to come up with a private alternative – a way of creating trust that transcended national boundaries. But, for now, it is easy to see the point with a more modern example that illustrates the power of corporate brand or identity in creating trust. When John Rockefeller incorporated his oil operations in 1870, he chose the name "Standard Oil" to convey to consumers that the kerosene it was selling was standardized, namely that it was free of the impurities that were common among rival sellers. It being "Standard" kerosene meant it could be trusted. The Standard brand was an early example of the power of corporate brands to deliver trust to the marketplace. Although "Standard" was just a label in some sense, in another way it was much more than that. Standard conveyed not only information but also a commitment. The idea was that the company stood behind the product and was in effect vouching for it. If the product was not up to the promise, future promises would be worthless and thus the brand, on which Standard spent a lot to develop, would be tarnished. In the absence of Standard standing behind its kerosene, one could imagine a government regulator testing kerosene or providing remedies for frustrated consumers through robust consumer-protection laws enforced in government courts. But, if the brand could be built and backed up by a costly promise, then some or all of this regulation would be unnecessary. Perhaps trust could be delivered to consumers more cheaply through brand, or some combination of brand and government.

Businesses deliver trust in a variety of ways, which we consider in more detail in the chapters that follow. For present purposes, two points of difference from government trust are worth noting. First, unlike government, which is a monopolist, businesses that provide trust have to compete with other businesses. This competition is not solely about trust, but it is a significant component of any product or service offered by a business. Every decision by a consumer is based on the question: "Can I trust that this product will work as expected?" Companies that cannot ensure that the answer to this question is "yes" will not find long-term success in the market. Business competition is generally greater than political competition, and thus competitive discipline is a larger feature of business trust than of government trust. This is not to say that competition always works to provide optimal trust or that government trust is always inferior. This is obviously not the case, as we explore later. Our point is that there are advantages in some areas for a competitive delivery of trust.

Second, because business trust relies on the profit motive, it may break down when the gains from cheating are large enough. Economists call this a "final period problem." Consider a simple example: a business and a consumer will engage in voluntary exchanges over five periods of time. In the first four, they will exchange $5 for an equivalent value of services, provided at a cost of $4. In each case, the business earns a profit of $1. In the final period, with trust being established through performance in the first four, they will exchange $100 for an equivalent value of services. The business will earn a $20 profit. If the gain for the business from defrauding the customer in period 5 – taking her $100 and delivering nothing – exceeds the profit the business can make by being honest, then the business might cheat. After all, the business in this case could earn an extra $80 "profit" from cheating, equivalent to four more $100 transactions or eighty more $5 transactions if it were honest.

There are much subtler forms of cheating or creating false trust. The history of business in the United States (let alone the rest of the world) is replete with examples of corners being cut, consumers being deceived, and information about the true nature of things being concealed. Just as government can overcharge for the trust it creates through regulators acting in their own selfish interest, so too can business act against the public interest by doing the same. Often, business lobbies government for monopolistic advantage (as we discuss later), creating cronyist barriers behind which businesses too may overcharge for the trust government creates.

On the other hand, government can reduce cheating by holding a business to account when it acts fraudulently. Prospective regulation of various kinds can also help, by screening for fraud before products make their way to market. Government standing behind the business as a sort of guarantor of the trust the business is providing is a potentially elegant solution to this problem – consider, for example, the FDA granting approval to a new pharmaceutical, attesting to its safety. The alternative, namely government owning the means of production, has proven in both its communist and its fascist incarnations to be antithetical to human flourishing. In a sense, government regulation of businesses to create trust is simply a core government function (resolving a collective-action problem) being outsourced to a more efficient provider.

But this system has problems too. Government enters the scene to protect individuals *from business* but may end up protecting business *from individuals*. Regulation can be a weapon of business, not just a shield from business aggression. For example, there is the possibility that relatively larger or more well-established firms might exert disproportionate influence on the regulator and manipulate it into imposing costs on relatively small or less-established firms. In such a way, regulation might also give rise to anticompetitive behavior.

To picture this, consider government regulation of an investment fund. There is a significant risk of fraud in investments, as the Bernie Madoff scandal and the financial crisis tell all too well. To address this trust gap, the government requires compliance with a set of record-keeping rules. Although these rules are justified on consumer-protection grounds, they have the potential to serve an anticompetitive function, by biasing the game in favor of larger competitors.

Suppose that compliance with a regulation carries both a fixed and a variable cost. A simple way to illustrate this is to imagine that the only cost of compliance is personnel in a compliance department. If we make the modest assumption that the number of compliance officers does not scale directly with the assets under a particular firm's management, then smaller firms will find themselves at a competitive disadvantage, all else being equal, owing to their greater compliance costs.

Consider two firms: one with $100 in assets under management and one with $1,000 in assets under management. If each compliance officer can oversee $250 in assets, but there is a minimum of at least one compliance officer, then the regulatory costs for the smaller firm are one, while those costs for the larger firm are four. But, on a per-asset basis, the regulatory costs are lower for the larger firm. Smaller firms in this kind of system must substantially outperform larger firms to maintain competitive parity. In this example, the smaller firm must outperform the larger by 60 basis points. (If each officer costs $1, the larger firm pays $4 out of $1,000, or 0.4 percent of its assets, while the smaller firm pays $1 out of $100, or 1 percent of its assets.)

Another example involves shipping milk. If your mom was like ours, she told you not to cry over spilled milk. But the US government has long taken a different view. Under the Spill Prevention Control and Countermeasure program (adopted in 1973), the Environmental Protection Agency required milk to be shipped in containers that were designed for the shipment of oil and other petroleum products. While undoubtedly defended on public-interest grounds – protecting the purity of milk seems noble enough – the impact of the rule, and thus its actual motive, was to be benefit large corporate dairies. After all, larger companies could spread the costs of shipment across a larger asset base than their smaller rivals, including new entrants. The logic is the same as in the investment fund example given earlier: small local dairies have a much harder time passing on the costs of industrial-strength oil shipping containers to their customers. A higher regulatory wall is much harder for David to scale than Goliath. The result is an economy with less competition, which harms the very consumers government purports to protect.

Consider another example ripped from the headlines. As of this writing, the New York City government is considering bills that would cap the number of Ubers and other ridesharing services operating at any time. In a news story about the proposed legislation, it was noted that "the New York Taxi Workers Alliance cheered the City Council's pledge to move ahead with the bills."[3] How shocking! The primary competitor of ridesharing services is cheering the government's attempt to hamstring them and

---

[3] "City Council aims to make New York first U.S. city to cap Uber, others," *Reuters*, July 27, 2018, available at: www.reuters.com/article/us-uber-new-york/city-council-aims-to-make-new-york-first -u-s-city-to-cap-uber-others-idUSKBN1KH2I4

reduce their value to potential customers. It would come as no surprise if the coffers of the city council are currently being filled by the owners of taxi medallions. Although it remains to be seen if such efforts at reducing competition will succeed, the point is made.

Business can also use government to serve itself when it comes to resisting changes in regulation. Here is a recent example. In May 2015, the SEC proposed that mutual funds be allowed to electronically deliver fund statements to investors by default (instead of on paper). The mutual fund trade association, the Investment Company Institute, estimated that moving nearly 300 million documents – of dozens of pages – online would save over $100 million per year for shareholders and save nearly 2 million trees per year. The gains for investors, society, and the environment were clear, but the rule was tabled in 2016 because of opposition from paper companies, envelope manufacturers, and the US Postal Service. These opponents objected not on selfish grounds, but rather out of concern that seniors and poorer investors might not have access to the internet. Economists call this kind of duplicity – saying "We are protecting seniors!", when they are instead just protecting themselves – the "Bootleggers and Baptists" phenomenon. Both bootleggers and Baptists favor laws restricting alcohol distribution – but for different reasons! – so bootleggers and Baptists find common cause with politicians who are willing to take money from the former while using the arguments of the latter to convince the unwitting public. And government agents that do the bidding of both bootleggers and Baptists may do so not because of any strong commitments to either but with regard to their own position of power and influence in society (see Figure 9). Bootleggers are proponents of laws limiting the sale of alcohol, but this doesn't make them Baptists.

This sort of interest group activity is at play in the realm of government services as well. An innovative startup called Outbox offered a service that allowed a customer to forward all paper mail to it, and its machines would open, scan, and email the customer all of the paper mail. The customer could then choose to have the physical correspondence sent to her, deleted, or (most importantly) unsubscribe from future correspondence from this sender. They had built a convenient platform for managing snail mail but also a filter for junk mail.

When Outbox's founders, Evan Baehr and Will Davis, were summoned for a meeting with the Postmaster General of the United States, they assumed it was to discuss a partnership to help serve the US Postal Service's customer base. Silly rabbit! The Postmaster General told the entrepreneurs that the government was shutting Outbox down. The lesson – the government's customers are not US citizens but rather a small group of junk mailers. To add insult to injury, taxpayers massively subsidize an army of mail carriers delivering catalogs for private companies in a process that destroys countless trees, emits huge amounts of carbon (from the fuel used for planes and other vehicles), and ends up filling landfills. (The post-script to this story is truly stomach churning. The government stole Baehr and Davis's idea, and about one year later rolled out their version of Outbox, which is now out of business. But, given the government's

FIGURE 9: People benefiting from laws banning the sale of alcohol[4]

incentives and its inexperience with rolling out new products, the government's version
is having much less impact than Outbox likely would have had.)[5]

Therefore, it is not surprising that lobbying is regarded as among the best investments a company can make. For instance, firms that spend more than their peers on
lobbying outperform the market as a whole. According to Strategas Research, an
index of the fifty most intensive lobbying firms (based on the ratio of lobbying
expenditures to assets) outperformed the market as a whole by more than ten
percentage points per year from 2002 to 2012.[6]

Looking at particular instances also shows the return on investment for lobbying,
and addresses questions of causation that lurk when comparing the returns of top
lobbyers with those of the rest of the market. For instance, pharmaceutical firms

4   New York City Deputy Police Commissioner John A. Leach (right) watching agents pour liquor into
    the sewer following a raid during the height of prohibition (digital file from black and white film copy
    negative), Library of Congress Prints and Photographs Division, Washington, DC, 20540, USA. Digital
    ID: cph 3c23257, available at: http://hdl.loc.gov/loc.pnp/cph.3c23257
5   Theo Priestley, "USPS Launches Exactly the Same Digital Service It Killed in Startup Outbox,"
    Forbes, December 8, 2015, available at: www.forbes.com/sites/theopriestley/2015/12/08/usps-launches-
    exactly-the-same-digital-service-it-killed-in-startup-outbox/#38de1e824622
6   "Money and politics," *The Economist*, October 1, 2011, available at: www.economist.com/node/
    21531014

spent over $115 million lobbying Congress about pricing when the prescription drug benefit was added to Medicare in 2003 – they saved an estimated $90 billion. The return on this investment was over 77,000 percent, compared with a return on investment of about 11 percent for the market as a whole over that period.

A burgeoning field of academic research also supports the claim, which should be apparent from the mere growth of the lobbying industry as a whole. For instance, Hui Chen, David Parsley, and Ya-Wen Yang found a strong correlation between lobbying intensity and stock price performance.[7] In a subsequent work, Chen, along with Katherine Gunny and Karthik Ramanna, tried to isolate causation by examining the impact of lobbying expenditures on tax savings arising out of the American Jobs Creation Act of 2004.[8] They found that an additional $1 million spent on lobbying returned over $32 million in tax savings for firms under the Act. Returns such as these compare favorably with developing popular new products or world-changing innovations, but they do not have the same advantages to the economy as a whole. These resources are expended largely to divide the economic pie rather than grow it. They may also undermine the public's confidence in government generally, thus potentially preventing government from doing things that it should be doing – namely the things that it is the most efficient and effective at doing.

The bottom line is simple. Government has grown enormously over the course of recent human history, and especially over the past hundred years, in large part to meet the massive growth in demand for trust infrastructure, which was essential to create the modern world. More recently, businesses have been created and innovated with new ways of offering trust that enable human cooperation. Government provided the foundation of trust – public order, courts to resolve disputes, etc. – and then business stepped in where it could efficiently provide trust. (We discuss this in more detail in the next chapter.) The positive results for modernity of trust creation by government and then by government plus business have been undeniable, as global wealth has increased enormously and global poverty and disease have fallen accordingly. From the Dark Ages to the Industrial Revolution, the wealth of the average person changed very little around the world. A recent book estimates that the economic output per person remained relatively unchanged from 1000 AD until the middle of the eighteenth century, rising from a few hundred dollars per year to a few thousand.[9] The Industrial Revolution changed everything. In Europe and the United States, where the Revolution flourished, GDP rose from about $1,000 to nearly $50,000 per person in just 200 years, dwarfing the gains since the dawn of mankind.

[7]   Hui Chen, David C. Parsley & Ya-Wen Yang, "Corporate Lobbying and Firm Performance," *SSRN* (2014), available at: https://papers.ssrn.com/sol3/papers.cfm?abstract_id=1014264
[8]   Hui Chen, Katherine Gunny & Karthik Ramanna, "Return on Political Investment in the American Jobs Creation Act of 2004," *SSRN*, available at: https://papers.ssrn.com/sol3/papers.cfm?abstract_id=2537079
[9]   Edd S. Noell, Stephen L.S. Smith & Bruce G. Webb, *Economic Growth: Unleashing the Potential of Human Flourishing* (2013).

But the costs of government action have also grown exponentially. As the government has moved to solve a problem, whether of its own making or created by businesses trying to provide trust (among other things), it has begat new ones, and the larger it has grown, the less nimble, less responsive, and less effective it has become. The simple result is that a dollar spent on government services – providing trust and otherwise – does not deliver a dollar in benefits to society.

So far, we have seen how government enables trust through the creation of the rule of law and through regulation, and how business can be deployed on the margin to create more trust at lower cost than the government could. But, we've seen that both these systems have tremendous costs. Government suffers costs because of public-choice problems and because the power of the state can be turned against the people too. As one political adage describes it: "A government big enough to give you everything you want, is a government big enough to take away everything that you have."[10] Even if government could improve on a particular transaction, empowering it to do so risks negative spillovers, since government agents will act for their own self-interest or in the interests of those with power over them, instead of in the public interest. Even when regulators are trying to act in the public interest, they will make mistakes. Sometimes, regulators will see a need to regulate when there is none (a false-positive) and sometimes they will not see a need when there is one (a false-negative). The problem is made worse because government has a monopoly on violence and thus will not be checked (other than by the clumsy political process).

Business suffers from similar problems. Managers of businesses are agents too – whether of stockholders, workers, customers, or society generally, depending on your views – and thus may act selfishly or in other ways that are not socially responsible when making decisions about creating trust or other things. The result is often significant harm to individuals and society. Just as history is littered with government failures, so too is it littered with exploding factories, inhumane working conditions, negligent oil spills, adulterated food or chemicals, and so on.

The point can be generalized – whenever we put our trust in others, including when doing so to create the trust we need to cooperate with others, we may be taken advantage of by selfish actors, be they in government or business. Thankfully, there is a supplement and perhaps an alternative to these two trust-delivery approaches.

PERSONAL TRUST

The third type of trust is the most familiar – personal or interpersonal trust. It is probably intuitive to us, perhaps because of its biological origins. We first trust our parents, not because they did anything to earn our trust, but because we are evolutionarily wired to do so. Human survival would be in doubt if children could

---

[10]   Used by various Republican politicians during the 1950s through the 1980s, including Barry Goldwater and Gerald Ford; there is no consensus about its origin.

not trust their parents, at least at the outset. After about nine months, the typical human child develops "stranger anxiety," meaning they start to differentiate between humans and between who they can and cannot trust. Children never develop such an aversion to their parents.

In the past and over time, the human experience expanded beyond the core family. Trust grew genetically and geographically, from parents to siblings to aunts and uncles and cousins, and further down the line of consanguinity. Eventually, an individual's human tribe came to include distant kin of unknown linkage. Even further in our evolution, a person's tribe came to include people who spoke the same language, worshiped the same gods, or had the same physical characteristics.

This type of trust is powerful. Personal trust still forms the backbone of civilization. You probably trust members of your family or your inner circle of friends with your life, and you depend on them without reservation or question. But we should not overstate the point. You also trust McDonalds and United Airlines with your life when you eat a burger or get on a plane. And you trust the US government, our courts and judges, and the policeman walking the beat in your neighborhood. Nevertheless, personal trust is deeply intuitive to us all, and we undoubtedly would like to see it expanded. After all, if our dear friends and family who we trust were in charge of the plane or keeping the peace or running the local burger joint, we would have even more trust in them, assuming they were up to the task at hand. Or, to put it another way, the vast social costs of creating the trust infrastructure that enables us to trust strangers might not be necessary. We wouldn't need the fiction of a corporation or the clumsy government regulatory system because we could trust the most intuitive thing of all: other people. One might think twice about eating at Chipotle (google "Chipotle and E. coli"), but probably not about eating at Grandma Ginny's or Uncle Phil's house.

The virtue of personal trust arises from the directness of its connection between people – you trust Grandma Ginny because you know her. Her ability to satisfy your demands is not intermediated by a stranger. She has built this trust up over time, and if she breached this trust, one of the most important things in her life – her family – might be lost to her.

In Figure 10, we take a stab at conceptualizing the various types of trust. Blue dots represent individuals in a particular society. These individuals want to cooperate, and they choose a mechanism to do so – through government, business, or other individuals. This is obviously a crude model designed to illustrate the differences in approaches. We recognize that all three types frequently work together to enable the requisite amount of trust.

In our model, if individuals choose government trust, each of them votes for a government, which then issues rules that they are each subject to. If individuals cooperate instead through a business, many different businesses arise that will offer them opportunities, interacting with the individuals and with other businesses in

	Government	Business	Personal
Expressions	• Rule of law • Regulatory state	• Guild • Brand	• Tribe • Platform
Mechanisms	• Violence • Sovereignty	• Shared incentives • Competition & profit motive	• Kinship • Ethnicity • Religion • Language • Reciprocity
Characteristics	• Fully centralized and top-down • Breaks down when gains from violence diminish	• Intermediary nodes structure • Breaks down when gains from cheating are large	• Fully distributed peer-to-peer • Hard to scale (if based on personal contact) • No obvious upper bound

FIGURE 10: Trust technologies

competitive markets. Finally, in the last column, one can see that interpersonal trust is distributed directly among peers and does not rely on agents or representatives. Compared with the graphics for government and business trust, there is no intermediary in personal trust. People trust people directly. This makes it less costly and more reliable.

But this also makes it difficult to use for more than a few transactions. An economist would say that personal trust is not easily scalable. It works at local levels – I can trust my friend to watch my daughter when I get stuck at work – but it doesn't work at distance or large scale – I won't trust someone in China to do the same thing. And, in order to expand the number of people I would trust to watch my daughter, I would need to spend vast amounts of time building personal friendships or rely on an intermediary such as a business (e.g. a nanny service) or the government (e.g. a license to be a nanny or mandatory insurance).

Consider something as simple as whether to trust the experience of a particular product. The recommendation of a complete stranger might not be worth very much. The person may be biased or have idiosyncratic tastes. Their experience might not be representative or highly predictive of yours. If that person is your friend, on the other hand, the recommendation might carry more weight. Your friend will know more about you and your tastes, leading to better matching. More importantly, the investment in the friendship they made in you is at stake, whether in a large or a small way, and they will care about protecting it from the harm of a serious error in judgment. They will care about the quality of the recommendation more than a stranger would, and therefore you can trust it more.

If the reliability of a recommendation is proportional to the amount of investment in the friendship – we'd expect better friends to know us better and care more – then this type of trust is costly. Putting aside the other benefits of friendship, it might not be worth the investment for recommendations about things such as products or restaurants or movies. It might be more worthwhile for a recommendation on which doctor is best to perform your heart surgery, but even then, it runs the risk of being too small a sample.

There is also evidence that humans have a fixed cap on the number of other people they can trust in this direct way.[11] Evolutionary psychologist Robin Dunbar posited that people apportion their limited relationship capacity out into groups of varying approximate sizes: 5 for intimate relationships, 50 for close friendships (the type of person you'd invite over for dinner), 150 for casual relationships (the eponymous "Dunbar number"), and 500 for acquaintances. We can think of this relationship capacity as a form of personal trust capital. Because personal trust is the most powerful type, this capital is tremendously valuable.

Basically, personal trust is too scarce to scale to the societal level. It is for this reason that personal trust has not been used to expand trust as society has become more complex. The more strangers we deal with, the better off we can be, but inherent in this is the difficulty or cost of deploying personal trust technology to solve this problem. We all know how time consuming, difficult, and fraught creating and maintaining personal friendships can be. The average person's friendship group looks much like Dunbar observed, which has remained fixed since we were cavemen.

Expanding our base of friends to include all of the people we need to live our modern lives would be impossible – if you wanted a car, you'd have to make friends with iron ore refiners, mechanical engineers, brand marketers, painters, automotive designers, and hundreds of others. In his famous essay "I, Pencil," Leonard Read describes the complexity of a simple pencil and how no single individual could possibly manufacture one on their own.[12] It takes the knowledge and expertise of tens of thousands or more to create something so basic. This is trust at work.

What separates us from our ancestors is not that we have many more friends we can rely on, but instead that we rely on millions of strangers because of intermediaries that form the trust infrastructure. In this way, technology has

---

[11] W.-X. Zhou, D. Sornette, R.A. Hill & R.I.M. Dunbar, "Discrete hierarchical organization of social group sizes," 272 *Proc. R. Soc. B* 439–44 (2005), available at: http://rspb.royalsocietypublishing.org/content/272/1561/439

[12] See Leonard Read, "I, Pencil," reprinted in: *The Cambridge Handbook of Classical Liberal Thought*, M. Todd Henderson (ed.), 73 (2018).

enabled social evolution, which laid the groundwork for the trust institutions (business and government) that got us to this point. But there was no physical evolution to accompany it, so personal trust never moved beyond its initial iterations.

This is changing. New technology has the power to scale personal trust beyond friends and acquaintances to the societal level and beyond. The huge advances in information technology over the past few decades – especially the consistent improvements to computer processors, the development of low-cost data storage, and the rise of the internet – have opened up the possibility of scaling personal trust. The exciting part about this possibility is not just that new efficiencies can be brought to trust delivery, but that, unlike intermediated trust – through either government or business – personal trust has no obvious limit on how much trust can be provided.

For small-scale trust decisions, such as whether to eat here or there, to choose a Chevy or a Ford, to see the Tom Cruise movie or the one starring the Rock, the information needed is discrete, small, and low-stakes. You don't need to be friends with someone to find out whether the experience was valuable. In fact, depersona-lizing and aggregating opinions, preferences, and experiences may be a far better way of obtaining the real value of an experience. It's simple math: as the sample size increases, our confidence about the average experience and the distribution of values – what the shape of the bell curve looks like – increases. We get a picture of not only the typical experience, but also the diversity of experiences. This will thus tell a potential user not only what their experience is likely to be, but also the chance of a great or terrible experience.

Columnist of *The New Yorker* James Surowiecki wrote about this in his book *The Wisdom of Crowds*.[13] He described how the law of large numbers is able to combine information in powerful ways – aggregating samples taken from a large number of relatively uninformed people yields better point estimates of true value than even expert judgments. The famous example is of a contest to guess the weight of a cow at a county fair. While the average person's guess is further from the correct weight than that of the average expert, the aggregate average of the non-experts' guesses is closer than the expert's guess. As long as the crowd has inde-pendent and diverse opinions, aggregating local knowledge of a large number of individuals can provide better information than any individual guesses, even better than the guesses of individuals with great knowledge and experience on the particular issue. The idea is intuitive, as it forms the basis for the market economy, but it has some surprising outcomes. As Surowiecki shows, businesses have used so-called "prediction markets," a specialized form of crowd aggregation, to outper-form expert opinions in a range of areas, such as forecasting the demand for products. A consumer who wants to know whether she can trust a product or

[13]   James Surowiecki, *The Wisdom of Crowds* (2004).

service would benefit from the use of prediction markets. A single expert is better than a single non-expert, but a crowd of non-experts is better than a single expert. This is true in guessing the weight of cattle, but also in determining whether or not a consumer will have a good experience.

Prediction markets function simply: a sponsor introduces one or more tradable contracts that provide for payment contingent on some future event. Each contract either pays off a fixed amount if the event resolves in a particular way (e.g. if a particular candidate wins an election), or pays off an amount that varies depending on some number that can be determined in the future (e.g. one penny per percent of the vote that one candidate receives). The prices at which trades occur provide at least an approximate market-based prediction of the event.[14]

Kay-Yut Chen, an employee of Hewlett-Packard Laboratories, and Charles Plott, an experimental economist, conducted the earliest apparent study of the prospect of using these markets to improve corporate decision-making. They hoped that prediction markets would provide a means of aggregating "small bits and pieces of relevant information [that] exists in the opinions and intuition of individuals who are close to an activity."[15]

Participants were given real money that they could use in the game. Each market predicted the future monthly sales of various products. Meanwhile, Hewlett-Packard continued to assign some employees to produce forecasts. Chen and Plott concluded that the consensus market predictions were a "considerable improvement" over official forecasts – beating official forecasts fifteen out of sixteen times in one experiment and six out of eight times in another – and that this result was robust to different possibility specifications of the method of calculating the probability forecast.[16]

This result has been replicated by dozens of companies and in a wide range of contexts. For example, drug maker Eli Lilly established an internal prediction market to estimate drug development success.[17] It allowed about fifty employees from a range of corporate areas to trade on six drug candidates; the market aggregated toxicology data, clinical trial results, and marketing data better than any existing mechanism, correctly forecasting the three most successful drugs. Similar successes have been observed at Intel, which ran an experiment

---

[14] For a discussion of prediction markets, especially their potential application in the corporate context, see Michael Abramowicz & M. Todd Henderson, "Prediction Markets for Corporate Governance," 82 *N.D. L. Rev.* 1343 (2007).

[15] See, for example, Charles R. Plott & Kay-Yut Chen, "Information Aggregation Mechanisms: Concept, Design and Implementation for a Sales Forecasting Problem," Social Sciences Working Paper No 1131, California Institute of Technology (2002), available at: https://authors.library.caltech.edu/44358/1/wp1131.pdf

[16] Ibid. at 12.

[17] See James M. Pethokoukis, "All Seeing All Knowing," *US NEWS*, August 30, 2004.

in which a prediction market outperformed existing mechanisms for allocation of manufacturing capacity;[18] at Siemens to predict a project completion date more reliably than official forecasts;[19] and at GE to generate new business ideas.[20]

Although these markets seem somewhat removed from the concept of trust we've introduced here, they are, in fact, also about trust. Think about the problem Hewlett-Packard was trying to solve when it deployed a prediction market – management wanted a better estimate of the true expected value of printer sales, in part because it could not trust the information or forecasts generated by individual employees. These individual predictions might be biased up or down for a range of reasons, say because sales people are overconfident or because division heads want to be sure they make their numbers in a given quarter. Individuals might not have accurate or current information. Or, any number of other reasons might create an atmosphere in which managerial decision-makers cannot trust the numbers. Prediction markets are in part about restoring this trust. They use as their central mechanism not an intermediary tasked with dispensing expert judgment or aggregating disparate views, but rather a decentralized, ask-the-masses approach.

The point is simple: if you want to know whether to trust something, and you could only ask one person, you should ask a friend instead of a stranger; but it is likely that you would get a better answer if you asked a hundred or a thousand strangers. It is better to deploy the wisdom of crowds. The information we get in peer-to-peer networks is averaged out over a range of experiences and tastes; it is updated in real time rather than being stale and static; and it can be weighted by intensity of preference. After all, people with experiences that are more impactful, both good and bad, are more likely to give feedback to the system.

* * *

We should pause here to take stock of our progress so far. We have established that there are three primary types of trust providers – individuals, businesses, and governments. In addition, each of these types operates and provides trust through different mechanisms. Personal trust is biological, but also linked to ethnicity and nationality, and furthered by language and religion. Business trust is based on shared incentives and the profit motive and is disciplined, to some extent, by competitive markets. Government trust is premised on sovereignty and violence.

Finally, both in graphical terms and in some description, which we extend on later, we have described various characteristics of these types of trust. Figure 10

---

[18]   See Barbara Kiviat, "The End of Management?," *TIME*, July 6, 2004.
[19]   See Alex Tabarrok, "In Defense of Prediction Markets," *RED HERRING*, September 23, 2003.
[20]   See Michael Totty, "How to Decide? Create a Market," *WALL ST. J.*, June 19, 2006, at R9.

provides an overview of the types of trust and examples of how they work and how we observe them operating in our world.

But we are getting ahead of ourselves. To make the case for the personal trust renaissance that we think is on the horizon, if not already upon us, we must first consider the history of trust. The human invention of the social technology of trust is one of our greatest, if not our greatest, achievements.

5

The Genealogy of Trust

There have been four main epochs of human history and new forms of trust have arisen in each. In fact, these trust innovations – what we have called "social technologies" of trust – have made the transition from one epoch to another possible. After all, *Homo sapiens* are thought to have outcompeted Neanderthals in large part because of our ability to communicate and transmit knowledge more efficiently than trial and error. Our social technologies of trust enabled our ancestors to communicate, to cooperate, to exchange, and to expand our locus of trust in ways that enabled the survival of our species.

Over time, no particular technology of trust was sacred. Humans demanded trust, not any particular mechanism for achieving it or for enabling increased cooperation. Accordingly, the ways in which we expanded trust evolved and changed. These trust innovations have adapted to the age in order to address human needs of the particular time and place. Language was needed at one point, law at another, merchant cartels at yet another. Corporations were necessary under certain conditions and internet platforms under others.

Importantly, these social technologies changed human society in ways unimaginable to their innovators, who were undoubtedly not thinking profound thoughts or about societal-level changes when they developed new technologies. As we explore in this chapter, however, these technologies opened up and expanded new worlds for humans that those living within the prior epoch could not possibly have imagined.

We do not know – and, in this book, do not try to determine – all of the social and technological conditions that generated the need for the particular type of innovation. That is beyond our scope. Each innovation probably arose from a mix of individual experiments, human genius, and independent technological change, as well as environmental and other social factors. For instance, law, one of the social technologies we identify, was invented over many millennia as the human need for cooperation demanded it. But no individual human, not even Hammurabi the Lawgiver, "invented" law.

External technological change of infinite variety also generated the need for innovation in the provision of trust. Consider refrigeration. The idea of preserving foods dates to Roman times or earlier, but it wasn't until the invention of Freon (by

Thomas Midgley Jr and Charles Franklin Kettering in 1928) and its deployment by Frigidaire in a self-contained unit that in-home refrigeration became widespread – 8 million had been sold by 1935. The scientists and engineers who did this work were not thinking about trust when they did this, but they did have a tremendous impact on the supply and demand of trust. They contributed to a social milieu, namely the period of large-scale industrialization and suburbanization in the United States, that fundamentally transformed human history, in large part through the creation of new forms of trust delivery. Refrigeration meant that food could be preserved as never before, opening up massive efficiencies in the production and distribution of food. But these efficiencies could be realized only if food were shipped long distances and purchased from suppliers that were remote and unfamiliar to consumers. Hence, the need for more trust. The lowly refrigerator set in place a chain of events that necessitated greater trust. As we will see, there were several options for how that trust could be supplied. For now, the point is simply that our goal in this book is not to conduct an anthropology of these innovations but is merely to describe them and their consequences.

The four broad epochs or periods of human history are: (1) the hunter-gatherer period (from the dawn of mankind until about 12,000 years ago); (2) the agricultural period (from about 12,000 years ago until the late eighteenth century); (3) the industrial period (from the late eighteenth century until the dawn of the twenty-first century); and (4) the information period (the twenty-first century).

Period	Trust innovation	Examples
Hunter-gatherer	Tribe	Family, language
Agriculture	Rule of law Guild	Basic government services, medieval guilds, religion, early corporations
Industrial	Regulatory state Brand	Alphabet agencies, advertising and corporate brands
Information	Digital tribe	Platforms

FIGURE 11: Trust across the ages

As shown in Figure 11, each period has brought us or has been characterized by a new type of trust-delivery mechanism. Our hunter-gatherer ancestors relied on kin or tribe or language to generate trust among the group, while agricultural societies relied on law and our twentieth-century ancestors relied on the regulatory state and corporate brands. We, and especially our descendants, will, we think, rely increasingly on internet platforms – on a scaled version of personal trust – and less on centralized forms of trust delivery, such as government and corporations.

This is not to say that the types of trust associated with a particular period are the only types of trust being used during that period or after. In fact, trust is cumulative, and forms of trust that were used by our ancient ancestors are still used today. The family or tribe used by the most ancient humans (and our ape and other animal precursors) is still a foundational brick in the human trust superstructure. But as a proportion of the overall delivery of human-to-human trust, it is trivial today.

Let us look at each of these periods in broad strokes. Our goal in this part is not to write an authoritative history, but instead is to offer a high-level perspective on the supply and demand of trust in these periods. We are philosophizing. Oliver Wendell Holmes Jr noted that "to philosophize is to generalize, and to generalize is to omit."[1] A similar point was made by Eric Hoffer in his book *The True Believer*. In a section of his book that sketched a broad history to make a general point, he noted:

> The reader is expected to quarrel with much that is said in this part of the book. He is likely to feel that much has been exaggerated and much ignored. But this is not an authoritative textbook. It is a book of thoughts, and it does not shy away from half-truths so long as they seem to hint at a new approach and help to formulate new questions.[2]

This is our ambition as well and his caution applies equally here.

HUNTER-GATHERER PERIOD

Human civilization started out as innumerable groups or tribes of hunter-gatherers. From the dawn of man until about 12,000 years ago, humans survived in small groups of less than fifty individuals, relying on foraging for wild vegetables and hunting game. Trust was limited to these small groups, which lived in constant fear of being killed by rival bands. Cooperation was limited to within the group, meaning that not much could be accomplished compared with what is possible today. In fact, life for these early humans was more akin to a reality survival show such as *Naked and Afraid*. None of us would want to spend more than a few days, if that, in the lives of our ancient forbearers. (And, looking at it from their perspective, if you told them someday about going to the moon and back – something we did nearly five decades ago – they would have thought the possibility ridiculous. Look up at the moon tonight and just try to imagine it. It is difficult to comprehend today, surrounded as we are by technological marvels. As you ponder, just imagine being huddled by a fire on the African savannah, fearful of everything, except your small troop, limited to an animal skin covering and a stone tool, and looking up at the same moon and contemplating your offspring going there in something they made.)

---

[1] See Benjamin Cardozo, "Law and Literature," In: *Selected Writings of Benjamin Nathan Cardozo* 341 (1947). Cardozo quotes Holmes but does not provide a citation.

[2] Eric Hoffer, *The True Believer: Thoughts on the Nature of Mass Movements* (1951).

Specialization probably arose quickly within these groups – some specialized in hunting, others in cooking or making clothing, and someone had to focus on "research and development" to invent shelter, fire, tools, and all sorts of other things we take for granted. But with only a few dozen people working together, only basic needs could be satisfied. Life was, in the words of one philosopher, "nasty, brutish, and short."[3]

Trust for hunter-gatherers was mostly biological. Individuals trusted others in their group because they were programmed in their DNA to do so. It was human nature. Expanding trust to include others, further afield genetically, was not. Humans had to invent tools to cooperate, just like they needed to invent bronze and arrowheads. A technology was needed, a social technology.

Reputation probably came first. Life in small-scale tribes is what economists call a "repeat play game." Everyone interacts with everyone else more than once, thus permitting individuals to earn a reputation for being faithful or not. For being trustworthy or not. Some individuals earned the trust of others because they cooperated and become known as cooperators. When Grog did what he said he would do – guarding the entrance to the cave all night without falling asleep – others in Grog's tribe were more willing to cooperate with him. Other people in the tribe got a reputation for shirking or cheating and were punished in some way, whether this was through not sharing equally or being cast out.

In the native tribes of the United States, for instance, very light sanctions were deemed sufficient to prevent misbehavior because of the power of tribal reputation. Consider the famous case *Ex parte Crow Dog* as indicative of this phenomenon. In 1883, a Lakota Sioux by the name of Crow Dog killed a chief named Spotted Tail. The punishment? The tribe made Crow Dog give some blankets and horses to Spotted Tail's family to pay restitution, and he was banished from the tribe for a time. The tribe viewed this as sufficient punishment because of the power of reputation within the tribe – the power of shame and social isolation were sufficient punishment in themselves. The tribe reasonably believed that this punishment would deter crimes such as *murder* because of the social sanctions of reduced reputation for Crow Dog and other would-be murderers. To be cast out of the tribe was enough.

The larger tribe involved in this case – the United States – deemed that the punishment given was anathema to justice, because reputation cannot work as well among a polity of tens or hundreds of millions. For that reason, when the Supreme Court upheld the punishment against Crow Dog, because the Court found it did not have the jurisdiction to do otherwise, Congress passed the Major Crimes Act (1895), which extended Anglo justice into Indian Country. They had to create trust our way – through formal law and the incarceration penalty method – because reputation-based sanctions would not enable sufficient trust for non-native settlers to sleep

---

[3] Thomas Hobbes, *Leviathan* (1651).

soundly at night. The non-natives couldn't trust their fellow inhabitants of the Dakotas with such a low sanction for murder.

While reputation can do a great deal of trust-creating work in certain environments, it is fragile. Reputation is always on a knife's edge, since there are incentives to shirk responsibilities or cheat once a reputation is earned. If the payout from shirking or cheating is big enough, reputation does not work to ensure cooperation. If one cooperates in four deals (what economists call "periods"), earning the trust of a counterparty, the payoffs of cheating in the fifth deal might be extremely rewarding. Knowing this, a counterparty might account for the possibility of cheating in future periods. Working backward, trust may not be created at all, because people know others may eventually cheat. Thus, while reputation provided some social infrastructure for early humans, and still does to this day, it was hardly enough to create the widespread, inter-tribal cooperation necessary for large-scale human flourishing.

There were probably trust innovators. They came on the scene and experimented. Why they did, we cannot know for sure. Maybe they were born that way. Maybe it was how they were raised. Maybe it was a mix of the social environment and these other things. But, whatever the causes, individual tribe members undoubtedly tried new things, such as trusting tribe members in new ways or trusting members of other tribes. They may have been in search of new opportunities, new lands, or new mates. It is likely that many of these innovators failed, just as most innovations today fail to catch on. The consequences were probably social ostracism or even death. But one or two worked, yielded results, and then were copied and caught on. Once members of a tribe learned to trust each other in new methods, there were probably tribes that experimented with trusting other tribes. It is likely that this worked sometimes and resulted in disaster other times. Lessons were learned. Strategies were developed.

Tribes got bigger, perhaps through personal bonds but more likely through conquest. They expanded beyond the fifty or so humans that seems to form a natural limit on close personal trust. Not only were friendships difficult to maintain at the new scale of 100, 200, or 500 people, but the coercive premise of conquest probably made maintaining friendships even more difficult. For these larger groups to be stable, whether across tribes or within a larger tribe, new methods were needed. While some tribes were inventing new stone tools, others were investing in technologies of cooperation.

Law came first. It was primitive, not written down, not well thought out, and based on violence. The head of a tribe used physical strength and cunning to assert dominion over the tribe. Deviations from tribal welfare, as defined on an ad hoc basis by the tribal leader, were punished. This generated trust within the tribe. People could trust that, if they didn't follow the rules, they would be punished.

Although we do not know the precise forms this took among our ancient ancestors, it isn't difficult to imagine. Perhaps there was early specialization, with strong males responsible for protection and hunting and females responsible for child rearing. If male hunters or female caregivers violated these norms – say by shirking their responsibilities or stealing – they would be punished with violent retribution. Trust that individuals would do their duties started to be established.

Importantly, this was based on fear, on the threat of physical harm. Although this may be very effective at generating compliance and trust, it is a very costly form of trust creation, since deviations from social norms (or errors about whether deviations actually happened) resulted in physical pain or worse for individuals. Over time, the built-in fear of violence could produce strong social norms that were able to obviate the need for the violence that brought about those norms in the first place. But violence, even if used merely to make the threats of violence more broadly credible, was still needed. And violence imposes large costs on society. It has a negative impact on individuals who suffer from it and, when there are errors in the application of violence, the consequences can be catastrophic.

Although the idea of compelling good behavior, and thus creating trust, through violence seems crude and antiquated, it is still the basis for the modern state. If you do not comport with the social norms ensconced in law, the state will use the threat of physical violence to deprive you of your wealth, your liberty, or your life. Every prohibition, from the lowly parking ticket to treason and murder, is premised on violence deployed by the state, just as it was for our earliest ancestors.

Social technologies of trust soon expanded. At some point, humans developed the ability to speak and create language. Language does more than just allow us to communicate and thus to lower the cost of coordination by making information easier to share and digest. In a world in which we are more likely to trust members of our own (national, regional, or ethnic) tribe, language is also a low-cost signal of in-group status. Two strangers can easily and immediately identify members of a particular tribe when they open their mouths to communicate. If one is predisposed to trust a fellow tribe member over an outsider, language is an efficient sorting tool. In fact, there is probably no other tool as effective at raising the level of trust between strangers than speaking the same language.[4]

Being able to speak Norwegian does not mean other Norwegians will trust you. It is not a sufficient condition for trust, but, at least historically, it was frequently a necessary one – Norwegians wouldn't trust you just because you spoke Norwegian, but if you didn't, they definitely wouldn't. For most of human existence, people had low levels of trust in complete strangers. But, when a stranger opened their mouth and showed they were a member of the particular tribe, trust rose a little, perhaps sufficiently to enable a transaction to happen, whether this was sharing a responsibility or engaging in trade. This is the marginal level of trust discussed earlier – the additional amount of trust necessary to enable voluntary exchange or

---

[4] It is not just raw language that serves this purpose; specialty patois also plays this role. If one has any doubt, just attend a faculty workshop in philosophy, economics, law, or any other discipline.

cooperation. Language, especially in the past but also somewhat today, is a tool that can help deliver it.

Although this example may be strange to modern, cosmopolitan readers, our ancestors, whether part of a small tribe on the African plains or a large country such as China, rationally felt they could trust people that were part of their tribe or nation more than outsiders to their particular polity. Developing a hard-to-learn language was a way of raising the costs of faking in-group status. This has been suggested as a reason why, for instance, languages have many long words despite not using up all the possible permutations of short ones. (E.g. in English, only three of the five common vowels make words when put between "c" and "t," and an optimally simple language would have found use for "cet.")

Despite its ancient roots, recent research shows that language is still crucially important in creating trust. There are a variety of studies with multinational corporations that demonstrate a strong correlation between language and trustworthiness. For instance, in a study of over 300 Finnish and Chinese subsidiaries, Wilhelm Barner-Rasmussen and Igmar Björkman showed that language fluency is crucial to developing inter-unit trust.[5] This line of research shows that even socialization in a corporation's values is not sufficient to create enough trust when there are significant language barriers. As one recent study of multinational teams of three German auto companies concludes: "language uniquely affects trust."[6]

While prehistoric trust started with the simple tribe, which was an extension of the core family unit, over millennia, our ancestors formed new and larger "tribes" to deal with ever-greater complexity and opportunity. These "trust tribes" come in all shapes and sizes. We humans trust members of our groups more than non-members. Historically, and still to this day, this means that we are likely to trust members of our religious sect, our club, our sports team, our workplace, our online community, or, regrettably, our race or ethnicity, more than non-members. Creating trust has both benefits and costs. Trusting people that look or talk or worship like you can help expand human cooperation, but the end result of that cooperation can be both good and bad. It can be the cure for polio or can lead to the Hundred Years' War.

Over time and space, the demand for trust has grown, and various entities or institutions have been created to supply it. The need for new trust mechanisms, for humans to expand the social technology of cooperation, often arose from advancements that were generated independently and thus not directly related to trust. The rise of agriculture was just such an exogenous event that begat a need for greater mechanisms of trust.

---

[5]   Wilhelm Barner-Rasmussen & Igmar Björkman, "Language Fluency, Socialization and Inter-Unit Relationships in Chinese and Finnish Subsidiaries," 3 *Manage. Organ. Rev.* 105 (2007).

[6]   Helene Tenzer, Markus Pudelko & Anne-Wil Harzing, "The impact of language barriers on trust formation in multinational teams," 45 *JIBS* 508 (2014).

AGRICULTURAL PERIOD

The first big leap in human advancement was the idea of agriculture. Instead of roaming around and eating wild grains and rice, and hunting for animals, humans in China, Mesopotamia, South America, and elsewhere independently started staying in one place and growing or raising their own food. The domestication of animals (pigs and sheep) and grains (rice, soy, wheat, and others) happened in various parts of the world between 15,000 and 10,000 years ago.

Agriculture created the possibility of centralization, providing enough food and resources in a small geographic area. Rather than a band of fifty people roving over long distances in search of unpredictable resources, more and more people could apply their labor to a concentrated area and have predictable access to food. The importance of place increased because, by building farms and durable housing, we invested in improvements that were worth protecting from invaders, unlike the ephemeral caves or temporary shelters of hunter-gatherers. With more and more people in a concentrated area, there was a massive increase in the demand for trust. This was the start of human civilization.

Law

Settling down in one spot begat the need for law. Nomadic hunter-gatherers did not need much law, since little or nothing was owned. The idea of property, especially regarding the land, was foreign to or less developed among such societies. If land is not owned, there is less need for sophisticated legal systems regarding ownership. Although ownership rights of various sorts were common in Native American tribes (and likely elsewhere), where scarcity demanded them and the costs of establishing them were not prohibitive, these property rights were more commonly established via custom rather than formal law. Contract law is not a necessity for nomads either. Without property there is little exchange, and therefore not much need for an organizing framework in which to situate transactions.

But once the productivity gains in food production from stationary existence were realized, the demand for law to create trust increased dramatically. Agriculture requires investments and thus well-defined property rights, as well as criminal and contract law. No one will invest today (i.e. plant seeds) for a payoff in several months (i.e. the harvested crops) unless they can trust that their demarcated land will be respected and that they will have the rights to reap what they have sown – whether to consume it or sell it at a fair value.

Although early humans had a form of this type of law, the scope and sophistication of law reflected the primitive conditions of human society at that time. Law needed to be regularized and formalized only when there was a dramatic increase in the amount of trust necessary for human society to function. The investment and time-horizon required to move to agriculture was just such a necessity.

The scope of law and the stakes today are different, but the basic logic is the same. Law provides important infrastructure for trust. At a basic level, a government is vital to keep the peace, which enables individuals to focus on things other than keeping their families safe. We can all get a good night's rest, since we do not have to take shifts guarding the door. Sound sleep begets creativity and productivity.

At large scales, government is necessary to collect taxes to provide for the common defense – what economists call a public good. We all benefit from government keeping the streets free of bandits and foreign armies wanting to harm our persons or take our property. Trusting that our homes, our factories, our farms, and so on, will be there tomorrow just as we left them not only saves individuals from having to provide defense themselves, but also encourages investments in them in the first place.

Paper and other forms of record keeping, initially developed for law and still vital to it today, are likewise largely about trust. A written contract is more easily enforced for a variety of reasons, and thus provides greater levels of trust that the obligations will be met. It is for this reason that the first uses of written language in Mesopotamia were contracts written on pieces of stone. Our modern mechanisms of verification – property records, bank account statements, securities settlement procedures, and, now, the distributed ledger or blockchain – are all just modern trust-delivery tools. As their use expands (in part because of innovations that reduce their costs), our ability to trust more people and to do more things with the people we trust expands.

An example of early law is shown in a clay cuneiform tablet from Ur in Mesopotamia from several thousand years before Christ (see Figure 12). According to scholars, this tablet records quantities of barley produced in various plots of land. The tablet is akin to a property record and contract document, in that it records investments and outputs, establishing them as a baseline against which social expectations of behavior are measured. A farmer could be assured that his investment in a field wouldn't be squandered by false claimants because a written contractual record existed. The innovations of writing, language, law, and portable records provided the trust necessary to create sufficient conditions for agriculture to take root. Documentation provided verification, limiting the risk of fraud. The story of trust technologies, as we will see, is intrinsically concerned with the elimination of fraud.

Farmers needed to also protect against thieves. Accordingly, trust was established via criminal law. In the Code of Hammurabi, the penalty for robbery was death: "If anyone is committing a robbery and is caught, then he shall be put to death."[7] A third party – the government, with a monopoly on violence – was needed to enforce this threat. If credible, farmers could be confident that their investments would not be wasted because of this risk, and therefore would be more likely to make them.

---

[7] Hammurabi Code Ex. Law #22. See: http://avalon.law.yale.edu/ancient/hamframe.asp

FIGURE 12: Clay tablet from Ur (Mesopotamia)[8]

Similarly, the specialization of agriculture required rules about fraud. While cavemen probably did most things for themselves, the move to agriculture meant that eventually specialists would be needed. This meant some humans would be principals (the owners or bosses) and some would be agents (the workers). As noted earlier, agency enables scale, which enables wealth and welfare to be increased exponentially. But it also opens up the possibility of cheating, shirking, and deviations from owners' interests, as well as the associated costs to reduce these indiscretions. Human innovators created law to reduce these costs (along with the fraud risks inherent in trading), thus permitting trust to be created more cheaply. An example can be found in the Code of Hammurabi: "If a herdsman, to whose care cattle or sheep have been entrusted, be guilty of fraud ... then he shall ... pay the owner ten times the loss."[9] This threat, backed by the threat of violence from the government, was designed to create trust. An owner of cattle or sheep could *trust* the individual they hired (or compelled) to manage their herd or flock, because that person knew they would have to bear the costs of any cheating or misbehavior. In fact, with punishments set at ten times the value at stake, they were assured of not being able to profit from wrongdoing. (Interestingly, the level of punishment may have been set that high because detecting all cheating back then may have been more difficult. The work of Nobel Laureate Gary Becker demonstrates how optimal punishments take into account the social costs of the wrong as well as the probability of detection

---

[8] Clay tablet with pre-cuneiform writings from the end of the fourth millennium BC, from the collection of the Louvre. Reprinted with permission of the Creative Commons: https://creativecommons.org/licenses/by-sa/3.0/deed.en

[9] Ibid. Ex. Law #265.

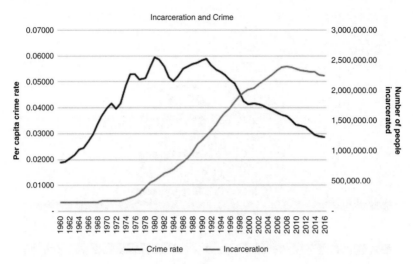

FIGURE 13: The growth and persistence of carceral trust control[11]

and punishment.[10]) Criminal punishments lowered the costs of agency, thus freeing up the owner to do other things. Cooperation was enabled, and this made everyone better off.

Creating trust didn't come cheap. The cost of this trust creation? Death. Or liability of ten times the amount stolen or lost. These are extreme measures. They are threats designed to scare untrustworthy people into trustworthiness. But the costs these measures impose on society are large, especially when mistakes are possible. Trust is created, but at a huge cost. (A similar point will be made later regarding advertising. It too can be used to create trust, but if trust could be created more efficiently through other means, then the billions spent on ads could be considered largely wasted.)

Consider the modern judicial system in the United States. According to the Bureau of Justice Statistics and the Federal Bureau of Investigation (FBI), in 2016, there were more than 2 million prisoners under state and federal jurisdiction. This is more than triple the per-capita rate of incarceration in 1980, when there were nearly five times fewer prisoners. The growth in carceral control was initially a response to an increase in the crime rate. As seen in Figure 13, starting in the 1980s, there was a boom in the prison population as a result of a jump in the crime rate, which reached epidemic levels by the 1970s. Politicians (especially Republicans, but, in truth, all politicians) responded to this increase in crime – driven by drugs, the flight of wealthier people to the suburbs after riots in several cities, and a variety of other factors – by passing legislation that increased mandatory minimum sentences.

---

[10]   See, for example, Gary S. Becker, "Crime and Punishment: An Economic Approach," 76 J. *Pol. Econ.* 169 (1968).

[11]   Data from the Bureau of Justice Statistics (www.bjs.gov/index.cfm?ty=pbse&sid=5) and the FBI (www .fbi.gov/services/cjis/ucr).

Getting tough on crime was a winning platform. The Rockefeller drug laws of New York were typical. The mandatory minimum sentences for crimes – especially drug crimes – that were previously considered low level dramatically increased. Although it remains to be seen whether the incarceration rate will fall in response to the drop in crime as expected, there are reasons to doubt it will. Being tough on crime is still resonating in US politics, with politicians playing on fear that is often divorced from facts on the ground. Moreover, there are other powerful actors with a vested interest in the status quo. Many states have privatized prisons to a greater or lesser extent, creating a lobby that will resist attempts to decarcerate the United States. Lest you think this is a problem created by outsourcing or privatization, government-run prisons may also experience the same effect. Prison guard unions are extremely powerful, giving millions of dollars to politicians, and they too have a vested interest in not reducing the population of US jails. At the end of the day, everyone involved is selling trust to US citizens, but their interests may deviate from the optimal because of the difference between the world we inhabit and the stories we are told about what we need. If the gap between the crime rate and the prison population lingers for reasons beyond the time-lag of sentences themselves, or new crimes are invented that continue to fill prisons, we can chalk this up to inefficiencies in the trust-creation system.

But maybe the argument can be made more simply. Consider two – that's right, two! – Chicago cops from the past several decades, Sergeant Ronald Watts and Commander Jon Burge. These men, charged with preserving the peace and building trust in the community, used their authority to send nearly 200 innocent men to prison. According to his obituary in *The New York Times*, "Mr. Burge and detectives under his command were accused of extracting confessions from more than 100 people while questioning them in the 1970s and '80s by shocking them with cattle prods, smothering them with plastic typewriter covers and pointing guns in their mouths while pretending to play Russian roulette."[12] Not to be outdone, Sergeant Ronald Watts framed untold numbers of men for various crimes for not paying protection money to him and his crew or simply because they crossed him. Nearly fifty Chicago men have been exonerated to date and dozens more cases involving Gates are pending.[13] Any reasonable extrapolation of these cases to the country and the world suggests that the human toll of such abuse of the trust-creation mechanism of government violence is staggering. This is the cost of trust, at least provided in this way.

[12]   Sam Roberts, "Jon Burge, 70, Ex-Commander in Chicago Police Torture Cases, Dies," *The New York Times*, September 20, 2018, available at: www.nytimes.com/2018/09/20/obituaries/jon-burge-dead.html

[13]   Jason Meisner & Megan Crepeau, "Charges to be thrown out against 18 more men whose convictions linked to corrupt Chicago cop," *Chicago Tribune*, September 21, 2018, available at: www.chicagotribune.com/news/local/breaking/ct-met-corrupt-ex-chicago-cop-charges-dropped-20180921-story.html

More abstractly, the point about the costs of trust creation was well made in the "Justice" episode of *Star Trek: The Next Generation*. The crew of the *Enterprise* find themselves on a seemingly idyllic planet in the Rubicun star system. There is no crime and there is a high level of trust on the planet, but the reasons for the peace and calm are mysterious. Then, a young crew member, Wesley Crusher, accidentally steps on some seedlings while trying to retrieve a ball, and the reason is revealed. Every deviation from the rules is punished by death. "Mediators" arrive instantly to inject Wesley with a fatal drug. Compliance – and thus trust and cooperation – were achieved through extreme legal sanction.

When Captain Picard intervenes to save the day (of course!), the lesson we are left with is that law has costs. If there are punishments without exceptions, especially when life is at stake, the unintended consequences can be large. Wesley didn't deserve to die. His death wasn't needed to create an orderly and prosperous society. Mistakes happen – no system of law is perfect. And mistakes regarding life can't be undone. Of course, the people of the planet were okay with the system – it seemed to work pretty well for them. They liked the society it created. The question that the crew of the *Enterprise* posed to them was whether there was a way of achieving the high levels of trust they had but at a lower cost.

We know from our own experience that, when the stakes of punishment are high, the response is not necessarily more compliance, but more evasion and costly legal procedures designed to ensure fairness. Consider the death penalty, the closest thing we have to the system of justice on the planet in that Star Trek episode. While, in theory, capital punishment should deter wrongdoing, the data are mixed. Innocent people have been sentenced to death. In addition, the potential for errors and possible bias in the system have led to a Baroque system for handling these cases that makes the litigation in Charles Dickens's *Bleak House* seem efficient. Capital cases take decades to work their way through the courts in order to ensure that mistakes are not made. The stakes of trust creation are extremely high, meaning the costs are extreme too.

The crew of the *Enterprise* considered the planet primitive, and Captain Picard referenced Earth's past (our present) primitive practice of capital punishment. The gist of this criticism is that the regulation necessary to achieve social trust at certain times and in certain places is unnecessary at other times and in other places. If we can achieve the same or greater levels of trust with better social technology, we should do so. If we could eliminate the death penalty, as the Pope just recently urged every society to do, but keep (or even increase) the current amount of social compliance with law, everyone would want us to do so.

The need for more effective trust-creation mechanisms increases as the size and scope of, as well as the stake for, a society increases. As agricultural societies experienced rapid growth as a result of specialization and increased cooperation, the need for additional trust became clear. Human communities grew bigger, expanding rapidly. Personal trust was no longer sufficient to maintain trust within a single human tribe. By 8000 BC, the city of Mureybet, in what is now northern

Syria, had 500 inhabitants (thought to be the largest city of its era). While this seems incredibly small – a typical New York apartment building has more residents – it took a tremendous increase in the social technology of trust to allow a human settlement of ten times the natural tribal size to function and be cohesive. The humans of 15,000 BC could never have imagined living in a community of that size, because they would have thought it impossible to trust that many people.

Religion

Religion was another social technology that played a big role in enabling the expansion of human societies and cooperation. Religion is a tribe. In fact, members of the Jewish faith even call themselves "members of the Tribe." And for good reason. We are more likely to trust individuals who share our core values, since they will be less likely to deviate from an agreed-upon (and arguably divinely inspired) set of rules and practices. Jews are likely to trust other Jews more than Buddhists or Zoroastrians or Catholics or Scientologists, all else being equal.

Of course, religion purports to be about a search for and answers to questions about morality and the ultimate purpose of humanity. Some religions also claim to be divinely ordained. We do not deny that these are reasons why religion exists. These claims may also be true – who are we to suggest otherwise? But, even if they are true, their manifestations on Earth have been used for other purposes, both good and bad. Relevant to our story is one of these – religion also may have proliferated as a simple means of tribal affiliation that enabled trust.

This is not speculation. The money men of pre-modern Europe were often Jewish, not just because the Catholic Church banned usury, but also because of the intra-tribal trust that was created by a common belief system. If subscribing to the tenets of the Torah made you a more trustworthy person to other subscribers of the faith, then it lowered the costs of trade. This was especially important in an era in which there were no alternative mechanisms for efficiently validating transactions. With credit scores and other technologies that enable instant verification, we do not need religion to play this role as much as in the past. It is perhaps in part for this reason that the percentage of college freshmen with no religious affiliation has increased by three times since the 1980s, from about 10 percent to more than 30 percent.[14] Today, religion's importance for answering cosmological questions is no less central, but it plays a smaller role in the overall supply of trust than it did in past centuries. The pattern emerges in the division of labor among trust providers themselves, with multi-use trust tools providing a great deal of trust and then declining into their niche as a new social technology explodes.

---

[14] Allen Downey, "College Freshmen Are Less Religious Than Ever," *Scientific American*, May 25, 2017, available at: https://blogs.scientificamerican.com/observations/college-freshmen-are-less-religious -than-ever

In terms of trust, this is a good thing. The new technologies – searchable paper record databases, the internet, blockchain, etc. – enable trust at lower costs and in ways that do not discriminate based on crude proxies, such as religion. History has taught us well the downsides to religious tribalism.

But the use of religion as a means of increasing trust is not ancient history. The notorious fraudster Bernie Madoff, whose Ponzi scheme defrauded investors of approximately $18 billion (the largest fraud in US history), targeted wealthy Jews and Jewish institutions in part because they were more likely to trust him (a fellow Jew) than they would have a non-Jew. The downside of trust – the ability to cheat members of a religion who inherently trust other members of that religion – is evidence of the power created by tribal trust.

* * *

As trust was created in larger groups – through shared language, religion, and primitive law – the gains from cooperation made even larger tribal groupings possible. A thousand years after the largest human settlement was made up of just a few hundred people, the town of Jericho reached 2,000 people. A few thousand years later, Susa, in modern-day Iran, reached 8,000 people and, shortly thereafter, Ur (which many believe to be the homeland of Abraham, the father of the monotheist religions), in modern-day Iraq, and Yin Xu, in modern-day China, had over 100,000 inhabitants. Tribes grew and grew. Carthage, the archenemy of Rome, reached half a million inhabitants by 300 BC, and Rome reached over a million inhabitants a century later. Several other cities, such as Baghdad and Kaifeng (China), reached a million people during the first millennium AD. Trust, enabled by law, by language, by religion, and by new social identities wrapped up in empire or the state, expanded dramatically.

Then the Dark Ages resulted in a widespread retrogression in the amount of trust in human society. As institutions, governments, and other trust mechanisms failed, social cohesion decreased, leading to declining social welfare. Individuals and communities became isolated. Cooperation at great distances, and even in local areas, declined dramatically. Less investment was made. Creativity, exploration, and expansion of human flourishing came to a screeching halt.

Over time, smaller human societies, ruled over by feudal lords wielding supreme power to create trust, started to rebuild cooperation on a larger scale. As the city states and proto-kingdoms of Europe started trading with each other across greater and greater distances, however, it would not be enough to use simple law, such as that found in Hammurabi's Code. Because of the retreat of institutions with global reach, such as the Roman Empire, the ability of governments to create trust across Europe was diminished. As a result, there was a need for new trust technology. A clever solution to business cooperation developed across Europe – the concept of guilds.

Guild

There were many guilds or trading groups in medieval Europe. The goal of a guild was simple: to create trust among individual artisans, tradespeople, merchants, or traders. (Of course, the guild structure did more than this, but trust creation was a major motivation.) To create trust, individuals or proto-businesses banded together to form an entity that would supervise individual members. Just as early humans created "governments" to mete out justice, so too did individual merchants create guilds to do the same thing in a more limited context. Governments and guilds (and, as we will soon see, corporations) are merely abstractions – legal fictions composed of human actors cooperating in new ways. These fictional entities were each created to generate more societal trust, and hence more interaction and cooperation, and therefore greater human flourishing.

How did guilds work to create more trust? By creating a separate entity – the guild – the artists or merchants could create a distinct and collective reputation for good behavior. Individuals that were part of a guild were able to increase the trust they delivered to others by having both themselves and the guild, as separate entities, stand behind their promise. Each time one of the members acted, the person on the other side of the transaction was relying not only on the individual's reputation, but also on that of the guild.

Knowing this, the guild would have strong incentives to police misbehavior on the part of members of the guild, since any cheating would diminish the reputation of the guild, and thus all members. In fact, this was the purpose of the guild. To picture how it worked, imagine that there are ten merchants selling mead (a honey-based beverage akin to beer) in a particular area of the Low Countries in the thirteenth century. Each of these merchants sells a nearly identical product – there was much less product differentiation then – and is unknown personally to most customers. They may have come into town, set up shop, and planned to move on to the next town in a few days. In addition, this was an age in which information was very costly to obtain, there were few identifiable brands for products, and policing misbehavior was extremely difficult – there were no warranties and the local sheriff was unlikely to be able to find, let alone discipline, most cheaters. It would therefore be logical for many customers to have a difficult time differentiating between mead merchants. With high information costs, customers having little ability to differentiate, and few remedies in the event that the product was not up to expectations, merchants had strong incentives to skimp or cheat.

But doing so would mean that customers might stop buying mead from merchants altogether, choosing instead to make their own or to be unwilling to pay a good price – they might discount the price they were willing to pay by the probability that the product would be watered down or of poor quality. If all the merchants were cheaters, then this would mean that each would be able to charge for only what they delivered, and if all the merchants were saints, there would be no cheating in the first place. But, if there were some honest merchants and some cheaters, then things become interesting. Without the ability to signal that they are of high quality, good merchants would be tempted to drop out of the market altogether. Imagine it costs two pfennigs to make good mead and one pfennig to make bad mead. Merchants selling watered-down mead can sell theirs for two pfennigs and make a profit, while the honest merchants can only break even at that price. This is the so-called market for lemons, which economists describe as any market in which the dynamics lead to only "lemons" (as in, a defective used car) remaining in the market.

The guild is an elegant solution to this problem. It might have started as follows. One of the honest mead merchants has an idea: why not start a club of mead merchants – Mead Merchants United (MMU) – that would admit only members who promised to uphold certain standards of production and to deal with customers honestly. The MMU might give out labels to such members as a way of signaling quality to customers. And, since it needs to maintain the value of the membership and the label, it would have to conduct inspections and hold members to account if they cheated. Notably, policing other mead sellers for cheating was likely cheaper and more effective than if they were policed by government (which had less information about good and bad mead, as well as limited resources to enforce any rules) or by customers (given the primitive nature of the markets).

In general, the idea is that, where it is difficult for individual merchants or the government to enforce standards of commercial conduct, it may be necessary to invent another mechanism – another way of creating the trust that is essential for voluntary exchange to happen on favorable terms.

The Hansa

Although many early guilds were small groups of artisans or merchants in a particular trade or craft, there were broader guilds that expanded the reach of the human tribe across vast distances. An example is the networks of traders known as the Hansa (also the Hanse or the Hanseatic League).[15] The Hansa, a group of loosely affiliated German trading posts, established the first trading network spanning all of Northern Europe. Through a formal institution – a sort of mega-guild – the members of the Hansa "tribe" were able to gain the trust of traders from London to Russia. Being a part of the Hansa guild meant that you could be trusted. Or, at least, trusted more – and perhaps just enough more – than non-guild members.

The Hansa developed a rigorous system for ensuring this trust. Consider the example of the Hansa outpost – called the German Kontor – established in Bergen, Norway, in 1360. The Hansa went there to provide a way of bringing cod fish from the fishing grounds of the far north (near the Arctic Circle) to the rest of

[15] Justyna Wubs-Mrozewicz & Stuart Jenks, eds., *The Hanse in Medieval and Early Modern Europe* (2012), available at: www.brill.com/hanse-medieval-and-early-modern-europe

FIGURE 14: The Hansa community of Bergen, Norway[16]

Europe. Without modern communications and international business transaction law, there was no easy way to get the fish across thousands of miles to customers demanding it, especially after the Pope declared Fridays to be meatless. The Norwegian fishermen in the Lofoten Islands did not have any knowledge of how to dry fish for shipment, how to ship fish, or how to build relationships with customers in dozens of countries and city states. The Hansa had all of these things, and could have served as mere intermediaries, entering into contracts for purchase (from the Norwegian fishermen) and sale (to the cities of Europe), while guarding their business secrets with intellectual property protections.

But the Hansa could not trust the Norwegian fishermen or their customers in Europe to live up to their bargains and not steal the business for themselves. There was no rich body on international contract law and no international arbitration forum to resolve disputes. There was no intellectual property law or other way to protect business methods or trade secrets. The fishermen or the customers could fail to fulfill their contracts, either in whole or in part. If the fishermen or businessmen in Bergen learned the secrets, they could oust the Hansa and take over the business themselves. There were no bonds between the Hansa and the Norwegians, whether they be national,

[16] Photo by M. Todd Henderson.

religious, or cultural, and law was too crude to provide trust, given the available technology. The German merchants, based in Lübeck, could have tried to conquer Norway, bringing it under military control, but this would have required huge costs (in both lives and treasure) and might not have been successful. Instead, they developed this system of early globalist capitalism, with trust created in a new way.

To ensure a steady supply of fish from source to table, the Hansa built their own network of agents to obtain the fish, dry it, and ship it to the heart of Europe. Hansa agents operated in the north to ensure supply, in Bergen to collect, dry, and ship the fish, and in the south to facilitate delivery throughout Europe. The secrets had to be protected through non-legal means, so the community in Bergen had to be closed to ensure that the agents could be trusted. Thus, the Hansa outpost was walled off from the rest of Bergen. Hansa agents were forbidden from intermingling with their Norwegian neighbors. Intermarriage was forbidden, allegedly on religious and cultural grounds but in fact it was about trade secret protection. To ensure allegiance and compliance, the agents were chosen at a young and impressionable age, and were reared entirely in the culture and values of the Hansa. The result was social isolation, imposing great cost on the Hansa, its agents, and the local Norwegians. But it was the only way of creating sufficient levels of trust.

The Hansa network worked for centuries – in Bergen it lasted for nearly 400 years – but it was an extremely costly system. Rigid social discipline and isolation had to be maintained; the monopoly enforced through threats. If it had been possible to achieve trust in alternative ways, the result would have been a welfare gain for everyone involved – the fishermen and customers could have achieved better value, the Hansa agents would have had better lives, and the society of Bergen would have had a more integrated society. Today, of course, there is no need for an elaborate and culturally isolated network of Hansa agents to get fish from Lofoten to Leipzig – we have built, with a mix of government and private law, mechanisms for ensuring trust that is sufficient to enable the cod trade.

The Hansa did eventually expand their trust tribe to include non-Hansa members in the communities in which they operated. After all, Hansa agents had to deal with locals, be they fishermen or suppliers of their walled-off communities. Trust was needed here too. And in a world in which trust was based mostly on identity, it was costly to establish. Monarchial decrees were useful to achieve this end, since they could expand the tribe. In the late tenth century, for instance, the king of England declared that the traders of the Hanseatic League that were doing business on the wharves of the Thames were "worthy of the good laws, like to ourselves."[17] The goal was to mitigate "commercial insecurity" – to create trust.[18] This helped bolster London (one of the first Hansa outposts) as a major trading center. Government

[17] Helen Zimmern, *The Hansa Towns*, 15 (1889).
[18] See, for example, Peter Stabel, Jeroen Puttevils & Jan Dumolyn, "Production, Markets and Socio-economic Structures I: c.1100–c.1320," In: *Medieval Bruges, c. 850–1550*, Andrew Brown & Jan Dumolyn (eds.), 107 (2018).

decree, or law, was necessary to create trust when the parties to a particular deal were not members of the same tribe. As such, those bound by such laws became a new form of tribe. The king's statement of law brought the Hansa tribe into the British tribe by decree.

The Law Merchant

Guilds or merchant clubs were one elegant solution to the trust problem created by the limitations of the age – limitations of the violence of the sovereign, of information for consumers, and so on. Another solution was a new type of law. Around this time, a body of informal law known as the "Law Merchant" arose across medieval Europe. The Law Merchant was a set of rules that crystalized out of customary trading practices among various merchants that regulated their conduct in many different places. There was no European Community or even many nation states then, and this made trade across political jurisdictions extremely costly. Foreign merchants – say Italians selling olive oil in Germany or Czechs selling salt in France – needed the protection of local laws, but there were no protections for them and there was a concern of local bias. They were not members of the local, geographic-based or linguistic-based tribe, and therefore had reason to worry about being taken advantage of or not protected. Enforcement across borders was also difficult, if not impossible. Customers, too, probably feared they would be cheated by people outside their tribe. (This concern still exists – in a clever experiment, economist John List showed that customers at baseball card trade shows got better prices from local merchants than from out-of-town ones.[19])

The merchants wanted to trust each other, but they needed a credible, external source of power to do so. Therefore, they created their own law and their own courts to regulate conduct at trade fairs across Europe. In England, these courts were called "piepoudre" or "piepowder" courts, after the French term for "dusty feet," which traders undoubtedly had after days at the fair. The courts were informal affairs conducted outside in tents at trade fairs. Over time, the Law Merchant developed into a rich body of commercial law, based on Roman law traditions, governing contracts, intellectual property, and all aspects of business trade. The Law Merchant created the trust necessary for human cooperation in business at a time when government was unable to do so.

Medieval Flanders

Another example of guilds arising as a substitute for (and thus a competitor to) government can be seen in the development of Flemish textile guilds in and around Bruges, in what is now Belgium. In the eleventh century, the development of

---

[19] John A. List, "Testing neoclassical competitive market theory in the field," 99 *PNAS* 15827–30 (2002).

Flanders, like in the rest of Europe after the collapse of Rome, was inhibited by rampant violence.[20] Various counts tried to "stimulate trade and urban development . . . by imposing a stronger system of justice," but the tools of government were insufficient to have the desired effect.[21] Government did not have the technology to assert itself over distances, and it did not have the status among citizens. In our lingo, it wasn't capable of creating an environment in which citizens could trust each other (private trust) or the public provider of trust (public trust). Information was too costly to obtain; instruments of violence were too crude; institutions capable of performing trust-creating functions were not mature or capable. For instance, during the Ottoman siege of Malta in 1565 (some four centuries later), it took six weeks for King Phillip in Madrid to hear news from his spies in Sicily about whether the so-called ravelin of Christendom was holding. The information technology of the era dramatically curtailed the potential of sovereigns to create trust.

During the next two hundred years, a mechanism of social control designed to improve the human condition among the burghers of Flanders – the guild system – developed organically. There was no princely command or Mongol imposition of authority based on conquest. Instead, countless experiments now lost to history were tried, most of which failed. However, over time, building upon the lessons of these failures, humans in this area (and across Europe) figured out ways of organizing themselves and coordinating their activities. They figured out a way to trust each other, in trade and then in other aspects of life among potentially hostile strangers.

One example comes from the early twelfth century: as early as 1113, there were societies of merchants "aimed at enhancing mutual assistance when traveling abroad."[22] In foreign lands, merchants might find themselves at the mercy of uncertain justice; likewise, locals dealing with these merchants might find themselves uncertain of whether or not they would be treated fairly. These merchant societies thus needed to protect merchants from two different threats – external threats from foreigners and internal threats from merchants whose cheating might have negative spillover effects.

These mutual aid societies probably worked to make things better for merchants, and therefore were copied and expanded. In the darkness and chaos of medieval Europe, individuals and groups of individuals learned how to create social structures of trust to fill the void created by the collapse of Rome. Cheating and violence were reduced as a result, allowing more opportunities for human cooperation, and thus the creation of wealth and human flourishing.

---

[20] See, for example, Peter Stabel, Jeroen Puttevils & Jan Dumolyn, "Production, Markets and Socio-economic Structures I: c.1100–c.1320," In: *Medieval Bruges, c. 850–1550,* Andrew Brown & Jan Dumolyn (eds.) (2018).

[21] Ibid. at 91.

[22] Ibid. at 107.

By the thirteenth century, trade guilds for specific industries (e.g. drapery, leather, bakers, and blacksmiths) grew into social organizations of great complexity and value. They were not merely places to meet over a mug of mead. They "combined economic, social, military, and also religious functions."[23] They served as mechanisms of "popular political representation," as a means of voting against princely interests in favor of the more corporatist commune, and as "tools of urban government, delegated with military, political, and legal tasks."[24] There was safety and community through the guild.

The guilds provided protection not only against the violence of outsiders, but also against the cheating of its members and the costs that such cheating imposed on other, non-cheating, members: "[G]uild members participated in the inspection of both production and marketing" of products during the late thirteenth and early fourteenth century.[25] At that time, if one cloth merchant cheated a customer in a transaction, say by providing low-quality products, the reputation of all cloth merchants in Bruges might be reduced. Dyers or traders from Genoa might buy their cloth from Ghent instead. The misbehavior of one might impact all. By creating a guild to represent the interests of all the merchants in a particular line of trade and geographic area, standards of good conduct could be enforced. After all, any individual merchant wouldn't have the incentives to police cheating by competitors – the costs would be born solely by them, but all other merchants would also benefit. This "free rider" problem plagues all attempts for individuals to act in the public interest. A mechanism of collective action is necessary. The guild was just such a mechanism.

The guilds' jurisdiction "extended beyond economic matters," and included means of integrating members into the political life of the time. But they were first and foremost a mechanism of social control.[26] Like governments then and now, to be effective, guilds had to do more to earn their exalted position as intermediaries of trust and human cooperation. They needed to create faith among members and non-members. This could be achieved in part, but not entirely, through good and honest decision-making. They also needed some goodwill – what we might call patriotism. Here is one account of their role in fourteenth-century Flanders, which is generalizable:

> Guilds were not simply economic and political organizations: the corporatist values they promoted encompassed other aspects of urban life. They regulated moral

[23] Ibid. at 95.

[24] Jan Dumolyn, Georges Declercq & Jelle Haemers, "Social Groups, Political Power and Institutions II, c. 1300–c.1500," In: *Medieval Bruges, c. 850–1550*, Andrew Brown & Jan Dumolyn (eds.), 268 (2018).

[25] Peter Stabel, Jeroen Puttevils & Jan Dumolyn, "Production, Markets and Socio-economic Structures I: c.1100–c.1320," In: *Medieval Bruges, c. 850–1550*, Andrew Brown & Jan Dumolyn, 96 (2018).

[26] Jan Dumolyn, Georges Declercq & Jelle Haemers, "Social Groups, Political Power and Institutions II, c. 1300–c.1500," In: *Medieval Bruges, c. 850–1550*, Andrew Brown & Jan Dumolyn (eds.), 278–79 (2018).

behavior according to the guild ethos of brotherly love and they organized charitable activities in ways that helped maintain social order. They promoted festive
social events and ceremonies to reinforce their solidarity... [T]hey established
a religious and architectural presence in the urban landscape.[27]

It is no wonder that guilds also used various imagery, including banners, and that,
when they were under siege from rival trust providers, the flags and uniforms of the
guild were the first target.

The various Flemish guilds operated at the level of a specific trade or industry, and
for a specific geographic region. By the start of the fifteenth century, fifty-four craft
guilds were operating in Bruges.[28] But there was cooperation across guilds to achieve
a broader, more regional impact. For instance, during regional trade fairs – known as
the Champagne fairs – the guilds of Flanders cooperated under the banner of "the
Hanse of the Seventeen Cities" to "coordinate Flemish trade at the fairs."[29] The
Hanse of the Seventeen Cities arose during the period 1180 to 1230 to enable broader
cooperation and to generate trust at a broader level than was achievable through
individual guilds in specific cities.[30] The guilds of Bruges, of Ghent, of Antwerp, and
so on teamed up to create a super-guild to represent a broader set of regional interests
vis-à-vis Italian or Middle Eastern traders. The effect was similar to the creation of
a proto-federalist system of government, with the local guilds akin to state or regional
governments, and the Hanse of the Seventeen Cities akin to the national government for Flanders.

The Champagne fairs were a series of half a dozen, six-week trading events
throughout the year in which buyers and sellers of all sorts of goods came together
in several cities in the Champagne region of northern France to trade. It was
a convenient location, between the cloth-production facilities in the Low
Countries (with raw materials already imported from England and Wales) and
the dyeing and exporting centers in Genoa. There were no national or international laws to create the necessary trust, and no police force or king to enforce the
rules. Instead, the various guilds built their own industry-specific rules and then
more general trading rules that were enforced through private law. While some
security was supplied by local governments – "[l]ocal and regional governments
secured the roads" – the trust necessary for trade was provided by the businesses
themselves.[31] The reason was that the merchants had the expertise and the incentives to be able to create enough trust at the lowest possible cost. The Flemish
Hanse, for instance, excelled at, among other things, "arbitrat[ing] ... conflicts

---

[27] Ibid. at 280.
[28] Ibid. at 281.
[29] Peter Stabel, Jeroen Puttevils & Jan Dumolyn, "Production, Markets and Socio-economic Structures
      I: c.1100–c.1320," In: *Medieval Bruges, c. 850–1550*, Andrew Brown & Jan Dumolyn, 99 (2018).
[30] Ibid. at 113.
[31] Ibid. at 105.

between members," all of whom paid a "high membership fee" to join the mutual trust society.[32]

While a full treatment of the history of the Flemish guilds is beyond the scope of this book, it demonstrates their quasi-governmental character and the dynamics of the market for trust. It is therefore worth briefly considering here for this reason. During the fourteenth century, there was frequent political turmoil in Bruges and throughout Flanders. At one level, everyday merchants, represented through the guilds, battled with dynastic oligarchs of the city, and the city battled with the existential threat of the incursion of French princes and kings. The four textile guilds – weavers, fullers, shearers, and dyers – were often at the head of reform efforts and attempts to assert the importance of self-regulation by resisting centralization of legal authority.[33]

Inevitably perhaps, the self-regulatory approach of the guilds morphed into more formal legal structures. They began to look more and more like formal government. For instance, in 1304, a principle was established that nine of the thirteen aldermen and councilors of Bruges had to be nominated by the guilds.[34] Although it was followed irregularly for many years, by 1360, the "Nine Members" concept was relatively fixed. These included one person to represent the commercial and landed elites, one to represent the textile guilds, one to represent the butchers and fish-mongers, one to represent builders, one to represent metal workers, one to represent leather workers, one to represent clothing workers, one to represent bakers, and one to represent brokers of all kinds.[35] In this way, the guild system began to morph into a governmental one. Self-regulatory bodies took on the role of representation in a larger, more generic rule-making body.[36]

As such, government power began to win in the market for trust creation. This evolution might have been a natural one because of the increased efficiencies that can arise with creating trust at scale. Maybe it was inevitable that self-regulation became government regulation. But perhaps instead the evolution was the result of the fact that certain individuals with political power tried to weaken the guilds by bringing them into a governmental format.

We have never learned which of these was a more important driver of change, because another form of competition in the market for trust resolved the matter in favor of centralized governmental power. A French noble – Philip the Bold of Burgundy – took control of most of the Low Countries through inheritance. On April 26, 1384, he imposed a charter on Bruges (through the threat of violence) that "eradicated the role of the guilds from the body politic . . . strip[ing] them of political

---

[32] Ibid. at 111.

[33] Jan Dumolyn, Georges Declercq & Jelle Haemers, "Social Groups, Political Power and Institutions II, c. 1300–c.1500," In: *Medieval Bruges, c. 850–1550*, Andrew Brown & Jan Dumolyn (eds.), 282 (2018).

[34] Ibid. at 288.

[35] Ibid. at 288–89.

[36] For a discussion of this in a more modern context, see William A. Birdthistle & M. Todd Henderson, "Becoming a Fifth Branch," 99 *Corn. L. Rev.* 1 (2013).

and military power."[37] The guilds were a competitor in the provision of trust and community; the new prince used sovereign violence to favor political power over its rival.

The competition between princely power and the guilds was not fought on honest and open terms, comparing the various pros and cons of various mechanisms of creating trust. Instead, princely government used a pretext. Philip the Bold wanted to get rid of the guilds, since they were a threat to his authority as monarch. The prince argued that the rival guilds were engaged in too much fighting and that this was undermining the security of Bruges. Governmental power, specifically princely power, was needed to stop the guilds from disrupting the peace. He used this as an argument to seize the guilds' banners and other instruments of power.[38] Government power displaced non-government power through a diversion set up to justify the threat of sovereign violence. As discussed in Chapter 8, governments today take a page out of Phillip the Bold's playbook. They are trying to thwart the likes of Uber with arguments about the safety of the public with fantastic anecdotes of passengers harmed, taxi-driver suicides, traffic or pollution increases, or the like. Although some of these may be real harms worth addressing, the point remains that the argument is being made, as it was in Phillip's time, without reference to the real stakes of distorting the market for trust.

Within a decade of Phillip's assertion of governmental power, there was legislation that changed the way aldermen were chosen – after October 26, 1399, alderman could be appointed only by "the princely commissioners of the renewal of the law, usually high ducal officials."[39] One history of Bruges notes that, during the first part of the fifteenth century, "the elites [of Bruges] began to turn against one another," and that this was the direct result of and encouraged by "the machinations of a new and more ambitious prince."[40] There was full-scale war in the market for trust delivery.

The princes did not win outright, at least not at first. In 1411, the guilds overthrew the successor to Philip the Bold, John the Fearless, and the regime he'd put in place in Bruges.[41] The guilds won back much of their political and economic authority. This too, however, was a brief and incomplete victory. During the fifteenth century, "ducal power was in the ascendant."[42] Undoubtedly this was related to a maturing of governmental institutions, which made them more attractive as mechanisms of trust delivery, but also to changes in technology that made information and people flow much more cheaply and to the development of new, more powerful weaponry that gave sovereigns the ability to project power further. Over the decades, the princes

---

[37] Jan Dumolyn, Georges Declercq & Jelle Haemers, "Social Groups, Political Power and Institutions II, c. 1300–c.1500," In: *Medieval Bruges, c. 850–1550*, Andrew Brown & Jan Dumolyn (eds.), 295 (2018).

[38] Ibid. at 295.

[39] Ibid. at 296.

[40] Ibid.

[41] Ibid. at 297.

[42] Ibid. at 298.

"gradually reinforce[ed] the power of the central institutions [they] created in Flanders."[43] This included building up courts – the judicial court of the Council of Flanders and the Chambre des Comptes – that "tighten[ed] [their] grip over urban justice."[44] The battle for the provision of trust was on.

Over the next several decades, the princes and the guilds locked horns repeatedly. In 1437, a revolt restored guild power: "The ideal of the commune, as a wider community of all burghers and guilds, had triumphed again."[45] But, according to one historical account, the "[t]riumph was fleeting."[46] Philip the Good imposed an economic blockade – in effect, he used the threat of violence to favor governmental power (him) over guild power in the market for trust. A "harsh repression" of the guilds followed his victory, and "[d]ucal authority, and its state apparatus," were largely victorious.[47] "The 'Burgundian state' was gradually reinforcing the power of the central institutions it had created in Flanders," such as various official courts.[48] Centralized law won over decentralized law.

The governmental provision of trust never won full control in Bruges, Flanders, or anywhere else for that matter. Pockets of other types of trust provision thrived in corners here and there. But, after the dukes brought the guilds to heel in Bruges and Ghent and across the Low Countries, the era of government, seemingly lost with the sack of Rome, was back. Here is how one group of historians of the period described it:

> The guilds would never completely lose their social and political power, but from then on, and throughout the sixteenth century, they were to be cowed by a political system that was elitist and oligarchic, ruled by local merchants, jurists, and nobles who were usually more unconditional in their loyalty to the Habsburg rules of Flanders than their predecessors had been.[49]

For the next several hundred years, government in Flanders and throughout Europe, the United States, and elsewhere was the primary provider of trust.

There are modern analogs, because even today government cannot always create the optimal conditions for trust between merchants or between merchants and customers. Legal scholar Lisa Bernstein has studied legal arrangements among traders in certain industries, finding that the creation of shadow governments to handle disputes and create bespoke law more efficiently creates trust. Here, she writes about the diamond industry:

> [D]iamond industry disputes are resolved not through the courts and by the application of legal rules announced and enforced by the state. The diamond industry has systematically rejected state-created law. In its place, the sophisticated

---

[43] Ibid.
[44] Ibid.
[45] Ibid. at 305.
[46] Ibid.
[47] Ibid.
[48] Ibid. at 298.
[49] Ibid. at 309.

traders who dominate the industry have developed an elaborate, internal set of rules, complete with distinctive institutions and sanctions, to handle disputes among industry members.[50]

The example of diamond merchants is replicated in many industries. We will consider one of these examples – the private regulation of stockbrokers and other Wall Street professionals – in Chapter 7.

It is important to note here an important point about the use of private regulation and what we've called the market for trust. As imperfect as private regulation may be in particular cases, it is vital that it be compared not with an ideal form of regulation, but with the next best alternative. For instance, consider the accreditation system of higher education in the United States. Although accreditation bodies – private, non-governmental actors – have been criticized as ineffectual or wasteful in some instances, those suggesting that we should do away with accreditation must consider that the likely alternative is not no regulation but rather government regulation of higher education. In other words, the existence of regulation most likely represents a demand for regulation – based on a need for trust – that must be satisfied by someone. What's more, private regulation may be superior. For instance, government regulation of higher education might be less tolerant of certain types of education, such as religious-based education, especially when political winds blow a certain direction. As in all cases discussed in this book, the choice is most likely between types of regulators, not between regulated and unregulated.

The logic of such regulation in many cases is straightforward: misbehavior has negative impacts not just on the people who misbehave, but also on others. This can happen directly and indirectly. Today, it is more likely to be an indirect harm arising in cases or industries where brand affiliation is low. If one is cheated at McDonalds, the obvious choice is to go to Burger King instead. But, if your stockbroker cheats you, you might distrust all brokers. In such cases, if a merchant cheats, all affiliated merchants may suffer a little because customers will be worried about being cheated. In some industries, there may be negative spillovers from cheating – customers might doubt all used-car salesmen or all mead merchants if they get cheated by one.

In the past, and in some instances today, the mechanism might be direct. In medieval times, foreign merchants were often subjected to collective punishment. For instance, during this period, Flemish merchants operating in England were responsible for the debts of other Flemish merchants.[51] "English creditors could seize the goods of any Flemish merchant to recover their losses on a transaction with

[50] Lisa Bernstein, "Opting out of the Legal System: Extralegal Contractual Relations in the Diamond Industry," 21 *J. Legal Stud.* 115 (1992).
[51] A. Grief, "Impersonal Exchange and the Origin of Markets: From the Community Responsibility System to Individual Legal Responsibility in Pre-Modern Europe," In: *Communities and Markets in Economic Development*, M. Aoki & Y. Hayami (eds.) (2001).

another Flemish merchant who had defaulted."[52] This rule probably arose as a means for encouraging self-regulation, given the limits on information and enforceability of law at the time. Neither the creditor nor the king might be able to figure out who the cheater was and, if they did, the cheater might have skipped town never to return. Without a mechanism to create the necessary amount of trust, there would be severe disruptions in trade, as creditors seized the property of unoffending merchants more or less at random. The solution was some sort of collective self-regulation to offset the collective liability. In this case, the creation of a guild with high membership fees to keep out the riffraff and to act as a bond against non-performance.[53]

More generally, everyone may benefit from higher standards imposed by punishing the cheaters. In this way, non-cheating merchants can credibly make promises to their customers. But there is a collective-action problem inherent in any attempt at disciplining cheaters. No individual merchant has incentives (or the power!) to regulate another merchant, since they do not receive all of the benefits of the discipline. Say it costs one merchant $10 to punish a cheater, and each of 100 merchants would gain $1 as a result. Clearly it makes sense for the group to punish the merchant (a gain of $90), but no individual merchant would spend $10 to gain $1. If the merchants could team up, they would engage in the discipline, but the costs of bargaining and coordinated action make this difficult.

Government is a typical solution to collective-action problems in this and other areas of regulation, but government cannot efficiently achieve this at all times. Today, in the diamond industry, it cannot. But in earlier times, the guild was a common solution at the initial stage of international commerce. The guild was the most efficient mechanism of collective action under the circumstances of medieval Europe.

But, the guild was not a silver bullet. There are no silver bullets or enduring solutions in the history of trust. Guilds were imperfect, maybe even perverse at times or in places. In a pioneering work on the subject, Sheilagh Ogilvie wields considerable evidence that guilds were often self-serving:

> [M]y own reading of the evidence is that a common theme underlies guilds' activities: guilds tended to do what is best for guild members. In some cases, what guilds did brought certain benefits for the broader public. But overall, the actions guilds took mainly had the effect of protecting and enriching their members at the expense of consumers and non-members; reducing threats from innovators, competitors, and audacious upstarts; and generating sufficient rents to pay off the political elites that enforced guilds' privileges and might otherwise have interfered with them.[54]

[52] Peter Stabel, Jeroen Puttevils & Jan Dumolyn, "Production, Markets and Socio-economic Structures I: c.1100–c.1320," In: *Medieval Bruges, c. 850–1550*, Andrew Brown & Jan Dumolyn, 112 (2018).

[53] Ibid.

[54] Sheilagh Ogilvie, *European Guilds: An Economic Analysis* (2019).

This is not surprising. The stockbrokers' guild we consider in Chapter 7 – known as the National Association of Securities Dealers (NASD) and New York Stock Exchange, and now FINRA – served the interests of its members in socially sub-optimal ways repeatedly over its two-century history. But even New Dealers knew how important it was as an instrument of regulation. The problem with any guild, like with any government, is that it is an intermediary that is subject to what economists call "agency costs." If the guild or the government is an agent of the people in the task of creating trust or enhancing human welfare, there is a substantial risk that it will serve its own interests rather than that of its principal. This is, as we argue later, a problem that we believe is going to be reduced by recent trust innovations. But, it is important to judge the guilds, of then or now, not by what would be the first-best optimal solution to the trust-creation process, but rather by what was the best available mechanism at the time, net of all the costs.

Of course, as times and conditions changed, and the demands of the marketplace morphed, new forms of trust creation were needed. The cost of guilds in general or for particular functions outweighed their benefits, especially relative to the costs and benefits of alternative forms of trust creation. One of the most significant in human history – the corporation – was the next trust technology that humans invented, and it largely, although not entirely, replaced the guild.

The Corporate Entity

A similar motivation and context to what made guilds effective and necessary in trust creation led to the creation of the first corporations. Corporations themselves are fundamentally a trust innovation. Corporations were initially created as separate legal entities that could act as a mechanism for enhancing the reputation (and thus trust) of the collective.

In England, two early companies that exemplified the legal provision of trust were the Company of Merchants of the Staple (royal charter in 1319) and the Company of Merchant Adventurers (royal charter in 1505). These "companies" were established to consolidate the various exporters of wool and cloth (respectively) from England to the European continent. The idea behind these "corporations" was to achieve economies of scale and to increase regulatory control over English tradesmen operating on the Continent. As noted earlier in the discussion of the Hanse of the Seventeen Cities, a form of collective action was needed to represent the interests of the group.

The various English traders brought under the new companies were based primarily in Antwerp, far beyond the reach of the English monarch. They could not be protected by the English monarch and they could not be easily disciplined by Flemish authorities either.

The merchants operated independently, but they were not fully independent – they could impose costs on each other. This might have been as a result of local rules about collective liability, such as the English law that made all Flemish merchants responsible for the debts of any Flemish merchant. Or it might have been more informal – cheating by one merchant might impose costs on other merchants because of lack of differentiation. The companies in question sought to provide a mechanism of collective action to overcome these dual problems. Their function was governmental – the policing of merchants through a sort of proto-self-regulatory apparatus to protect the merchants from others and from themselves.

For instance, the twenty-four directors of the Company of Merchant Adventurers did not dictate the strategy of the various English tradesman operating in the export business; instead, they promulgated rules and sat in judgment of their alleged misbehavior.[55] They were not business corporations as we think of them today, but rather government-sponsored trade associations. FINRA, the private regulator of stockbrokers, is a better analogy to these early firms than Google or General Motors.[56] We discuss FINRA in Chapter 7.

This approach to early corporate governance happened in parallel in continental Europe. In the sixteenth century, several of the provinces of the Netherlands were engaged in trade with the East Indies. In 1602, these provincial trading companies were consolidated under the single umbrella of the Dutch East India Company (Verenigde Oostindische Compagnie or VOC). The VOC was a cartel. Like all cartels, it was established to limit competition and set prices, as well as to better police misbehaving traders. After all, one province treating its partners in the East badly might have an impact on all Dutch traders, even the ones that had not done anything wrong. Economists call these "negative spillovers," and reducing them is a core function of government. It is also a core function of "corporations."

Traders in the East Indies were able to have greater trust in the VOC than in individual, provincial trading firms because of the governmental role played by the VOC as an institution. Dutch traders could also trust that other Dutch traders' behavior did not harm them. The corporation called the VOC created both internal (among Dutch traders) and external trust (between Dutch and East Indian traders). At this time in history, the VOC was more effective than the Dutch government could have been. The company was invented in part to enable more efficient trust than the alternatives.

Today, our system of corporate governance, built over decades by courts, legislatures, and private associations acting in loose concert, delegates enormous regulatory oversight to corporate boards in much the same way. While in the old days it was about the ability of government to extend its reach, this is not the reason for delegation of regulatory authority today – no one doubts the ability of the government to exert control over corporations if it wanted to. Instead, the use of boards to play this role is based on ideas about efficiency – who can provide a given level of

---

[55] Ibid. at 125.
[56] For a brief history of FINRA, see William A. Birdthistle & M. Todd Henderson, "Becoming a Fifth Branch," 99 *Corn. L. Rev.* 1 (2013).

regulatory oversight and compliance at the lowest social cost – and perhaps some concerns about the proper extent of government power.

Although this "monitoring" model of the board predates the work of Melvin Eisenberg in the 1970s, it was his scholarship that formalized our modern understanding of the monitoring board.[57] Eisenberg noted that the statutory obligation of boards was to manage, but observed that in practical terms – in the real world – boards were passive. He therefore proposed that the principal function of boards was to select and monitor the company's CEO.[58]

The American Law Institute (ALI), which drafts model rules for various legal fields, embraced Eisenberg's monitoring model. The ALI's "Principles of Corporate Governance, Tentative Draft No. 1" required that a majority of the board of publicly traded companies be made up of independent directors. The goal was to put in place a robust monitor or overseer of management. As noted earlier, the idea behind this move was to identify the most efficient regulator of managerial conduct in the first instance. If boards could be deployed, or rather redeployed, to monitor CEOs and other managers, this would save the government having to do as much monitoring work. Not only would this mean a smaller government role, it would also arguably mean a more efficient regulatory approach.

The trade-offs are fairly clear in the choice between either corporate boards or the government as the primary regulator of corporate conduct. Board members would have more business expertise than government regulators. They would also have more information about the business at lower cost. Finally, being inside the firm, investigations and regulation of activities by board members would probably result in less push back and defensive crouch by managers, compared with the same work being done by the government. On the other hand, boards might be expected to be less vigilant than government monitors, given their personal and monetary affiliations with the firm.

This trade-off might net out in favor of boards as the primary mechanism of social control, especially since government regulators stand ready in the event of board failures. In this sense, monitoring boards are a form of self-regulatory organization (SRO), in that they face the same trade-offs as SROs for entire industries. As in the case of SROs, the situation could be improved if board members could be imbued with public mindedness that would reduce some of the potential risks of incentives and capture or group affiliation that might cause board members to turn a blind eye to unlawfulness or excessive risk taking. The cases establishing relatively strict fiduciary duties for directors and the push for independent directors can be seen in this light. Directors being tasked with a monitoring/regulatory role cannot be

[57] See, for example, Melvin Aron Eisenberg, *The Structure of the Corporation* 139–41 (1976).
[58] Douglas G. Baird & Robert K. Rasmussen, "The Prime Directive," 75 *U. Cin. L. Rev.* 921,937 (2007) (arguing that scholarly emphasis on executive compensation is misplaced, and that the board's primary duty is to pick the right CEO, rather than to worry about her compensation).

inside directors, since in that case the above-mentioned costs would swamp the benefits.

But this transition in the role of the corporate board is not an unalloyed good. If directors become monitors that are effectively serving a government function, then they necessarily lose the ability to play other roles for the company. In analyzing the net effects of this role for boards, one must ask the same question we have asked throughout this book: When it comes to trust – the board here serving as a mechanism of ensuring shareholders can trust the executives to make good decisions – who is the most efficient provider?

In answering this question, it is important to focus on both of the quasi-regulatory roles played by boards. A corporate board may act as an agent of government, policing executives' behavior to ensure they comply with broad social norms and rules. But, more fundamentally, the board acts as a regulator of executives on behalf of shareholders. Good governance can create trust among shareholders, especially minority shareholders. Knowing they are less likely to be ripped off or abused by executives, minority shareholders will invest on terms that more closely resemble the fundamental value of the company. (If they think they might be taken advantage of, shareholders will discount the value of shares accordingly.) The protection of the minority in this way lowers the cost of capital for firms, and thus permits them to engage in more projects and engage in less socially wasteful spending. The result is greater economic growth and opportunity for everyone.

Of course, government is essential here too. Governments provide courts in which minority shareholders can bring claims of abuse, and this then lends important credibility to promises of majority shareholders and executives that they will not abuse the minority. Government could, however, do much more. We could displace the board, substituting it with government monitoring instead. Government agents could audit executive decisions, bringing civil or criminal lawsuits with large penalties in the event that minority shareholders are oppressed. How this would work in practice and whether it would be superior to the current board-based system are open questions. The key point for our purposes is merely to recognize that these options exist, and that the appropriate question to consider is which of these would be the most efficient regulator or provider of trust.

Law, Generally

Over time, law in general became more sophisticated, providing increased certainty through written codes, formalization, and professionalization of the bar and courts. But all of these legal tools were different means to the same end – expanding the number of people who could engage in various transactions at low costs because they could trust that the transactions would be mutually beneficial.

We sometimes think of law as a mechanism of social control, but in this telling, it is instead (or in addition) a mechanism of trust creation and contracting facilitation. Law is about making cooperation less costly. Making law better in this sense means providing trust at the lowest cost possible, including decision costs and error costs. Contract law, property law, tort law, criminal law, and so on are all trust-delivery tools. They each enable us to trust in our fellow man and the promises they make, both implicitly and explicitly. Each of these areas of law, and their more sophisticated cousins, such as financial regulation, are needed only to the extent that they provide the requisite level of trust better than alternative mechanisms. For example, in a society in which trust is perfect, say because of familial bonds, there is no need for most contract law. There will still be contracts, of course, but the legal apparatus needed to support these contracts will be unnecessary.

But this is just the start of the ways in which law enables trust. The rich body of contract law built up over the centuries provides assurance that bargains that are struck will be carried out to their terms. Specialization requires cooperation – Henry Ford merely assembled the Model T; the Dodge brothers, Horace and John, supplied all the parts, except the seats and the tires. Without the ability to enforce contractual promises, businesses would have to be fully integrated, making every-thing from the rubber for the tires to the integrated circuits that power modern control systems. Although private remedies could be available, and are used to supplement law today, the fact that the sheriff is willing to use violence to enforce contractual terms in ways that contracting parties find acceptable enables trust to be delivered at very low costs. We cooperate. This makes us richer and better off than we would be if we did not.

We could go on and on. But for our present purposes, let us give just one more example of the way in which law builds trust. Another ancient body of law, the law of accidents or torts, creates incentives (through a system of rules and damages) for each of us to take the efficient level of precautions as we move through the world. If we drive recklessly and cause an accident, the law provides a remedy for the victim. The person who suffers personal or property damage can sue in court and, if they prove the accident was not their fault and that the accident caused the damage, they can recover the costs from the other driver. In theory, this remedy-after-harm approach makes the victim whole again and, by penalizing the wrongdoer, creates incentives for drivers to take care.

But lawsuits are expensive and uncertain, and sometimes juries or courts make mistakes. Plus, some victims cannot be made whole. It is cold comfort for someone killed by a reckless driver to have monetary compensation paid to their heirs. Moreover, some wrongdoers cannot pay, because they can't be located or don't have the money. Lawyers call this the "judgment-proofness" problem. This means that less than optimal deterrence may be provided by this type of law, and therefore levels of trust (on the roads) may be too low.

Law thus provides other means of creating the necessary trust. The government requires drivers to have a license as a means of ensuring minimum quality. It regulates cars too, requiring features (such as seatbelts and airbags) that reduce the expected damages from accidents. Mandatory insurance is another form of government regulation designed to create trust. And so are the roving packs of government agents in squad cars that pull over and punish speeders or other scofflaws. All of this regulation – from drivers' tests and the highway patrol to courts and product liability law – is designed to create trust in other drivers. Without it, we would not drive casually down the highway at high speed just feet away from other drivers.

But this trust comes at a very high cost. There are the administrative costs of staffing and running the highway patrol and of the testing and monitoring of apparatus for drivers. In addition, the police may exceed their mandate of trust creation, engaging in racial profiling for ulterior motives. The recent cases of murder committed by police during traffic stops are just the tip of this particular iceberg. These are the very unfortunate collateral costs of this trust-creation mechanism. Finally, there are the dollars spent on evasion by drivers, such as radar detectors and the like. These are examples of social waste necessitated by an inefficient trust mechanism.

Of course, all of these costs of creating trust are unnecessary in a world where intelligent machines do the driving for us. If artificial intelligence can control vehicles with dramatically lower risk, then we do not need the DMV, drivers'-education classes, the law on traffic accidents, or the highway patrol. Someday, we may all get into vehicles and trust, without law doing a fraction of what it has to do today. Technology will displace not just the way we drive but the social technology governing the way we drive. The police and others with an interest in the status quo won't go away without a fight, however, since they enjoy not just the gains from their jobs but also the fringe benefits of power granted to them by the importance of their trust creation.

As we consider next, changes in thinking and technology, coupled with changes in social technology, brought humanity out of this period, and the human tribe continued to grow. By the first quarter of the nineteenth century, London had reached a population of nearly 1.5 million people. During the period of the industrial epoch, human society grew as never before. Tokyo today has more than 30 million members of its tribe, and this understates the true scope of the human tribe. The massive growth in the size of the human tribe and the complexity of the work they were doing and the transactions among them necessitated new forms of trust creation.

* * *

For millennia, humans existed in hunter-gatherer tribes of less than one hundred people. The invention of agriculture and the domestication of animals offered a massive potential for increases in human wellbeing, but it required cooperation at scales impossible for clan-based tribes to achieve. Humans invented law (among other things) as a means of achieving this cooperation. Law, like language and writing, was a social technology that was an essential ingredient in the leap in human progress that came with the rise of agriculture. Without this social technology, the other technological advancements that followed would not have been able to unlock human potential.

The agricultural period lasted for thousands of years. There were innumerable advancements along the way, but the next big leap in human society did not come until the invention of powerful machines, such as the steam engine. These technological achievements created new possibilities for human advancement, but they were not enough. Humans needed a way to trust these new-fangled machines, to trust the strangers who would make them and operate them, and to trust the people all around the world who they now had the potential to cooperate with. It is to the industrial period that we now turn.

INDUSTRIAL PERIOD

The Industrial Revolution of the eighteenth and nineteenth centuries transformed the human tribe, just as the rise of agriculture had done thousands of years earlier. Over two hundred years, the agrarian and rural societies of Europe and the United States became industrial and urban. Although well into the twentieth century, most humans worked as farmers – in the United States, as late as the 1940s, nearly half of the workforce were in farming – the impact of the move to industrialization remade human society. Today, less than 2 percent of US citizens work on farms or ranches. There are about as many lawyers and accountants as there are farmers.

The Industrial Revolution dramatically expanded and improved the human tribe. There were huge increases in population. The population of Europe increased fourfold to nearly half a billion people during the two centuries of the Industrial Revolution. Just as the shift from hunter-gatherer economies to agrarian ones created infrastructure that supported increased density, industrialism dramatically increased the number of people that could cluster into the city unit.

Trade across countries also expanded tremendously. The Standard Oil Company, as an example, had a larger business outside the United States in the 1870s than it did inside the United States, exporting kerosene to Europe, China, and throughout the world. Human welfare also increased. According to the economist Robert Lucas, "for the first time in history, the living standards of the masses of ordinary people [began] to undergo sustained growth."[59] While there were undoubtedly large transition costs, social unrest, and various social failings during the transition from farm to factory, the net effect was eventually a society that was wealthier, lived longer, and worked much less than its predecessors.

Government was not prepared for the social transformation of widespread industrialization. The laws that worked for a localized, rural, agrarian society – basic

---

[59]   Robert E. Lucas, Jr., *Lectures on Economic Growth* (2004).

criminal law, enforcement of contracts, clear property rights – were not enough. In the agrarian era, most people lived in villages where their families had always lived. Thus, non-legal tools did a lot of work to regulate behavior. Reputation was a powerful deterrent to misbehavior. But when farmers left the fields for the factory, moving into cities where everyone was a stranger, this changed. The social norms of small communities encouraged prosocial behavior without the need for as much law or regulation. When these communities broke down, the social norms broke down with them. In the relatively anonymous world of the city, one's reputation was more resistant to damage. There were simply too many people to keep track of on any city block, let alone within the few miles of home or work. In addition, the number of people meant that any reputational losses could be reset by leaving one community within the city and moving to another. Strangers living together need to rely on people they don't know. This increases their options, but it also means that opportunities to cheat expand, as personal networks break down. This change alone necessitated a huge increase in law.

The machines, chemicals, and processes of industrialization also exposed workers and customers to dangers unimaginable to their immediate ancestors. As railroads and canals enabled goods to be shipped across long distances, people no longer relied on themselves or the local farm to provide their food. People in cities did not grow their own food. They had to rely instead on distant strangers. And, as the population soared because of the efficiency of industrialization, so too did the volume of food that needed to be produced. As humans learned how to mass produce everything, the working conditions and products brought new risks, and demand for trust grew rapidly. A new trust technology would soon rise to meet it.

The Regulatory State

In his 1906 novel *The Jungle*, Upton Sinclair told a story that provided the impetus for the regulatory state. Sinclair based the tale of Jurgis Rudkus, an immigrant working in the Chicago meatpacking industry, on months of investigation. The detailed descriptions of the unsanitary conditions shocked US readers. Meat purchases fell. Sinclair wanted to expose oppressive working conditions – what he called wage slavery – but the big takeaway for readers was disgust at industrial food production. As Sinclair said, he "aimed at the public's heart, and by accident hit it in the stomach."[60]

Other muckrakers, such as Samuel Hopkins Adams, wrote about the fraud involved in the production and distribution of medicines and other consumer products. Congress moved to action. Multiple pieces of significant legislation followed quickly, including new regulatory powers, such as the Meat Inspection

[60] Upton Sinclair, "What Life Means to Me," *Cosmopolitan*, October 1906.

Act and the Pure Food and Drug Act. This was the birth of the regulatory state. But it was only the beginning.

The Progressive Era of the early twentieth century expanded government regulation to increase US citizens' trust in what they were putting in their bodies, where they were working, and what they were paying for things. People could no longer trust that they would be fairly treated by the local store, their boss, or the people they traded with. The store owner was not a friend of the family, their boss was not a parent or uncle, and the typical exchange was with a stranger.

The problem was not just at a small scale involving only individuals, it also plagued business to business transactions as well. Businesses need to trust that they are being treated fairly, just as individuals do. If they cannot trust those they deal with, they will engage in wasteful expenditures to protect themselves or will suffer losses when cheated. Economists call these dead-weight costs – meaning social expenditures that could be avoided without sacrificing the quality or quantity of output by a business. After Ida Tarbell wrote scathingly about the Standard Oil Company's side deals with and control of railroads, which were a source of contention and distrust among businesses, Congress created the Interstate Commerce Commission to regulate the roads and anti-trust laws to break up monopolies. The goal was to increase trust, and thus decrease the costs of doing business, and therefore to increase the amount of human cooperation.

The new economic order of the Industrial Revolution created dislocations and interrupted the fabric of trust, and government saw an opportunity to use legislative and regulatory action to restore the eroding confidence in business.

Over the next few decades, the government grew tremendously. In 1900, government expenditures were about 5 percent of the size of the economy (measured in GDP terms). Excluding war time, government doubled in relative terms over the next three decades, rising to nearly 10 percent of the economy by 1930. The election of Franklin Roosevelt transformed the role of government in the lives of US citizens. The gradual rise of the government in the first three decades of the twentieth century was replaced by an immediate transformation of the state. Within just a few years, the government went from consuming 10 percent to nearly 17 percent of the economy. After World War II, the government returned to a new equilibrium – nearly 22 percent. Since then, the state has grown consistently, regardless of the party in power in Washington, DC, and the several states. Today, government spending in the United States is over 40 percent of economic output – more than an eight-fold increase over the past hundred years.

While President Franklin Roosevelt's New Deal established the government as the world's largest insurance company, it also expanded the role of government in the regulation of economic and other formerly private activities. The New Deal brought us the first big burst of so-called alphabet agencies – the SEC to regulate stocks and bonds, the Federal Deposit Insurance Corporation (FDIC) to regulate banks, the National Labor Relations Board (NLRB) to regulate workers, and so on. This era marked the creation of a new branch of US government not found in the Constitution – the administrative branch – which took its place alongside the executive, legislative, and judicial branches the Founders gave us.

The idea was straightforward: modern life had grown too complex, too dangerous, and too opaque for the old ways of regulation to work, and thus a new approach was needed. Put another way, the old trust infrastructure was insufficient to handle the burden of the new industrial economy, and a new infrastructure was needed to ensure the requisite levels of trust in society. The approach involved creating new agencies of government, staffed with experts in particular areas, that would issue detailed regulations based on broad goals set by Congress. Law professor Cass Sunstein called this the "second rights revolution," the first being that of the Founding. In his book *After the Rights Revolution*, Sunstein articulates a robust defense of the commitment by the national government, which started in the Progressive Era, accelerated in the 1930s, and culminated in the 1970s (with the creation of the Occupational Safety and Health Administration [OSHA], the Environmental Protection Agency [EPA], the FCC, the Federal Election Commission [FEC], the Consumer Product Safety Commission [CPSC], and more), with the promotion of safe and useful products, a clean environment, healthy working conditions, and so on.[61] We needed to "change remedies" to get the results we wanted and Roosevelt, as seen in Figure 15, had many options for us.

Critics of the Progressive Era, the New Deal, and the Nixon regulations of the 1970s view these extensions of government as unnecessary and worse. Richard Epstein, a classical liberal law professor at the University of Chicago and NYU law schools, is perhaps the most prolific and articulate critic. In a series of books and articles, Epstein piled scorn on the New Deal's command-and-control approach to the economy and regulation, calling instead for a return to the simple principles of government of the prior era, namely a limited role for government in policing against force and fraud, while defining property rights clearly so as to permit voluntary exchange. Sunstein and Epstein, both former teachers of ours, were fundamentally arguing about the best way to create the requisite amount of societal trust.

Each view has its merits. On Sunstein's side, there appeared to be a massive trust gap created by a new economic reality that the old trust systems seemed unable to solve. Government was the fastest and easiest way to fill it. At the turn of the twentieth century, it was difficult for consumers to know what or who they could trust. Information costs were high. Old reputations, linked as they were to micro-locations, were no longer sufficient, and new ones were not yet established. For instance, there were not yet national brands that customers could use to make choices about which products to buy. Legal remedies lagged, having been designed

---

[61] Cass R. Sunstein, *After the Rights Revolution* (1993).

FIGURE 15: Editorial cartoon from the New Deal era[62]

for the old world of risks, not the new one. Information about products was costly to obtain. There were no consumer advocacy groups, no *Consumer Reports*, no five-star rating system on Amazon or eBay. In their place, government stepped in. It had the brand, economies of scale, and a monopoly on legal violence – it had the ability to enforce its will with the idea of helping out those who could not help themselves given the state of the world.

On Epstein's side, there were practical and theoretical objections. There was no doubt that things were changing, but businesses, courts, and other institutions were moving in to fill the gap. Meat was already being inspected in 1906 by multiple local, state, federal, and corporate inspectors.[63] There were private,

---

[62] Drawing by Clifford Kennedy Berryman that was probably published in *The Washington Star* in 1934. Credit: Granger Historical Picture Archive/Alamy Stock Photo.

[63] Gary D. Libecap, "The Rise of the Chicago Packers and the Origins of Meat Inspection and Antitrust," 30 *Econ. Inquiry* 242 (1992).

market-driven attempts to improve food safety, to inform consumers, and to improve quality levels and trust. When government stepped in instead, it risked crowding out these alternative solutions, which may have been more efficient – that is, less costly for the trust provided. There is always the possibility that a large and powerful actor, with a monopoly on violence, would fill a void prematurely and less efficiently than its competitors in the market for trust. The concern is that, in response to a crisis of sorts, government would create a cumbersome and imperfect mechanism for the provision of trust. The twentieth-century history of failed or abused government interventions provides significant support for this view, leading Epstein and others to criticize government intervention in the first place.

However, whether you believe that the regulatory state was an imperfect but necessary response to a changing world or a premature and misguided usurpation of private rights in the face of uncertainty, it is clear that we are undergoing another such shift. We do not seek to answer the question of whether or not the regulatory state was the optimal trust provider – it is clear that it was the dominant one in the twentieth century. We argue later, however, that it will cease to be the dominant one in the twenty-first century and beyond. It will continue to have its place (and an important one at that), but just like the social technologies that preceded it, it will settle into its natural niche while new technologies rise to prominence. Just as the Hanseatic League diminished in importance and the Holy Roman Empire's primacy waned, we believe government will come to focus on the areas where it has a competitive advantage.

In a recent piece, Richard Epstein calls for the New Deal era to come to a close. He writes: "It is time for the New Deal, which has championed cartels and massive, unsustainable wealth transfers in the name of the public good, to be brought to its long-overdue end."[64] Here we find we are in agreement with Epstein. It is becoming clear that government is no longer the most efficient supplier of trust across a range of areas, and that these areas are growing over time, both by growing into new territory and cannibalizing old domains. We will return to this later.

But the spirit of our critique about government today can be seen by looking at the other great trust innovation of the industrial era: the corporate brand.

Corporate Brands

The idea of brand is not new. The word derives from "brandr," the Old Norse word for "fire" or "burn," as in the burn mark put into the hides of animals to signify ownership. The idea of marking a product with a burn mark seems to have originated in the early nineteenth century, as the first wave of global trade sent products

---

[64] Richard A. Epstein, "The New New Deal," *Hoover Digest*, January 25, 2013, available at: www .hoover.org/research/new-new-deal

all around the world. Producers sought to differentiate their products from those of their competitors, in terms of both ownership and quality assurance.

The idea is simple. If you believe you have a superior product, which would command a higher price or greater demand, you need to be able to provide a way in which users of your product can distinguish it from your competitors' products. If they cannot, they will not pay the price of the superior product, paying instead a blended average of the superior and inferior product. Customer loyalty is not just a way of one company winning in the market – it is a means of raising the overall quality of goods and services. By enabling companies to distinguish themselves, good companies can thrive and bad ones can fall by the wayside. Overall quality rises over time.

But the idea of product differentiation is even more ancient than the growth of brand in the nineteenth century. In 1266, King Henry III (1207–1272) required bakers to use distinctive marks to distinguish their bread from other bakers. There were probably many reasons for this, but trust was unquestionably one of them – through this differentiation, bakers' reputations could be established and bakers could be brought more easily under control. Regulating bakers was easier if the government could tell one from another. If a person became sick or was disappointed or cheated, the recourse was easier. Of course, some of the work of "regulating" the bakers would be from the king's men, but other "regulating" would be done by customers. There is less need for government regulation if customers are making smart and informed choices.

Many long-standing brands exist in Europe, such as the Löwenbräu lion, which has been in continuous use since 1383. Once brand became an important regulatory tool for customers and for governments, there were attempts to undermine it. After all, a brand that distinguishes a quality company or product makes that company or product more valuable than alternatives. This value can be expropriated by an inferior product that is able to cause confusion in the minds of customers as to whether they are buying the superior or the inferior product. Consider the case of a widget that costs $5 to produce and for which the seller charges $10. If a knock-off can be made for $2 but can be sold for the same $10, because it has misappropriated the brand, the cheat can earn greater profits. The trust in brands, which was important for creating trust in the first place, can be eroded.

Government stepped in to solve this problem – to restore trust in the market. To make the market work efficiently. Trademark law establishes rules, enforcement mechanisms, and penalties for this kind of cheating. Although private market solutions to this problem are possible, the government may be uniquely positioned to provide a low-cost regime to create trust in investments in brands. The knock-on effects are large in terms of creating trust in the marketplace and, ironically, reducing the size and scope of government, which is necessary to create trust in other ways.

Formal trademarks, recognized under law, are a creature of the 1870s, both in the United States and England. Congress passed the first trademark act in 1870,[65] and the UK passed the Trade Marks Registration Act in 1875. The global boom in trade during this period made the trademark system an integral element of the trust infrastructure. The nineteenth century saw the "death of distance," as inland transportation costs fell over 90 percent between 1800 and 1900.[66] All of a sudden, products could be shipped to consumers everywhere from anywhere, from strangers to strangers, all over the globe.

But it was the opening of the Suez Canal in 1869 that catapulted global trade. In the following thirty years, shipping costs fell 60 percent, and exports expanded at nearly double the pace of global GDP growth.[67] By 1870, world exports were about 5 percent of global GDP.[68] They rose to nearly 10 percent on the eve of World War I, but then did not reach that level again until the 1960s. By the turn of the twenty-first century, exports were nearly 20 percent of global GDP.

Companies such as Standard Oil (incorporated in 1870) did more international business than domestic business in short order. As the importance of distance died, the importance of brand differentiation increased, because government regulation became more difficult. While in the old days, everyone bought products from the local merchant, now dangerous items such as kerosene were shipped around the world and the people buying Standard kerosene in China knew nothing of the producer, shipper, or retailer, and would have little legal recourse if things went wrong.

This was the origin of the modern brand and it served as an alternative trust mechanism to government. In fact, when Rockefeller named his company in 1870, he chose the name "Standard" to express to his customers that his kerosene was free of impurities, in contrast with rival producers. This term was prescient, as much of the value of brand in general is in offering uniformity, predictability, and standardization.

Brand remained important as a trust mechanism, both globally and domestically, during the next several decades, but the economic depressions of the late nineteenth century and the wars of the early twentieth century resulted in a drop in global trade and economic output more generally. It wasn't until after World War II that the power of brand as an alternative to government regulation was fully realized.

From 1950 to 1970, global trade doubled. In the United States especially, this period saw the emergence of global corporate brands: Dunkin' Donuts (1950),

---

[65] The Supreme Court held the 1870 statute unconstitutional in the *Trade-Mark Cases*. Congress passed a replacement statute eleven years later, citing different constitutional authority. The statute was revised in 1905 and then was ultimately replaced in 1946 by the Lanham Act.

[66] Nils-Gustav Lundgren, "Bulk trade and maritime transport costs: The evolution of global markets," 22 *Resources Policy* 5 (1996).

[67] Angus Maddison, *Development Centre Studies: The World Economy: A Millennial Perspective* (2001).

[68] World Trade Organization, "World Trade Report 2013," 2013, available at: www.wto.org/english/res_e/booksp_e/wtr13-2b_e.pdf

Holiday Inn (1952), Denny's (1953), H&R Block (1955), McDonalds (1956), and Pizza Hut (1958).

These global brands had a profound impact on government. Brands signaled quality. They created trust. If one could trust that a room in a Holiday Inn would be of a certain quality because it was in a Holiday Inn, this decreased the need for additional government regulation that would have been necessary otherwise. Corporate brands, such as McDonalds, offered trust to consumers – one can trust that a Big Mac is a Big Mac, whether it is in Boston or Biloxi (and, ultimately, in Bucharest or Bangalore). The rise of brands, starting significantly in post-War USA, offered an alternative at the margin that prevented the need for additional government regulation.

Brand as a form of reputational trust creation is a substitute for government regulation. In the absence of brands, we would have less trust in the people who sell us things, since the reputational bond provided by the brand would be doing less work. Every time a corporation with a brand sells us something, it is betting its brand on the transaction. There will be mistakes – brands are not perfect defenses. Bad products and service still exist. But the power of brand is that it offers incentives for better performance on the margin. For example, if you purchased a computer from an individual on Craigslist, you would be less likely to believe in its quality if it did not bear the logo of a reliable brand, such as Apple or Dell. This same logic applies when buying directly from producers of products.

And yet people would still demand businesses to sell them things. What would substitute for brand? The answer is the old trust technologies employed by merchants (as opposed to producers of goods): warranties or money-back guarantees.

But, as noted earlier, these promises might not be easily enforced or might simply be second-level scams. Warranties are just promises and fraud is much easier with a promise than a product. In addition, for some harms, the judgment-proofness problem might be too large to prevent the transaction from happening. Going after a small merchant might not provide relief to a wronged customer. Government regulation, in the form of lawsuits (after a harm has occurred) or prescreening/ licensing (before a harm has occurred), might be necessary. In short, the government would have to be much larger and more powerful in a world without brand and other private trust provision. Accordingly, we can think of brand as a provider of trust that prevents the need for all sorts of other government regulation.

Consider McDonalds. It built a reputation (through investments in standardization and billions spent in advertising) that permitted trust at levels that in the past would have required government intervention. One could trust in a McDonalds experience across the United States in the 1960s, not because the government stood behind it, but because "McDonalds" and its golden arch logo did. Yet we can also imagine how new government regulations – such as inspections, insurance requirements, certifications, tweaked tort rules, and so on – could have had the same effect, namely could have created the requisite levels of trust necessary for individuals to eat hamburgers from roadside restaurants anywhere in the nation or world.

Local governments could have tried to create local trust. But how would consumers driving from New York to Florida have known whether to trust the government of Richmond or Charlotte or countless small towns along the way to provide efficient restaurant regulation that they could trust? State governments could act, and surely they did. But as with local governments, they enjoyed a monopoly over restaurant regulation, and thus might be captured by the regulated entities. After all, a restaurant that served mostly non-local customers would be very unlikely to face lawsuits or reduced traffic from bad food, and might therefore find buying off politicians cheaper than complying with strict regulations. The federal government could solve these problems to some extent, given its size and scope and control over all territory along the way. But there are problems here too. Remote in Washington, DC, and with many other issues to address, regulations may be slow to arise, clunky, ill-fitting to local conditions, and so on. The size of the federal bureaucracy needed to enforce restaurant quality across the vast continent of the United States would be enormous. And, as noted earlier, the slack created by the multitude of issues and the tribalness of parties would allow politicians to take advantage of it to line their own pockets. This isn't to say that government regulation of burger joints is crazy or unwarranted, but that it might not be the most effective method.

McDonalds provided most of this trust through the bond created by its advertising and through its own supply-chain regulation. McDonalds invested tremendously in guaranteeing a minimum level of quality and predictability into products bearing its logo and was compensated for this by consumers' willingness to eat there or pay a premium where they saw the logo.

Brand, in this way, became a guidepost for quality, a new type of proxy for information about a given product that a consumer could obtain without having to rely on government, reputation, personal experience, or the like. To be sure, the government also plays an important supporting role here, providing courts, legal causes of action, some inspections, and so on, and these have expanded as the private provision of trust has expanded. The point is merely that they have expanded less than they would have without the private supply of trust. The government we have today is smaller than the government we would have without brand. Every advertisement you see on television is an investment in less government.

Viewed in this way, warranties offered by businesses are also a substitute for government regulation. Both inspire trust and therefore enable transactions that would otherwise not occur. These warranties can take many forms. Explicit warranties may be noted on a product. L.L.Bean, for example, famously permits any product to be returned at any time for any reason.[69] Customers can therefore trust that they will be satisfied, since they have a money-back guarantee. Customers of outdoor apparel in North Korea or the old Soviet Union, by contrast, had to rely on

---

[69] For a humorous account of the ways people will use (or abuse) such policies, see this bit from the radio show, *This American Life*: www.thisamericanlife.org/radio-archives/episode/591/transcript

government violence alone to ensure that producers of outdoor wear and camping supplies provided quality products. If you didn't like your parka or tent or rain boots made by Factory #4 in Irkutsk, you could complain to the boys in the Kremlin, but that probably wouldn't have been a good idea. Better to take your lumps. Which explains why consumer goods were not exactly abundant or functional in the Soviet Union.

Another way to guarantee something is through an implicit warranty. Implicit warranties arise through reputational sanctions. Word of mouth has put many companies out of business, and thus creates incentives for the supply of valuable goods and services. The more powerful reputation is, the less need there is for either explicit warranties or government intervention, whether it is before the fact (e.g. inspections or licenses or certifications) or after the fact (e.g. litigation over defective products). The power of reputation is, in turn, determined by the costs of creating it. In a small village, reputation is easy to earn or lose, and therefore may be sufficient to create the incentive for good behavior. Reputation is therefore a pretty clumsy way of creating trust.

* * *

The machines invented during the industrial period created the potential for cooperation at a scale unimaginable to our ancestors of the agricultural period. Distance died (for the first but not the last time), as trade became globalized. Workers evolved from craftspeople to cogs in assembly lines. Cities grew enormously, meaning the average person was more likely to deal with total strangers on a daily basis than with their kin. The inventions and activities of the age also created new risks – both to life and to the environment.

As in the agricultural period, social technologies were an essential element of the progress humanity achieved during the industrial period. The growth of more sophisticated law and of corporate brands enabled humans to cooperate efficiently at unprecedented scales.

While in the late nineteenth century, reputation might not have been sufficient to obviate the need for aggressive law, the story we tell in this book about the rise of information technology may be enough to change that calculation. As we explore in the following section, in a world in which reputation can be produced and transmitted at low costs, the United States may come to resemble relatively closed communities such as the Lakota Sioux more and more.

INFORMATION PERIOD

Distance has died many deaths. It did when ships left Europe and China in medieval times, when Columbus and Magellan and other explorers opened new worlds to international trade, when steamships starting traversing the Atlantic, when railroads and canals started to crisscross England and the United States, when global shipping prices dropped dramatically after the US Civil War, and during the surge in global trade following the World Wars.

The response in each instance was innovation in and adaptation of our trust infrastructure. Real technology – be it a ship or a train or a canal or the telegraph – made the human community larger, and we needed a way to project trust across this larger distance. Sometimes it was done with government, sometimes it was done with business, and most often it was done with a mix of both. But it never involved large-scale expansions of personal trust. The rise of the information society, the emerging era we are on the leading edge of, is the first time in human history that personal trust is becoming scalable.

Since readers are probably familiar with the way in which computer technology and the internet have killed distance yet again, this time perhaps for good, it is not worth spilling much ink to make this point. But it is worth capturing some facts that demonstrate the way in which this process is transforming our world.

What we call the "internet" today had its origins in the development of computers in the 1950s and packet networking research by the United States, Britain, and France in the 1960s. But networking did not take off until the 1980s, when projects at US universities (funded in large part by the US Department of Defense and National Science Foundation) and at CERN in Switzerland developed hyperlinked documents accessible from any network node. The "World Wide Web" took off slowly. In 1993, only about 1 percent of telecommunications information was transmitted on the internet. But the growth curve was steep from there. By 2000, the amount rose to more than 50 percent, and within the decade it was approaching 99 percent.[70]

With smartphone penetration now at nearly 3 billion users, projected to be about 6 billion by 2020, the ability to access information and connect with other individuals is staggering. While our grandparents marveled at the transition from horses to cars to airplanes, the wonder of our time is the transition from shelves of encyclopedias to Wikipedia, from friendships to Facebook. When we were kids, if we wanted to know whether to see a movie, we asked our friends on the playground; today, every kid knows about Rotten Tomatoes's fresh rating or the significance of three versus five stars on iTunes. Likewise, if we wanted to know whether to buy a Sony or a Philips television, we might have found an issue of *Consumer Reports* at the library; by contrast, CNet or Amazon rankings are now a click away. Would you trust an acquaintance who said to buy that or eat there or stay at this resort or that one? Or would you immediately google it, relying on consumer ratings, be they on TripAdvisor, Amazon, Yelp, or countless other sites?

---

[70] Martin Hilbert & Priscila López, "The World's Technological Capacity to Store, Communicate, and Compute Information," 332(6025) *Science* 60–65 (2011).

The move from personal friendships to Facebook is, during this time of transition, viewed by many as a social retrogression. Articles decrying the move from person-to-person friendships to a more diffuse set of social media friends or touchpoints abound. Just google "Facebook destroys friendship," and you will see hundreds of relevant articles, such as the 2009 *Wall Street Journal* article entitled "How Facebook Ruins Friendships,"[71] or the piece from the *Daily Mail* in the UK entitled "Is Facebook RUINING your friendships?"[72] In the *Daily Mail* piece, Sara Cox answers the question in the affirmative, comparing going online to being on illegal drugs.

One common reason cited for this conclusion is the cognitive limit on social connections. Robin Dunbar has hypothesized that personal human interactions are limited to less than about 150 people. This is called the "Dunbar number." Here is how it is described in a recent paper: "Community sizes [in utopian communities of the nineteenth century] of 50, 150 and 500 are disproportionately more common than other sizes; they also have greater longevity. These values mirror the natural layerings in hunter-gatherer societies and contemporary personal networks."[73]

There is, it seems, a natural limit on the ability of humans without social technology to create cooperative groups. This is apparently true of primitive tribes, utopian communities in our modern society, and among our personal networks today. It is perhaps for this reason that many businesses find that expanding beyond this size requires more bureaucracy and process to maintain order. It was probably also the case that, as human tribes grew, from groups of 50 to the primitive cities of 500 by 8000 BC, the need for law kicked in around the Dunbar number. Various social technologies, such as courts, contract law, criminal punishments, bureaucracy, and a host of intrafirm organizational structures arose to allow cooperation among many thousands or millions of humans across space and time.

With Facebook, however, the average person has about 350 friends, or more than twice the natural cognitive limit for the typical human. If we take seriously the Dunbar number, this presents a problem. Perhaps Facebook and other social media tools are spreading us too thin, and preventing us or distracting us from forming deep and meaningful relations with other humans. Or, at least, this is the claim.

But the 350 number surely underestimates the typical social network of the member of the modern digital tribe. Facebook is just one application. The average person most likely uses many more, such as Instagram, Snapchat, Twitter, and so on. But these too are only the tip of the iceberg. As noted earlier, when we use Yelp,

---

[71]   Elizabeth Bernstein, "How Facebook Ruins Friendships," *The Wall Street Journal*, August 25, 2009, available at: www.wsj.com/articles/SB10001424052970204660604574370450465849142

[72]   Lucy Waterlow, "Is Facebook RUINING your friendships?" Mail Online, February 15, 2016, available at: www.dailymail.co.uk/femail/article-3444196/Is-Facebook-RUINING-friendships-Sara-Cox-investigates-social-media-really-affects-relationships-finds-going-online-addictive-Class-drugs.html #ixzz4i7QgZUNY

[73]   Robin Dunbar & Richard Sosis, "Optimising Human Community Sizes," 39 *Evol. Hum. Behav.* 106–11 (2017).

TripAdvisor, Rotten Tomatoes, eBay, or Amazon, or any other online platform, we are taking bits of friendship (or at least reaping some of the rewards typically associated with friendship) from each of the reviewers or commenters or participants who enrich the platform. We may come to rely on some of these people more than others but, by and large, these platforms permit us to consume "friendship" in tiny bits from thousands or even millions of people in ways that would have been impossible just a decade ago. Our social network is quickly becoming the population of the Earth, or whatever subparts of it we decide to participate in.

Strangers are now our "friends," or, at least, they provide us with many of the things we used to rely on our friends to provide. The result may be a more efficient state of affairs. Time and emotional connections are scarce, just as everything else is. Let's say you have thirty hours to spend cultivating friendships per month. If you need to have friends you can rely on to drive you to the airport, recommend things to you, and provide other types of support, you might have to allocate these hours across dozens of friends. But, if you don't need a friend to drive you to the airport anymore – Uber will do it instead – you can invest in fewer friendships but more deeply.

Internet platforms make personal trust scalable. As shown in Figure 16, each basic type of trust – personal, business, and government – exists in both a small and a large (or, at-scale) version. The basic version of government is what we call the "rule of law," namely a basic government provides courts, enforces rules that clearly define property rights, and tries to limit the use of force and fraud. When technology and returns to violence made scaling government possible, we got the modern regulatory state, with its centralized, expert-based mix of ex ante and ex post regulation. Similarly, the early trust provided by business took the form of the local guild. At scale, business provided trust across the globe based on brands and the discipline of supply chain management.

Personal trust was inherently limited since the dawn of mankind because we had not developed a technology that enabled humans to shatter the glass ceiling of cognitive functioning expressed in Dunbar's number. Until now.

	Small	Scaled
Personal	Tribe	Digital tribe
Business	Guild	Brand
Government	Rule of law	Regulatory state

FIGURE 16: Trust types by scale

Today, we are connected as never before and are able to access an amount of data that would have been unimaginable even a few years ago. According to data compiled by Northeastern University, in 2013, the world had approximately 4.4 zettabytes of data stored on the internet. (One zettabyte is a trillion gigabytes.) And humans are adding about 2.5 billion gigabytes per day to this total. That is the equivalent of 250,000 Libraries of Congress being added to our collective data every day! At this rate, humans will have access to over 44 zettabytes of data by 2020. For a sense of scale, way back in 2013, IBM estimated that 90 percent of the data in existence had been produced in the preceding two years. Even if most of this information is junk, the possibilities for technologies to be able to mine it for value to increase human flourishing are amazing to imagine.

Not only is the concept of scalable personal trust a mechanism for having the best of both worlds – a decentralized, human-to-human network at large scale – but there is no upper bound on the potential for the amount of interpersonal trust that can be created. The more nodes that are added to a network of information about a particular subject or transaction, the more information that that system generates. The population of the planet provides the only natural limit on the scale of the digital tribe.[74] In contrast, business and government forms of trust creation are naturally limited as they grow in size and the amount at stake increases. Size begets the need for delegation to agents; delegation to agents gives rise to agency costs (the costs of controlling agents, the costs of agents signaling their allegiance, and the inevitable wedge between what the principal wants and what the agent delivers); agency costs beget the need for technologies, such as bureaucratic rules to limit agency costs; and bureaucracies beget attempts to override them or manipulate them, such as in the case of lobbyists or others trying to capture governmental bureaucracies. These forces are not necessarily present or even needed for the creation of interpersonal trust, when created through an internet-based platform or otherwise.

The declining relative importance of geography for cooperation has aided the rise of post-national trust technologies. Digital platforms allow us to trust in a way more like our hunter-gatherer ancestors, in large part because of technologically enabled abundance. Unlike our agrarian and industrial ancestors, who were anchored to a particular place because their farm or factory stored all of their economic value there, modern humans can roam freely, much like our hunter-gatherer ancestors. And modern humans can flee, not because there are no factories to protect, but rather because the modern analogue to the factory is intellectual property stored in the cloud and accessible everywhere. Put another way, you can steal my smartphone, but you haven't stolen the real economic value, which resides in cloud-stored intellectual property. You could confiscate the servers, but because computing

---

[74] Artificial intelligence is a potential way to raise this limit without having to increase the number of human inputs.

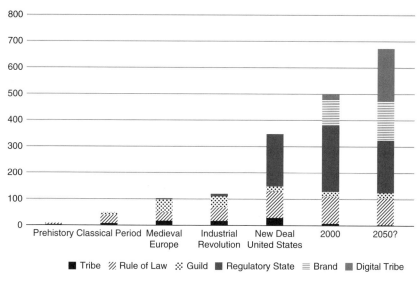

FIGURE 17: The growth and composition of human trust

power is increasingly fungible and plentiful, it wouldn't be hard to move digital assets to safety. As assets are increasingly digitized, the threat of physical confiscation is less devastating. This reduces the returns to violence, and thus the power that the state can wield.

SUMMARY

The story of trust suppliers that we've told in this chapter, while not perfectly linear, is one of continuing growth and change. When you go on a business trip, you trust a cab driver, a pilot, an airline, a hotelier, thousands of architects and contractors, at least one nation state, and many others. We place vastly more trust in countless more people than our tribal ancestors, who regularly interacted with fewer than a hundred people. The supply of trust has increased dramatically. We provide a rough projection of the sort of shift we have described in Figure 17. Note that this is meant to be illustrative rather than an accurate or authoritative depiction of the dislocations on the supply side of the trust market.

To chart the growth and change in trust provision over time, in Figure 17, we divide history into seven crude buckets – prehistory, the classical period, medieval Europe, the Industrial Revolution, New Deal USA, the year 2000, and a few decades into the future. We divide our three types of trust into its small- and large-scale versions: (1) tribe and its scaled version, the digital tribe, (2) rule of law and its scaled version, the regulatory state, and (3) guild and its scaled version, brand. The amount of total human trust in each period is shown by the height of the columns, and the composition of each period is roughly estimated by the size of the bars that make up the columns.

In the prehistory period, there existed familial or tribal trust, as well as some primitive law, such as those later codified in the Code of Hammurabi or the Ten Commandments. The rule of law became more important and more well developed during Roman times, as the Empire spread to cover the entire Mediterranean and the complexity of life increased tremendously. This period also saw the rise of guilds and other private regulation of behavior for the first time by businesses.

According to Plutarch, Numa Pompilius (the second king of Rome) invented the idea of a corporate entity that would be distinct from the persons themselves.[75] In Plutarch's account, Numa's goal was to reduce the power of two rival factions – the Romans and the Sabines – by further dividing them into groups of tradesmen of all kinds. Whatever its origins,[76] the idea of corporate separateness was used initially by towns, but then quickly thereafter by priests, artisans, temples, and ultimately the state writ large.[77]

Nevertheless, there was another device that permitted the isolation of liability in a way that is reminiscent of our modern concept of limited liability. A Roman citizen could grant a slave or family member power over some amount of capital or property. This interest was known as a *peculium*, and it was separate from the assets of the citizen that established it.[78] The assets remained the property of the founder of the *peculium*, and it could be revoked at any time. But the person running the business or deploying the assets could make decisions as if they were their own. Importantly, a creditor of the *peculium* could institute an action – an *action de peculio* – against its founder/owner for an amount up to that invested in the enterprise.[79] In other words, individuals could achieve certain business interests through agents and limit the extent of their liability to the investment in the business.

There were other Roman precedents for the concept of limited liability. The Roman sea loan, *nauticum fenus*, was designed to attract capital for risky voyages. The party supplying the capital was liable only for losses at sea and received a fixed return on the capital investment rather than a share of profits.[80] In both cases, limitations on liability arose not from the identity or status of the parties, but rather from an instrumental view

[75] William Blackstone, 1 *Commentaries on the Laws of England* 468 (1765).

[76] But, of course, others claim the idea was of Greek origin or, according to Sir Henry Maine, originated from primitive societies. Angell and Ames argue that the Romans borrowed the idea from the Greeks (see Joseph K. Angell & Samuel Ames, *Treatise on the law of private corporations* 35 (1st edn) (1861)). Maine argues that primitive societies thought of groups, such as families or tribes, as "legally" distinct from their constituent parts (see Henry Maine, *Ancient Law* 183 (4th edn) (1906)).

[77] Friedrich Carl von Savigny, 2 *System des Heutigen Römischen Rechts* 86 (1840).

[78] See Reinhard Zimmerman, *The Law of Obligations: Roman Foundations of the Civilian Tradition* (1996).

[79] M. Kaser, *Das romische Privatrecht* (2nd edn) 606 (1971).

[80] See John H. Pryor, "The Origins of the Commenda Contract," 52 *Speculum* 5, 7 (1977).

about the linkage between liability and control. When capital providers are in control, they can take affirmative steps to reduce their liability, but when they are not, either because they are too diffuse or because the actions take place too remotely, they cannot do so efficiently. And, in any event, the concept of corporate personhood and of limited liability was justified on grounds that private interests could more properly and efficiently regulate behavior than government could.

The later period of medieval Europe saw a rise in the level of trust, as trade expanded even further and covered more goods. Life was more complex in Renaissance Italy and the Low Countries of Imperial Spain than it had been for centuries, and the rise of guilds and the Law Merchant provided much of the trust that made it function.

Trust grew steadily again as industrialization swept across the UK, the United States, and eventually continental Europe. The regulatory state emerged here and there toward the end of the nineteenth century, especially in Bismarck Germany and in the United States, but by and large the era of canals and railroads and the first big boom in international trade was regulated by the basic aspects of government and by increasingly powerful guilds and cartels.

Then, as seen in Figure 17, the regulatory state arising out of the New Deal and the several decades that followed dramatically increased its share of trust supply. Regulation of food, consumer products, the environment, workplaces, and so on transformed the United States and eventually the global marketplace, supplanting other trust providers in these domains and creating whole new domains of regulation. Financial regulation became an international affair with the Bretton Woods Agreement, and global institutions, such as the United Nations, the World Bank, and the International Monetary Fund, all enabled an exponential increase in the size of the human tribe.

By the turn of the twenty-first century, the mix changed again. Corporate brands – Apple, Nike, Starbucks, Mercedes-Benz, Coca-Cola, and countless others – had assumed a significant role in regulating our world. The regulatory state had expanded too, although less than it would have otherwise had to in order to enable the amount of human cooperation that was possible, as brand did some of the work. At this time, the internet also entered the scene, enabling human cooperation and trust to enter a new realm.

The last column of the figure, our crude prediction for 2050, shows a growth in brand and a slight reduction in the regulatory state as a result of what we call the "digital tribe" becoming a more prominent mechanism of trust creation. Although (for the reasons that we consider in the next chapter) we expect most government regulation to persist, there will be areas in which we expect the digital tribe to be able to unring the bell, so to speak, and reduce the scope of government regulation. But, by and large, we expect the emergence of the digital tribe to have the primary effect of adding to the total global trust level, enabling human cooperation at an unprecedented level.

   All of this points to the fact that there are a variety of different providers of trust, each with its own attributes. Trust is, in effect, a product like any other for which there is demand and supply. Individuals demand trust so that they can engage in mutually beneficial exchanges, and other individuals form institutions or create tools to enable the delivery of trust. In the next chapter, we will look more closely at this market. An appreciation of who supplies trust and how they interact in the market for trust is essential to understanding how trust is likely to evolve. But, perhaps most importantly, this appreciation is essential for understanding how the incumbent providers of trust are likely to respond to and resist the trust disrupters who threaten them but hold great promise for the rest of us.

6

The Market for Trust

Trust is valuable. We need it to make our lives better. Therefore, trust is something that humans demand. We don't really care who provides the trust, so long as there is no breakdown in trust. When you walk down a dark street at night, it doesn't matter whether the security guards are public or private, so long as you can trust that you will not be robbed, or worse. The Chicago Police Department patrols the streets where we live, but so do private police officers of the University of Chicago Police Department, as well as neighbors. All of them make us feel safe to stroll the streets of our Hyde Park neighborhood. (Of course, they aren't perfect, and crimes do happen. But no system of trust is perfect, and when comparing them, we must not fall prey to the Nirvana fallacy. Humans cannot achieve Nirvana, so we must choose between second-best solutions based on trade-offs. When it comes to social policy, there are no solutions, only trade-offs.)

It isn't just where we live. Consider walking the streets of Main Street, USA, in Walt Disney World. The police of Kissimmee, Florida, are nowhere to be seen; instead your safety is supplied by the Walt Disney Company. If the Mouse Police are as equally skilled, trained, and equipped as the Kissimmee Police Department, who is paying them or setting their rules shouldn't matter. What matters is that you can trust. In fact, many people may be more inclined to trust Disney in this regard than the local police department.

The choice of trust providers is also evident when you buy goods and services. Disney stands behind its merchandise with warranties. The courts of Florida are also available if you are cheated at the Main Street Emporium. But Disney and Florida aren't the only trust suppliers. American Express stands behind purchases made using its credit card. In addition, Disney employees are subject to discipline when they cheat. They are disciplined by law, by their employer, by their fellow employees, and by their social network. All of these people, institutions, and companies contribute to the trust necessary to buy a stuffed mouse doll or grab lunch in Cinderella's Castle.

Whether for safety or in business transactions, we want a trust supplier that will deliver the amount of trust we need at the lowest possible cost. Often, this is an amalgam of trust providers, but there may be a dominant one. If American Express didn't guarantee against fraud and if, for some reason, Walt Disney World's reputation was immune from tarnish, if customers were cheated, humans would demand that courts or other governmental approaches (such as licensing or other ex ante regulation) get involved to enable voluntary transactions.

We do not care whether the performance or a promise is guaranteed with a private bond (such as a warranty) or by the prospect of suing in court, assuming the costs and outcomes would be the same. What matters is the probability of being compensated in the event that we are harmed. If the probability of private relief is equal to or greater than the probability of public relief, then we should prefer private relief. And, vice versa.

Say you are cheated in a commercial transaction. You pay $100 for an item and it turns out to be defective. What are your options? The retailer might give you a refund. Or, your credit card company might not charge you. The government can act too, either before the transaction (by setting quality standards) or after, by giving you a place and rules to make your case in court, backed by the threat of violence (by the sheriff) to make the seller pay.

Imagine that you have an 80 percent chance of obtaining private relief (in the form of a return or refund through a warranty) and you will get $100 back if you are successful. That is worth $80 in expectation, and serves as a type of insurance. If this is as good as you can get in the market by choosing among different suppliers, the transaction risk might be worth it and the transaction will happen. If the chance that the product will be defective is very small, then an 80 percent chance of getting a full refund if it is defective might be good enough to make you trust enough to do the deal.

Public relief is an alternative. You might be able to sue and get your money back, although lawsuits are expensive and, at least in the United States, each side usually has to pay for their own lawyers. Small claims courts offer some relief on the expense and delay of litigation, but only for small claims, and even these do not operate with a paragon of efficiency.

Another type of public relief is possible – ex ante regulation in the form of product quality standards coupled with government fines against defective products serve to incentivize producers to make high-quality products. But it is difficult to measure the cost of ex ante regulation – standards set by government regulators – in part because they are spread across all taxpayers. There is also the issue of cross-subsidies. All taxpayers pay for this type of insurance on every product, but only consumers of a particular product are using it. The same issues arise with courts. And lawyers cost money, making the sue-in-court option particularly unattractive. In the absence of ways of aggregating claims, even a multi-thousand-dollar loss might not be worth pursuing. And even when claims are aggregated, as in the class action system created by Federal Rule of Civil Procedure 23, the result in most of those cases is lots of money for the lawyers and pennies for millions of class members.

Returning to the above-given example, if the probability of public relief in either case or in a combined case is 70 percent, and you will get $100 back (ignoring lawyer fees), this is worth $70 in expectation. Compared with the $80 in expected value in the event of a defect from the private option, this is inferior. If an individual consumer had the option to choose, they'd take the private warranty over the public option. In this hypothetical, the private option is more efficient and should always be preferred.

But, of course, one cannot easily (if at all) opt out of the public system, even if it is inferior. We all pay for courts, even if we don't use them. We all pay for regulation, even if we don't need it. And, it follows that, when these systems are abused by selfish lawyers or power-hungry regulators, we are all made worse off.

The same logic applies to private warranties to some extent – if you never break things or return them when they do break, you pay for a warranty for those who do. But private markets admit more options. Some products can be bought without a warranty, although the government may persist in offering you one – an "implied" warranty – even if you'd rather not pay for it. Competition in private regulation and law would provide more optionality and tailoring to meet the demand for regulation, if only legal mandates by government would get out of the way.

Of course, our numbers in the previous example were made up. We can easily make the opposite case – one that favors government regulation over private alternatives. Imagine that the dispute is about a lot more than $100. A defective product risks your life. Even if the seller promised some relief, the seller might be unable or unwilling to pay. Limited liability means that, even if you sued the company and won, your recovery would be limited to the assets in the company, and this may not be enough. The money may also be of little comfort to your family and, of course, you'd rather not be dead.

How can you trust in a case like this? You might rely on the company to purchase insurance in the private market or on a regulator such as the government to conduct inspections or threaten criminal liability in the event of wrongdoing. In the latter case, government might be the more efficient provider of trust.

We can thus see that there is not a single provider or type of provider of trust, but rather there is a market for trust in which many types of entities offer many different mechanisms for creating trust. Trust is supplied in many ways, some of which are inherent and some of which are explicit. When we say that there is a market for trust, we do not mean to suggest that trust is provided only by third parties or that it has published prices, as in the market for cantaloupes or computers. As previously discussed, we trust in part because we are humans, and humans have learned that trusting is (mostly) a good thing.

So, in all transactions, we bring a reservoir of goodwill that enables trust to be achieved at relatively low cost. Our concept of a market for trust is thus focused mostly on the margin, that line between not enough trust and just enough to enable a transaction to happen. There is competition among trust suppliers to provide that marginal or sufficient amount of trust to enable a particular deal to be done.

In this way, the marginal amount of trust is a product like anything else: individuals demand it and producers of trust supply it in competition with each other. Unlike most other products, which can be self-produced, trust is something that only external parties can provide (at least when the parties do not know each other personally). One person can trust another on faith, but unless the other person to the transaction, or some neutral third party, is willing to in some way certify or guarantee the performance, that faith is likely to be shaken on occasion. Blind trust is usually foolish, so providers of trust began providing verification techniques that make all participants in a transaction better off. This valuable service has enriched (and in turn expanded) the universe of suppliers.

We trust each other more today in part because we can easily understand one another, because there are paper or digital records, because we can communicate cheaply around the world, and because the courts and police stand ready to enforce our system of rules. Human society has seen an exponential growth in the amount of overall trust over the past century as these technologies have been adopted and spread. The result has been an enormous growth in wealth and wellbeing: worldwide GDP per capita has increased nearly 7,000 times in the past four centuries.[1] In more recent times, the increase in trust among people in China – trust in the fact that they could freely trade and interact with each other – which was brought on in part by the move away from Maoism toward capitalism, has brought over 600 million people out of poverty.

Although religion, language, and other ancient forms of trust provision still exist and do important work – just as the family, churches, temples, and mosques, and other associations do – there are two primary suppliers of trust today that make the global economy possible: government and businesses of various kinds. They have not supplanted other trust mechanisms entirely, but they do most of the work today. For the bulk of today's economic activity, traditional forms of trust have been marginalized by the government and businesses.

THE RECIPROCITY GAME AND THE IMPORTANCE OF INTERMEDIARIES

What qualities of the market for trust makes intermediaries so important? The problem is that person-to-person trust is extremely costly to produce and difficult to maintain. As noted previously, non-kin-based trust arises only with large amounts of information sharing. This investment in trust is not scalable at a personal level,

---

[1] Angus Maddison, *Contours of the World Economy, 1–2030 AD: Essays in Macro-Economic History* (2007).

meaning reservoirs of trust take a long time to fill. They are also potentially leaky, given the possibility that those you trust may take advantage of you.

Economists developed a simple "reciprocity" game for illustrating these points. The setup is as follows. The game involves two people who are completely anonymous to each other and do not interact in person, instead interacting only online. The game lasts one round, after which the players will not play again. Their identities will never be revealed. The game takes place in two steps. In the first step of the game, Player 1 has to send some money to Player 2, say between $0 and $100. Player 2 then receives the money. In the second step of the game, Player 2 decides to send back some product of a given value, also between $0 and $100.

If the game is played by coldly calculating actors and they believe the rules of the game are as described, economists predict a strange result: nothing will happen. After all, if Player 1 sends some non-zero amount in step 1, say $50, then Player 2 can respond by sending over nothing (a product valued at $0). Player 2 ends up with a net of $50, while Player 1 ends up with nothing despite sending $50. Knowing this, Player 1 will send over nothing, since the player knows they will be cheated, and Player 2 will send over nothing in return. In other words, in a world in which Player 1 cannot trust Player 2, mutually beneficial transactions will not take place.

There are three ways in which sufficient trust can be established to permit gains from trade. The first way that trust can be established is through evolved human nature. Humans may have some mix of inborn traits (such as altruism or fairness) that work to create sufficient amounts of trust for the transaction outlined above or similar transactions to take place. If people are inherently "fair" in their dealings, then if someone sends you $50, you will send them back a product worth $50, even if you didn't "have to" and wouldn't "get caught" if you didn't. For instance, maybe you'd feel guilty – you couldn't live with yourself if you didn't – and this cost might be enough to get you to act. This purely internal cost might outweigh the benefits of cheating.

The source of inherent fairness might be biological and linked to species survival. We may all be pre-programmed to cooperate (at some minimum level) because cooperating is a way of getting things done, and getting things done enables humans to thrive. Our biological baseline might then be to trust more than other species, and this is an advantage we have.

Some laboratory experiments with college students purport to demonstrate this result.[2] When playing the reciprocity game, college students act "fairly" – that is, those acting as Player 1 send over a non-zero amount of money and those acting as Player 2 send back goods of equal value. This is a desirable outcome and, if true, says a great deal about the uniqueness of humans. Of course, if it were true writ large and outside the laboratory, then we would not need much law. After all, what use are

[2]   For an overview, see Ernst Fehr & Klaus M. Schmidt, "The Economics of Fairness, Reciprocity and Altruism – Experimental Evidence and New Theories," In: *Handbook of the Economics of Giving, Altruism and Reciprocity*, Serge-Christophe Kolm & Jean Mercier Ythier (eds.) (2006).

courts to enforce contracts in a world in which no one breaches a contract, and what use are police where no one steals?

But these results have been criticized in field experiments that presented real-world tests of the inherent-trust model. Consistent with the traditional economic theory, in non-laboratory settings, altruism or inherent trust is insufficient to create enough trust to enable even relatively low-stakes transactions. In one such experiment, the economist John List found that what the deal testers would get from baseball card dealers at card shows depended on the likelihood that the dealer could get away with cheating.[3] This comports with most people's intuitions about the world – in commercial transactions, if the other party can cheat at very little or no cost, they are very likely to do so.

It is surprising that such rebuttals are necessary. The failure of every society that has been predicated on inherent fairness is a testament to the fallacy that inherent fairness is enough to make society function at a high level. The Marxist ideal – "from each according to his ability, to each according to his needs" – is a prominent example of such an approach, and it has never worked in practice. In fact, relying on it, and the central planning and coercion necessary to enforce it, led to hundreds of millions of premature deaths from violence and starvation. Every communist society has failed, despite their high ideals.

There is no doubt we have large levels of inherent trust – and thank goodness we do – but we need more to create the level of trust required for society to thrive.

A second way that trust can be established is through the use of legal sanctions. Consider the reciprocity game again. If Player 1 knows that if she sends over $50 and receives nothing in return she can sue in court (or assert some other form of dispute resolution) and receive her money back, then she is more likely to do so than in the absence of such a guarantee. But, for the reasons discussed earlier, law is a costly means of enforcing bargains to create this trust. Lawyers are expensive and courts are slow. This reduces the value of voluntary transactions for everyone, but especially for poorer people, who may be unable to afford the time and expense of a court fight. Juries make mistakes and may be biased. Again, this has an impact on everyone, creating a kind of tax on every transaction, but it may disproportionately affect individuals who do not look or act like a random selection of six or twelve citizens.

A third way trust can be established is through non-legal means. If the reciprocity game is played in multiple rounds, participants can earn a reputation for fair dealing. If Player 2 cheats in the first round, then Player 1 will be able to retaliate in the second round by not engaging in a transaction. Knowing this, Player 2 is more likely to play fair in the first round, and Player 1 is therefore more likely to trust Player 2 in the first round. Economists who study game theory describe the retaliation

[3] John A. List & David Lucking-Reiley, "Demand Reduction in a Multiunit Auctions: Evidence from a Sportscard Field Experiment," 90 *Am. Econ. Rev.* 961 (2000).

strategy as "tit for tat," and conclude that it can lead to more cooperation than in single-round games.

But every multi-round game has a final round in which cheating becomes valuable – perhaps even more valuable once a reputation for fair dealing has been established. (After all, a player who earns a reputation for fairness might be able to defraud Player 1 in a way that would be unlikely in a single-round game.) Other non-governmental approaches are available to address this problem. As noted earlier, Player 2 could post a bond that would be payable to Player 1 in the event of cheating. Third parties might also be available to provide certification. *Consumer Reports*, the Good Housekeeping Seal, and the Better Business Bureau are good examples of non-governmental entities providing certifications that stand in for government regulation.

The basic point is clear: more trust equates to more value creation. In a reciprocity game with 10 groups of players and $100 each, a no-trust "society" equates to everyone leaving empty handed, and an optimal trust model leads to $1,000 being apportioned throughout the group.

* * *

So far in this chapter, we have seen the ways in which trust can be conceptualized as a "product" that is demanded and supplied in a market for trust. We have also examined the theoretical framework for the supply of trust by third parties deploying various social technologies. In the next section, we consider the ways in which the market for trust is similar to and different from markets that we are more familiar with. As it turns out, the market for trust is much more fragile than other markets, since it is one of the few markets in which one supplier (the government) is also a regulator in the market. This conflict of interest can be a significant impediment to the advancement of human wellbeing.

MARKET DYNAMICS

We have described why there is a need for intermediaries to provide trust and how various types of trust providers work together and compete with each other to provide the marginal amount of trust necessary to make a transaction happen. Now, let us turn to some of the ways in which the market for trust differs from other markets.

Direct versus Indirect

First we will consider how we measure the value of trust. The market for trust is unique because trust is delivered differently by different providers in the market. In most markets, the providers bring their products and services to market in more or less similar ways. Trust, however, is supplied by both for-profit business, which brings trust to the market in one way, and the government, which brings trust to the market in another way. Specifically, for-profit businesses supply trust directly as part of a bundle with a product or service. Trust is linked directly with a particular product or service. In contrast, governments provide trust indirectly and often it is not linked with a particular product or service.

For instance, if you buy a Toyota Camry, the trust component of the purchase is part of the transaction, whether it is a warranty, the brand, or another feature. This direct link means that the decision to purchase the Camry necessarily includes a valuation about the trust element provided by the business.

The government's contribution to the trust component of the transaction for the purchase of the Camry, however, is indirect and not as easily evaluated. As discussed earlier, the government provides safety rules for automobiles, including the Camry, as well as oversight of manufacturing facilities by the National Highway Traffic Safety Administration (NHTSA), OSHA, and other federal agencies. Government also provides courts and a rich body of products liability law that helps ensure consumers can trust that their purchase will live up to its promise.

Because the governmental aspects of trust are provided indirectly, they are more difficult to evaluate. Do you know how much of your tax money goes to paying for the services provided by the NHTSA? Do you know the value provided by the NHTSA that would not be provided by the market in the absence of the NHTSA? Are these government programs worth it? It is difficult to measure and we cannot be sure whether they are worth it or not simply by observing customer behavior. This means that any evaluation about the competitive position of government versus private suppliers must take account of the direct versus the indirect nature of the way in which trust is provided.

To consider the impact of this, one need look no further than the taxi market. Cabs in a particular jurisdiction are fairly regular in design, and changes to cab services are slow and clunky. The cabs we ride in today are not much different from those we rode in as kids, and any innovations in service are applied in every cab, regardless of customer preferences. Does anyone watch the video screens in some cabs that show commercials and clips from the news? Or have you ever seen a cab offer bottles of water, charging ports, and magazines and newspapers, like many ridesharing drivers do? Uber drivers innovate at a local level, based on their customers' preferences; innovation in the taxi business emanates from a centralized body – the taxi commission – which is more removed from customer experiences than Uber drivers and applies a one-size-fits-all approach to service.

The issue can be a matter of life and death. A few years ago, students from our law school were involved in a horrible crash while riding in a taxi. They were not wearing their seatbelts; one of the students died and the other spent years in various medical facilities. We don't know whether these students chose to not wear safety belts or whether the belts were, as we frequently experience, missing or buried under the seats in the back of an outdated taxi. We have each had thousands of cab rides and have never reported a missing seat belt to the local taxi commission; we routinely report such conditions on the Uber app.

Prices versus Taxes

Another difference between the market for trust and other markets is how we pay. In a typical market, say the one for hockey sticks or hotel rooms, customers pay a price for a product or service. The price mechanism aggregates information about producer costs and consumer preferences, causing resources to be allocated in ways that reflect social value. The things that consumers value will be produced and at levels that satisfy consumer preferences or demands.

This general framework applies to the supply of trust by for-profit businesses. As we set out in the definitions of these markets, part of the price customers pay for goods and services includes paying a little for trust. The trust might be built into a brand, a warranty, or another element of the product or service. But consumers pay for it with cash as part of the purchase price.

As a result, the company will bundle the trust at the efficient level, dictated by a competitive market. If too much trust is provided or at a price that exceeds the value of the trust, customers will choose rival products or change their consumption patterns. The tendency will be for trust to be provided in an amount equal to the value of the trust supplied. The price mechanism will provide information to producers and consumers of trust and will, over time, lead the market for trust toward efficiency.

It is true that there may be distortions in this market driven by cognitive bias toward or against risk. For example, people may irrationally overpay for trip insurance or extended warranties that are unlikely to be worth what the consumer spent. But this also reflects a well-functioning market that allows opportunities for different types of consumers to build their own unique risk preferences into a transaction. Importantly, the ideal amount of trust may vary by consumer, which makes private-market competition even more valuable to consumers.

But, unlike most markets, the market for trust includes government as a competitor, and governments do not provide trust through prices, but instead pay for trust through taxes. The aspects of government trust described earlier, such as ex ante licensing and regulation, as well as ex post litigation in government courts, are paid for through general revenues. This means that there is no direct linkage between the amount of trust provided and the preferences of the individuals consuming or utilizing the trust. To be sure, some costs of regulation and litigation and other aspects of government trust provision are borne by business, which then may pass them along to customers. But this is not true for all government costs. The "price" of products liability is factored into product prices, but the costs of the NHTSA or OSHA are not. The residual will be disconnected from market transactions, and therefore may be provided in excessive or insufficient amounts. For example, a complex and expensive conflict-resolution system for international commodity transactions may be of little value to a dog groomer in Chicago, but the groomer will pay for it through her taxes just as a grain trader will, who will benefit greatly from such a system.

In addition, the fact that government trust is funded through taxes instead of through prices means that the typical feedback system of the price mechanism will be missing for government trust. Without this feedback, it is difficult for government and taxpayers to evaluate whether the efficient level of trust is being provided.

For instance, consider the taxi market. Government regulation of taxi cabs is done through the taxi commission, which is funded through general tax revenues of the city. If the government spends too much money on taxi regulation, the tax bill of the typical citizen will be higher than it should be, but by an amount that will be trivial. A few dollars per citizen extra will permit a regulator to waste millions on inefficient levels of trust creation (or self-serving behavior) by regulators.

It will be more difficult for private trust providers to be able to get away with this, since they have to operate in competitive markets. There will be instantaneous feedback if the price they are charging, inclusive of the cost of trust, is too high. Although the signal may be noisy and imperfect, over time, competition can be expected to push the provision of trust in the direction of greater efficiency.

Tailoring

A closely related point to these first two is that business trust can be narrowly tailored to the needs of individuals, while government trust operates at a society-wide level. The point is a familiar one. Consider the insurance for products provided by business versus that provided by government. For instance, imagine buying a chainsaw from Home Depot. The manufacturer or retailer might offer you a warranty for defects or some other type of insurance. One would expect risk-averse buyers to opt for the warranty and amateur or clumsy users to buy the additional insurance. Other buyers – risk-neutral and adroit ones – would choose to pay a lower price, forsaking the insurance. Prices would reflect consumer preferences about risk and trust. If you trust the manufacturer without the insurance, you will opt out; if you don't, you will pay for it in the market price.

Government also might offer insurance in this case. Products liability law is available for users who are injured by products, and its scope is broad enough to cover many accidents that are not based on obvious defects. Importantly, however, products liability cannot be waived by customers – everyone *must* buy it, in effect. The reason for this is because one of the points of products liability law is to transfer wealth from one group (non-injured users) to another group (injured users) with the aim of encouraging safer products. (This is why we keep referring to the government as an "insurance company.")

Mandatory government insurance may be justified in some or all cases, but it demonstrates that trust tailoring is more difficult to achieve when there are multiple goals being pursued by government actors. Business is trying to sell a product; government is trying to do many things at once, some of which have nothing to do with the transaction at issue.

Unless government works well, the result of government attempts to achieve these various goals through products or services may generate large inefficiencies. Products liability law, for instance, often has very little to do with the risk of actual harms to adept users of products. The famous case of the multi-million-dollar judgment for spilled coffee at McDonalds is just one example of how products liability cases can often be thought of as merely transferring wealth from one group (consumers) to another group (unlucky victims), irrespective of the relative fault of the parties. Often the judgments reflect a view that "rich" companies should pay money to "poor" consumers. In such cases, law professors Steven Shavell and Louis Kaplow have shown that we could do better by limiting the legal system to a focus on efficiency and by having transfers such as these achieved through a tax and transfer system.[4]

There is also a temporal element at play here. Competition ensures that tailoring happens quite fast in business, but the political process means that supplying such trust happens more slowly at the government level. Voting is costly for individuals and society, and therefore happens only episodically. This is true for voters picking representatives, but also for the representatives. The legislative calendar is extremely busy and getting floor time on the US Senate to consider any change in law is a significant task. The public mind must be motivated to want change as well and, most of the time, it is difficult to move people's attention from their daily lives and frivolities to matters of political importance. This means that, at some points in time, we will get too little law making and, during crises especially, at other times we will get too much law making.

However, government is not only slower on the uptake, but it is also more likely to produce trust that will outlive its usefulness. When a particular product falls out of use, so too do the trust elements sold alongside it. However, in the government system, the trust mechanism remains in effect until there is strong incentive to change it. Because political action requires a great degree of consensus and expending political capital, it is easier to leave old regulations on the books, even when the business models they were meant to work alongside are outdated or even obsolete. We will discuss this burden later.

Government trust is also applicable to everyone equally because government operates by rules and a tradition of equal treatment. This is the nature of bureaucracy. It is impossible to write rules that apply to individuals, as this would be both extremely costly and viewed as unfair and potentially corrupt if done by political actors. One-size-fits-all is the nature of government action and this means that, in the

---

[4]   See Louis Kaplow & Steven Shavell, "Why the Legal System Is Less Efficient Than the Income Tax in Redistributing Income," 23 *J. Legal Stud.* 667, 669 (1994).

delivery of trust, the outcome will be too much trust in some places and too little in others.

Some taxi riders will be okay with a light-touch regulatory approach, while others will want much more. The taxi commission can only provide the service demanded by the median rider (and it is only guessing at what this service is, without receiving much feedback about whether it is getting this right). For the reasons discussed earlier, there will not be much information about where the rules overshoot and where they undershoot and, in any event, there is not much that the public can do about it even if there was good information. A cab is a cab.

The rise of alternatives expands the regulatory possibilities that can make everyone better off. Those with a demand for more regulatory oversight can choose companies such as GoNanny, which promise a ride safe enough for small children, while those who are less picky or more trusting can ride with an Uber driver. Within that platform, the star-rating system means that riders can decide what level of service they want – a few friends will not ride with drivers with anything less than a 4.9, while we happily plumb the depths of the 4.5s of the world.

As this book is headed to press, new innovations are being rolled out. On August 3, 2018, Uber announced a new program designed to enhance the effectiveness of its community-generated trust. Called "Rider Preferred," the program will designate some drivers as excellent based on receiving the best feedback on the highest percentage of their trips. These drivers will receive a "seal of excellence," and other benefits, with the main goal being to make riders trust more in the system of feedback. Whether the program works or not depends on whether people – riders and drivers – find it useful. Our point is not to suggest that it is a good idea or that it will be beneficial. Instead, this is merely an example of a trust-based innovation arising from an increasingly competitive market for trust.

Government as Producer and Regulator

Another key aspect of the market for trust is that the government is both a producer of trust and a regulator of other providers of trust. In almost every other market, the government is not a producer, it is only a regulator. With the exception of some communist and fascist governments past and present, governments generally do not own the means of production. This means that the production of most goods and services is done by private, for-profit businesses. Government regulates these businesses in a range of ways, including how they are governed, how they raise money, how they treat their employees, how they distribute information to investors and customers, and, of course, how they design and sell their products.

In the market for trust, however, government is both a supplier of trust and a regulator of other trust providers. This means that there is the potential that the government, as the regulator, will be biased in favor of itself and against its competitors supplying trust. We discuss this more in Chapter 8 in our discussion of the regulation of the ridesharing market.

The key takeaway, however, is simple to appreciate. If the government is supplying trust for a particular activity – say, riding with a stranger – it is probably doing so through a bureaucratic system in which there are jobs, careers, and interest groups with a vested interest in preserving the status quo. If a rival emerges, offering a potentially superior trust-delivery service, just as Uber and other ridesharing companies arguably have, this status quo is threatened. The government agents who currently provide trust may be out of a job; the taxi companies who have invested in the current system may lose their competitive advantage gained through investing in it; and politicians who have been able to use government power to extract professional and private gains will also lose out. All of these individuals may therefore react to the threat of a rival trust provider by regulating it to minimize its impact or even to knock it out of existence. As discussed previously in the discussion of bootleggers and Baptists, it is likely that this attack on a competitor will use the lofty rhetoric of the public interest as the reason – "Protect the poor taxi driver!" or "Uber is dangerous!" – but the actual reason will be about protecting the benefits of incumbency.

Individuals who are generally in favor of a significant role for government or governmental regulation in our lives might also reflexively object to disrupting government control over a particular trust market, such as taxis, because they are afraid of spillovers or slippery slopes. We have in mind here an individual who, if honest, would characterize the rise of Uber as a net positive for social value, but worries that, if Uber disrupts the government monopoly on taxi regulation, this would cause a cascade of privatization of governmental activities that would then, on net, be socially negative. While this is certainly possible, we reject the general use of slippery slope arguments to rebut clear welfare improvements. They are simply too easy to deploy in nefarious ways and, after all, we do not know if the slope will be slippery or even if the descent down such a slope would necessarily be negative once we learned more.

There are other perversities at play. The City of London recently banned Uber. This was no doubt because of the relative power of the highly concentrated taxi cab industry compared with the diffuse interests of Uber drivers. But, the typical public choice story had a dark side as well. London cab drivers are overwhelmingly older and whiter than Uber drivers in the city, who typically come from immigrant communities. The use of allegedly public-spirited legislation to discriminate, to protect entrenched interests, and to step on less-powerful rivals has a long history in the United States and elsewhere. The Davis–Bacon Act (1931) set prevailing wages for construction work in the United States, and its primary purpose was to protect Northern (white) workers from lower-cost Southern (black) workers. In the north especially, law was often the vehicle of racism in the workplace. When Frederick Douglass sought work as a caulker on whaling ships in New Bedford, Massachusetts, in the 1830s, the white workers did not resort to violence, like his former masters in the eastern shore of Maryland had, but instead turned to the racist and protectionist impulses of local politicians. What became federal law in the Davis–Bacon Act a century later was the lived experience in countless northern communities for black workers subject to local laws limiting their freedom.

The racist underpinnings of much legislation that was seemingly public oriented was evident in other countries as well during this period. When a minimum wage bill was being considered in Massachusetts during the Progressive Era, a member of the state commission on the topic, Arthur Holcombe, described a similar law in Australia as designed to "protect the white Australian's standard of living from the invidious competition of the colored races, particularly of the Chinese."[5]

Although most markets do not suffer this particular type of potential distortion – the regulator being a participant and thus regulating itself and its competition – there are a few others in which it occurs. The market for altruism is one.[6] Consider the ways in which we help other people. Although altruism can be self-produced – you can help the little old lady cross the street – we can do a lot more good when we act collectively. For this reason, most altruism is intermediated through entities. The Sierra Club, the National Rifle Association (NRA), Planned Parenthood, the Red Cross, Goodwill, and countless other charities are obvious examples of how people banding together to a common cause can increase their impact.

But it isn't just charities that do charitable work. There is in fact a market for altruism in which three types of entities – governments, NGOs, and for-profit businesses – compete in a way to provide ways for individuals to help other individuals. Government collects taxes and invests in public goods; NGOs collect donations and put them to good use; and businesses engage in a lot of socially responsible behavior, including donating to charity or producing social products such as fair-trade coffee or cars that are more environmentally friendly than is required by law.

In general, people can act in three socially responsible ways when using these entities to project and amplify their altruism: (1) cash contributions (i.e., taxes, contributions, or investments); (2) work (i.e., volunteering for an NGO or working for the government or a socially responsible company); and (3) consumption (i.e. buying products from an NGO or company that is committed to the public good). By giving money to one of these institutions, working for them at a lower wage than one would otherwise demand, or buying goods or services from them, one can help others.

Think about buying fair-trade coffee. The purchase of fair-trade coffee is in fact the purchase of regular coffee plus a donation to help a coffee farmer in a poor country. This bundling of a regular product (coffee) with a contribution to the poor

---

[5]   Arthur N. Holcombe, "The Legal Minimum Wage in the United States," 2 *Am. Econ. Rev.* 21 (1912).

[6]   M. Todd Henderson & Anup Malani, "Corporate Philanthropy and the Market for Altruism," 109 *Colum. L. Rev.* 571 (2009).

(the extra money that Starbucks pays for beans sourced from certain growers) is a way in which for-profit businesses can compete with other providers of altruism. One could instead pay taxes to the government, which could then give foreign aid to the country, which could then (perhaps) use it to help the poor coffee farmer. Or, one could donate the money to an NGO that is committed to helping the poor in that particular country. All three of these may be worthwhile and effective, but the advantages and disadvantages of each should be easy to identify.

How these pros and cons net out is, however, uncertain. In the absence of a clear advantage for one versus another, the sensible approach for the government regulator would be to not favor one over the other. After all, if government writes rules that are biased in favor of government, or makes donations or consumption of fair-trade coffee unfavorable, then it may crowd out this type of altruism in favor of more government. If this is justified on the grounds that the government is *better* at intermediating altruism, as it surely is in some areas, such as national defense, then the bias is acceptable. But, if not, then we should view the tilting of the playing field in favor of government skeptically.

The rules of the game for altruism are largely determined by tax policy. The tax rules are biased against corporate delivery of altruism. For instance, a donation to a charity to help poor farmers in Ethiopia is tax deductible, while the portion of fair-trade coffee that is a donation to help poor Ethiopian farmers is not. There are many other examples of how tax policy may distort the market for altruism in ways that are not obviously justified by the relative efficiency of altruism delivery.[7]

The key point is simply that government must be extremely careful when it acts as both a regulator and a participant in a market, lest it adopt policies that bias the market in ways that are not justified by fairness or efficiency, and instead serve the selfish interests of the makers or beneficiaries of government policy.

Thoughtful observers of government regulation of other trust providers should thus cast a skeptical eye on government policies that limit innovation in the provision of trust. They should also look through purported rationales for government eliminating a competitor in trust delivery – be it about safety, the rights of certain workers, or fairness – and demand hard evidence that the innovation will be bad for society as a whole in the long run. It should not be enough that the government promised the particular company or industry a monopoly. If this reason were sufficient, the result would be less innovation, less consumer satisfaction, and less tailoring of regulation (in both directions). It would also reward both governments and private businesses in ways that would encourage businesses to seek and governments to grant monopolies in the first place. This is undoubtedly a bad thing, except in the narrowest class of cases. If the history of trust that we previously discussed has taught us anything, it is that advances in the delivery of trust often disrupt existing suppliers, but are beneficial in enabling new levels of human cooperation.

---

[7] Ibid.

Bundling and the Social Welfare Conundrum

Another aspect of the market for trust is that choices in the market reflect a combination of both trust and the underlying goods and services. While this is true for nearly all goods and services – buying an Apple computer instead of a Lenovo computer involves a valuation based, in part, on brand, warranties, and other aspects of trust – where the trust element is a predominant factor in a consumer's choice, the stakes of the market are greater. This is because providing trust is a core government activity and, when a rival threatens this directly, it may be difficult to unpack the bundle of things delivered by the non-governmental provider. When a private business, such as Uber or eBay, establishes a platform in which it can deliver trust, it is also offering other features, such as a user experience, a payment mechanism, and so on. Thus, trust providers offer a bundle of services. So, when we evaluate the efficiency of trust delivery, the challenge is to consider trust along with these other aspects. This complicates an analysis of the market.

Our approach to evaluating the market for trust is what economists call a "welfarist" approach – we are for policies that increase social welfare and against those that decrease it. This type of approach tries to take a deeper consideration than higher level modes of analysis, such as liberty or fairness, in order to focus on the specific goal of human flourishing. In our view, "liberty" and "fairness" are just short cuts for achieving that end. Those who subscribe to them believe that protecting liberty or achieving fair distributions will, at the end of the day, be the approach that best achieves human flourishing. Instead, we are open to liberty, fairness, or any of a number of other approaches if, and only if, they can be shown to increase human wellbeing and happiness.

While our approach is good in theory, when we analyze the market for trust, the social welfare objective can become a trap of sorts. The reason is the complexity of human interactions and society-wide valuations of welfare. Consider the case of Uber again. The value of Uber to its customers and society seems obvious: its valuation in the tens of billions of dollars speaks directly to this. But a social welfare calculation considers not just the benefits, but also the costs, including the displacement of alternatives and distributional issues. When these considerations are included, the question about whether ride sharing is better (from a social standpoint) than government taxi regulation is more difficult.

We still believe that the net social welfare gain from ride sharing is positive (in fact, strongly positive). The point is simply that we cannot take it as a given just because individuals choose to use ridesharing platforms instead of taxis. After all, individual choices may be selfish and may not reflect the broader social value of collective action. The theme of this book is how trust-delivery mechanisms enable greater cooperation, and we need to be mindful that this is in fact what alternatives to government trust delivery are doing.

This competition with government distinguishes the market for trust. Choosing to use Uber instead of a taxi may appear, to a consumer, to be the same as choosing In-N-Out Burger instead of McDonalds, but if we are thinking about trust, it isn't. Moving your burger consumption habit from McDonalds to In-N-Out may cause a business to falter and even go away, but the broader social impact is minimal or zero. But putting the government out of the trust business in a particular field or area is different. As we saw in our earlier discussion of the history of trust, this can be a socially beneficial thing, but it can also potentially be a bad thing. The stakes demand scrutiny.

What should this scrutiny look at? We will consider this in more detail in Chapter 8. But the analysis should consider not only the welfare gains for individuals using ridesharing services, but also the impact that moving away from government trust provision may have on users of alternatives. In addition, an analysis of the value of Uber and its ilk should consider the gains that may result from getting the government out of the ridesharing regulation business. After all, the money currently spent on taxi regulation could be put to better uses, such as education, feeding the poor, lowering taxes, and protecting people from force and fraud. While our own view is that, when this analysis is done, the gains from private trust provision in this area will be clear, we leave that to your determination after finishing the book.

The Life Cycle of Social Technologies

Another aspect of the market for trust is the interplay between the gains from economies of scale in trust delivery and the agency costs and other limiting factors that also increase with the size of the trust-delivery mechanism. Let's unpack this.

On the one hand, the bigger the enterprise that is helping to deliver trust, the more efficiently that trust can be delivered. Consider the government during the turn of the twentieth century. No business or non-profit at that time had a national or international reputation and, therefore, if one wanted to provide the trust for financial transactions or consumer products, the best option was most likely the government. Economies of scale simply mean that the cost of delivering trust (or anything else) becomes less on a per-unit basis as the scale of the enterprise increases. It is cheaper on a per-car basis to build 1,000 cars than it is to build one car. The same is true of trust. It is much cheaper to sell 1,000 units of trust as part of a particular transaction than it is to sell one unit, on a per-transaction basis.

On the other hand, as the scope of the enterprises delivering trust increases, the potential for other costs, broadly defined, to seep into the system also increases. In the previous chapters, we introduced the concepts of agency costs and public-choice economics, both of which demonstrate how large institutions insulated from instantaneous market feedback can drift away from efficiency because of the selfish acts of the human decision-makers that control them. For instance, as the government or a business grows by virtue of returns from economies of scale, it needs to delegate more authority to agents, who can act with more autonomy. If these agents, be they political actors, bureaucrats, or corporate managers, are not subject to intense oversight, they may choose actions that benefit them and not the public or the particular stakeholders of their enterprise. Knowing this, large organizations have to devote substantial resources to ensuring that agents don't run amok. This too is a cost.

One way in which large firms and governments respond to increasing agency costs is to use bureaucracy as a means of preventing and policing abuse. Procedures and rules designed to limit discretion are the means by which government tries to ensure that cheating and selfishness in the application of government power will be reduced. Bureaucracy, whether it is at a government agency, in a business, at a university, or in another entity, is essential to run any organization. But, however efficient bureaucratic processes are at managing these costs, a downside of this approach is that it deters innovation. The point was captured (perhaps a bit too enthusiastically) by Honoré de Balzac in *Les Employés*:

> No one comes or stays in the government offices but idlers, incapables, or fools. Thus the mediocrity of French administration has slowly come about. Bureaucracy, made up entirely of petty minds, stands as an obstacle of prosperity of the nation; delays for seven years, by its machinery, the project of a canal which would have stimulated the production of a province; is afraid of everything, prolongs procrastination, and perpetuates the abuses which in turn perpetuate and consolidate itself. Bureaucracy holds all things and the administration itself in leading strings; it stifles men of talent who are bold enough to be independent of it or to enlighten it on its own follies.[8]

Balzac's point is also true for large for-profit businesses. Look at the US innovations of the last few decades and you will find them emerging from startups in garages in Silicon Valley more than from industry stalwarts such as IBM or Cisco. The point can be overstated. Walmart's innovations in supply-chain management have revolutionized business in the United States and there are more examples that can be mustered. But the general point remains: if you look at the most valuable US businesses today – Apple, Google, Microsoft, Amazon, Facebook – they did not exist even thirty years ago. Big isn't necessarily bad, but it isn't exactly known for always being cutting edge.

Another cost of large enterprises is the gains from cheating that increase with scale, as was discussed earlier when considering the reciprocity game. As an organization gets bigger, the size of the transactions it can successfully engage in increases as well. This means that the potential gains from fraud are bigger for larger organizations than for smaller ones. The federal government can squander billions or trillions, while the local government can waste dollars only in the millions; executives at big banks can steal much more from their customers than executives at smaller banks.

---

[8] Honoré de Balzac, *Les Employés* ("The Bureaucracy") 20 (1899 edn) (1837).

The net result is a sort of natural equilibrium. Organizations grow, while the returns to scale outweigh the rising agency costs and other negatives of size. The difference then levels off as the costs rise to equal the gains from adding additional units of size. Finally, the organization shrinks as the costs of additional expansion exceed the gains. This is the typical life cycle of a firm, whether it sells tractors, tuna fish, or trust. This form, common in the business literature, captures the cycle of the typical business enterprise. We are merely extending it to the more general case of government and other mechanisms of cooperation or, as we call them, social technologies.

We think that this model also describes the life cycle of the social technologies of trust. A crude diagram of this is seen in Figure 18. On the X-axis is time, starting with the earliest age of humanity and extending to the present and into the future. The Y-axis represents the amount of total trust in human society. The three lines represent the types of trust – personal, government, and business – and how they have changed over time. All three types are present, more or less, at all times. The curve on top at any particular time is merely the predominant form of trust for that particular period.

These curves are merely illustrative – they represent the relative level of the supply of trust by various types of trust providers over time, based on our read of the history. As detailed in Chapter 5, at first, personal trust in the form of tribe was the only type of trust that humans had. Starting from the left-hand side of the chart, we see that the predominate form of trust was personal or kin-based trust. There was no government or business trust, as we know them today. As humans began to move away from a nomadic existence, we developed the rule of law. It started with the move toward permanent settlements and the growth of agriculture and domestication of livestock. Relatively quickly, law or government became the primary mechanism of trust. It is

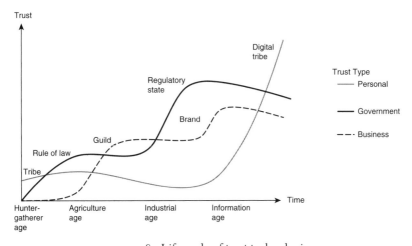

FIGURE 18: Life cycle of trust technologies

not that people trusted their kin less, but instead the portion of the total amount of trust in society, which had grown enormously, that was supplied by personal trust fell as other types of trust technology were deployed. But, as the law enabled more cooperation, humans expanded their activities in size, manner, and geographic scope in ways that dramatically increased the complexity of human behavior. The monarch or regulator could no longer control activities at great distances, with highly uncertain impacts, or based on information unknown to the government. Time, space, and complexity were all barriers to the efficient provision of trust by government. Governments were unable to keep up with the expansion in geography and complexity of interactions because the ability to project violence (the basis for all regulation) was limited by the technology of the era. The rule of law got about as far as it could before leveling off in efficacy.

Guilds, the first type of business trust, then arose to enable these transactions, creating self-governance and the Law Merchant, for example. For the first time, business trust predominated.

But then, in response to the increasing need for trust in the industrial age, new technologies for projecting violence, as well as changing social conditions, led to the creation of the regulatory state. This innovation in the delivery of government trust changed the shape of the curve, reinvigorating government trust. Business life cycles can do this too, as old established firms can avoid maturity and decline by developing a shape-changing innovation.

The story we tell then sees the rise of brand, because business developed a new mechanism that increased the efficiency of delivering additional trust in the post-World Wars era. Reputational trust, which was the basis of all trust in the prehistoric period, was rebuilt in corporate form. Humans imbued artificial entities – such as the corporation – with personalities, and gave these personalities content through massive investments in branding. These brands became bonds against misbehavior, just as a person's reputation did in the era before humans left their clans or small towns.

After this, as we move into the information age and project these curves forward, we see a maturation and decline of government and business trust. Government becomes less effective at creating trust for all the reasons we discussed earlier. We see this in the polling data and feel it in our everyday lives. Government is too big and political fights are too contentious to believe that we are anywhere else on the curve other than in a decreasing marginal efficiency of government.

The same is true for brand. While brands remain as essential at delivering trust as government, the move to online shopping is indicative of how internet platforms are changing the power of brand as a means of further increasing trust. Many shoppers are more inclined to trust Amazon's aggregation of the preferences of the digital tribe than they are to develop a particular affiliation with a brand. Or, to use a starker example, consumers used to choose airlines based on brand, but today platforms such as Kayak and Priceline have offered consumers a portal to force these brands to compete on the factors that are most salient to consumers (because the experience of flying is so tightly regulated, most competition occurs on price). Just as platforms have come to discipline brand in the provision of trust, as we will see, we believe that they will ultimately discipline government.

As we project into the future, we see the inexorable rise of the digital tribe. What is notable is how the curve for personal trust does not follow the typical life-cycle curve. While other social technologies for trust delivery are naturally limited by agency costs and the costs of bureaucracy, this is not true for personal trust aggregators. The digital tribe is decentralized, so there is no bureaucracy and no agents. The more members of the digital tribe that are able to be aggregated, the greater the information generated by the system. While there are costs to adding additional members and the gain from additional information may decrease at some point, there is no reason to suspect that the harnessing of trust from disperse individuals will decline in the way that government and business trust did, because personal trust is not subject to the same natural limitations.

We can imagine, for instance, a network of individuals connected to each other directly, perhaps using sensors of various kinds to measure utility or wellbeing of some sort. Perhaps our bodies will be connected with small implants that measure and transmit a measure of happiness, and this will be used to transmit to others an aggregate satisfaction level for a community having a particular experience, be it the use of a product or the experience of a concert, a restaurant, or the like. This kind of trust technology – a heat map that shows how the human tribe enjoys this or that – is scalable and the network effects of it are limitless. While the information even in this example is not perfect, we are only at the beginning of an explosion of personal trust technologies.

While it is true that we still need someone to create a platform – even the most decentralized network needs an intermediary of some kind to establish the turf and rules of the network – the bureaucracy to manage a platform pales in comparison with the organization needed to run all the nodes of a platform. Fewer employees, fewer decisions, and less power means lower costs of intermediation. An example is the New York Stock Exchange, which we consider in the next chapter; it is a platform, an early predecessor to the internet-based platforms we discuss in the rest of this book. The costs of operating the New York Stock Exchange do not scale to the size of the transactions that take place under the exchange. If anything, the greater the number of transactions on the exchange, the smaller the size of the platform's costs (all in) on a per-transaction basis.

Obsessive focus on customer experience is the core principle that drove Amazon to prominence and is one of the hallmarks of Lean Startup methodology,[9] a popular strategic toolkit for startups. While not all of the information about customer

---

[9] Eric Reis, *The Lean Startup: How Today's Entrepreneurs Use Continuous Innovation to Create Radically Successful Businesses* (2011).

satisfaction is directly about trust, it is bundled. To paraphrase Tolstoy, all happy customers were the same (they had trust plus they liked the product), but unsatisfied customers were unsatisfied for different reasons. A happy customer implies that both trust and product were sufficient, while an unhappy customer may be unhappy for either reason. As our platforms for gathering information continue to compete and improve, so too will our ability to efficiently provide trust. And as our ability to provide trust becomes more efficient, the more we will move away from crude, one-size-fits-all trust provision toward nimble, customized provision.

SUMMARY

Trust is something that we demand because it increases our ability to improve our lives. Humans have inherent levels of trust that have been crucial to our ability to cooperate across non-kin groups. But at large scales and in complex transactions, these levels are probably insufficient. Government can address these shortcomings, but government operates inefficiently and can be blunt. It may also, inadvertently, be biased in favor of the wealthy and in ways that tilt the scale against minority populations of all kinds. Private means of trust creation thus become vital. Where government regulation does not work for whatever reason, this private regulation becomes essential for creating trust. And where government regulation not only supplies trust but also regulates the private trust providers that it competes with, it is critical that we find a way to reverse this monopoly and create competition in the trust market. The regulation of stockbrokers provides a great example of how this has worked in practice. It also provides lessons for how well-established government regulations that we are all familiar with may be undone in ways that will enhance human welfare. It is one the United States' first examples of a regulatory hack and we will consider it in the next chapter.

PART II

In Part I of this book, we introduced the concept of trust as something that enables human cooperation. We also characterized familiar things, such as language, writing, law, corporate brands, and internet-based platforms, as social technologies that create trust at scale, thus enabling cooperation. We then considered how trust is provided in a market in which various entities compete with each other to supply the trust that individuals demand in order to cooperate. This market, as we describe it, is unique in many respects, especially because the government is both a provider of trust and a regulator of trust providers. The potential conflict of interest may cause trust innovations to happen less often and less quickly than they otherwise would, especially as government has grown larger and more powerful over time.

In this part, we present two case studies that illustrate these general points and the evolution of trust innovation. In Chapter 7, we tell the story of how the New York Stock Exchange was invented to solve a trust gap in the brokerage business. The gap arose from a legal lacuna created by a statute that effectively foreclosed access to courts for brokerage clients. With law suddenly foreclosed as a trust-delivery mechanism, the brokers needed to create a substitute that would deliver the necessary amount of trust to meet the demand of customers. Cooperation among brokers and clients would not happen without trust, and brokers had to build their own alternative to government. Although founded in the eighteenth century, the New York Stock Exchange is strikingly similar in its conception and approach to the platform companies such as eBay and Uber that we are all familiar with today.

In Chapter 8, we look in greater detail at the regulation of taxi cabs and the evolving ridesharing market. The key insight from this analysis is how technology influences the choice between potential providers of trust. We show how the cab market cannot function effectively without regulation, and how government served this role to create a vibrant ridesharing market. But, the use of government to provide this trust came with shortcomings. Regulators created a cartel to solve some market problems and this led to inefficiencies. Regulators were also insulated from political pressure and the nature of government regulation meant regulations were not tailored to users' needs.

Economists knew for a long time about these deficiencies and there was eventually a political movement to deregulate. It failed. Without the technology provided by the internet, there was no way to efficiently provide the trust necessary to make a vibrant ridesharing market. Uber and other platform companies solved this problem and, today, we have viable alternatives to government-supplied trust in ride sharing.

7

Private Trust and the Regulation of Stockbrokers

Self-regulation sounds like an oxymoron. Parents do not go out to the opera and leave their kids alone – they hire a babysitter. But there is a powerful logic to self-regulation in some cases (although not for children). In this chapter, we look at the regulation of stockbrokers, which, since the 1700s, has primarily been accomplished through various self-regulatory organizations (SROs). These SROs, while not perfect, provide an interesting case study for the broader points we are making in this book about the role of non-governmental providers of trust. We do not believe, and do not claim, that these providers can accomplish their trust-creating job without government. We live on planet Earth, not on some libertarian fantasy world. Instead, our goal in this chapter is merely to demonstrate how private trust-creating forces can operate in lieu of, but yet supported by, government regulation.

* * *

The idea of private law doing the work of trust is illustrated by the regulation of stockbrokers. The New York Stock Exchange is also one of the first examples of a startup creating a private regulatory system to create trust between a producer and a supplier of a product. The alternative to government regulation that was established by the exchange largely regulates Wall Street to this day, providing one of the most important and long-lasting regulatory hacks. The banks and stockbrokers that serve as intermediaries in the purchase and sale of stocks and bonds are regulated by a system built up as an alternative to government regulation. The New York Stock Exchange may have preceded Uber and Airbnb by over 200 years, but their stories are largely the same.

ORIGINS

The story starts in January 1791, when a broadside was published that called for "a meeting of the dealers in the public funds in the city of New-York held at the Coffee-House."[1] At this meeting, a group of dealers in government debt, the first type of publicly traded securities in the United States, agreed to be bound by fourteen rules,

[1] Stuart Banner, *Anglo-American Securities Regulation: Cultural and Political Roots, 1690–1860*, 250 (2002).

FIGURE 19: Brokers meeting under the apocryphal buttonwood tree in Manhattan[2]

including a prohibition against dealing with non-participating brokers and a limitation upon the number of securities that could be sold in a given day. This early attempt at organization failed after a crash in the public debt markets in that same year.

Several other attempts to build an exclusive exchange followed. Later that same year, twenty-four brokers agreed to fix commissions, at one-quarter of 1 percent. Known as the "Buttonwood Agreement," popular mythology holds that this agreement was signed under a buttonwood tree near the corner of Wall and Pearl Streets and that it grew into the New York Stock Exchange (see Figure 19). Both of these myths are untrue, and the agreement proved equally untenable.

A third agreement by brokers tried to create an exclusive club of members for the trading of securities. Known as the Tontine Coffee-House, its members included John Jacob Astor and future Supreme Court Justice Brockholst Livingston. This trading group had many rivals, some in specific categories of securities, and no single group of brokers was able to dominate early trading. In fact, because much trading happened outside the exchanges, that is, literally on the street, it was known for years as the "curb" market.

---

[2] Gottscho-Schleisner Collection, Library of Congress (Washington, DC), available at: www.loc.gov/pictures/item/93845488/

These original attempts at creating a stock exchange failed, in part because they were not vital to the success of the brokerage business or to Wall Street. The government might not have been a perfect regulator, but it provided sufficient trust in the form of state contract law – if a broker cheated a customer, the customer could sue to get their money back. The legal system was not perfect in this regard, but it was apparently enough to create the necessary amount of trust in the market. At this point in time, an exchange was merely an attempt to form a cartel – to raise profits by limiting competition through the use of fixed commissions and exclusive dealing requirements. As much as some brokers would have liked to create and enforce the cartel, it was unsustainable.

But, later that year, the circumstances changed sufficiently such that creating an exchange became vital to the survival of the brokerage business and of Wall Street. An exchange was needed not to limit competition, but to enable it. The law, which had provided trust, went away, and without trust, the brokerage business was impossible. This happened when the New York legislature passed the Stockjobbing Act of 1792. This law made contracts for the sale of stock owned by others unenforceable in New York courts. This meant that those dealing with stockbrokers could no longer trust that they would be treated fairly or that they would not be cheated. After all, if the courts were unavailable to enforce brokerage contracts, customers who were cheated would have no recourse other than the reputation of the broker. Reputation in the market was important, but it was thought not to be enough to create sufficient trust at that time. The government regulatory system was thus insufficient and so the brokers decided to create an alternative. What was needed was private law, not to supplement or tailor public law, but to replace it entirely.

Several exchanges were established to try to build the trust that was necessary, including the predecessor to the New York Stock Exchange. Their approach was simple. Create a separate entity – a club – that would not engage in brokerage services, but instead would serve as a gatekeeper between brokers and customers. We call it a "club" because that is what they called it at the time – William O. Douglas called it "a private club [with] elements of a casino."[3] But it was just a platform, the same as eBay or Uber. The club would admit members for a fee, screening them to ensure that they were reputable members of the community with good business records and sense. Then, the club would promote its members as brokers who could be trusted. But it was not enough to screen them; the club created incentives to ensure that its members did not cheat – it held their membership fee as a bond against any wrongdoing. As a leading historical account describes, the early exchanges provided "a refuge for securities traders vulnerable to the popular suspicion of their profession."[4] Just as eBay created a platform – that is, for user-created

---

[3]   Joel Seligman, *The Transformation of Wall Street* 73 (2003).
[4]   SEC Historical Society, "The Institution of Experience: Self-Regulatory Organizations in the Securities Industry, 1792–2010," available at: www.sechistorical.org/muse um/galleries/sro/sro02a.php (accessed September 24, 2013).

buyer and seller feedback – to create a reputational force that disciplines sellers ex ante, so too did the exchanges try to police broker cheating through private law making and enforcing. This is what Uber, GoNanny, Feastly, and countless other companies are doing today.

The early exchanges were somewhat successful, but a vibrant "curb" market thrived for many years. However, in 1817, a group of nearly thirty brokers formed the New York Stock and Exchange Board. The Board grew and changed as the market for securities increased over the next few decades. As more securities were traded, the Board increased the formality of its membership processes and the rules by which it conducted its business. By 1860, the Board dominated securities trading in New York, in part because its reputation allowed it to determine the prices at which other trades would happen most effectively.

The Board built this reputation through the creation of a miniature legal system that included rules governing trading and disputes among brokers. A majority vote of the Board's members originally determined the outcome of disputes. As its membership grew and the number of disputes accumulated, subsets of the Board took on this quasi-judicial role and the decisions in individual cases took on the nature of precedent. This was the organic creation of courts, administering rules developed by private bodies. This extra-governmental regulation increased public confidence in brokers associated with the Board and therefore attracted business. Think eBay for a modern analog.

New York's highest court explicitly blessed the non-governmental character of this system in its decision in the case of *Belton* v. *Hatch*, decided in 1888.[5] In *Belton*, a broker who was suspended from the Board for unsound practices sued to recover the value of their seat, which was sold by the Board to another broker. Denying the claim for recovery of the sum, the court enforced the contract between the broker and the Board, holding that the Board could use the privilege of membership as a regulatory tool.

THE NEW DEAL REVOLUTION

This system of private regulation, as an explicit alternative to government regulation, lasted nearly 150 years, from 1792 to 1933. During this time, the Board, and its sister exchanges, were the sole regulators of brokers. The stock market crash of 1929 and the subsequent economic depression led many, including President Franklin Roosevelt, to conclude that the cause of the crash, and thus of the depression, was unregulated speculation in securities. Accordingly, the Roosevelt administration drew up legislation that would largely displace the private regulators by, among other things, requiring that government bureaucrats approve all exchange rules and

[5]   *Belton* v. *Hatch*, 109 N.Y. 593 (1888).

regulations. Here we can see the market for trust in action. Not only is the government an alternative regulator *in* the market, it is also a regulator *of* the market.

The government's attempt to regulate the regulator was tantamount to a declaration of war on Wall Street, and led to an intense lobbying campaign by brokers to kill the bill. The compromise that was reached in the Securities Exchange Act of 1934 was the creation of the SEC, which had the power to write and enforce new rules, but with the pre-existing regulatory apparatus largely in place.

Private regulation was also expanded. During the early days of the SEC, Chairman James Landis proposed that private regulation be used as a way of efficiently policing the nearly 6,000 securities dealers in the over-the-counter market. The problem of government regulation in the absence of a private supplement was "a little bit trying to build a structure out of dry sand."[6]

To create the "cohesive force" that would bind the sand together, Congress amended the Securities Exchange Act with the Maloney Act of 1938. It authorized the creation of one or more private regulators for the over-the-counter market. Chairman, and later Supreme Court Justice, William O. Douglas defended the Maloney Act to the Harford Bond Club, as follows:

> By and large, government can operate satisfactorily only by proscription. That leaves untouched large areas of conduct and activity; some of it susceptible of government regulation but in fact too minute for satisfactory control; some of it lying beyond the periphery of the law in the realm of ethics and morality. Into these large areas self-government, and self-government alone, can effectively reach.[7]

Douglas's argument is recognition of the fact that government, because of the manner in which it must operate – that is, under the civil service rules and constitutional limitations necessary to prevent tyranny – is necessarily limited in the scope and efficiency of its regulation. There are socially undesirable acts that government simply cannot reach, but private regulators – because of their agility, expertise, information, and lack of constitutional constraint – can.

THE CASE FOR PRIVATE REGULATION

Consider the doctrine of suitability. Securities brokers are under an obligation to ensure their recommendations are "suitable" for their customers. A broker who sells a poor widow a speculative penny stock will probably lose their license and be barred from the industry. This is true even if the widow asked to be exposed to the risk and the broker's actions did not rise to the level of fraud. This is far beyond what we normally see in routine contracts – in the absence of coercion, incapacity, or (sometimes) extreme bargaining power asymmetries, contracts are generally enforced. But for brokers, other members of the industry will throw them out of

[6] Joel Seligman, *The Transformation of Wall Street* 185 (2003).
[7] William A. Birdthistle & M. Todd Henderson, "Becoming a Fifth Branch," 99 *Corn. L. Rev.* 1 (2013).

business because of "unsuitable recommendations." This is because all brokers suffer from the presence of bad apples in the industry, and they therefore rationally want to raise the standards of behavior. If it were left to government to police this transaction, brokers would ironically have much greater leeway to recommend unsuitable securities, since fraud is much more difficult to prove than a lack of suitability. The Supreme Court's opinion in *Ernst & Ernst* v. *Hochfelder*[8] requires an intent to deceive for securities fraud, and the threat of government action unquestionably puts defendants into a greater defensive posture than private regulatory action.

The ability to use suitability to police bad (but non-fraudulent) behavior is just one example of the ways in which private regulation can be more powerful than government regulation, and it has particular appeal in the securities industry, where consumers may be particularly vulnerable. For instance, the study of financial literacy mandated by the Dodd–Frank Act recently concluded that "investors have a weak grasp of elementary financial concepts and lack critical knowledge of ways to avoid investment fraud."[9] Or, consider FINRA's 2009 "National Financial Capability Study." It found that only a slight majority (52 percent) of respondents understood that mutual funds provide a safer return than investing in a single company stock.[10] This is like saying that only 52 percent of people believe in gravity. And this may be a reason for greater paternalism here, and for that paternalism to take the form of tailored self-regulatory enforcement, rather than more Draconian, brittle, and less informed government regulation.

The logic for the private regulation of finance is based on the rational self-interest of market participants. Industry professionals have strong incentives to police their own, since many of the costs of misbehavior are borne by all members of the profession, while the benefits are felt only by the misbehaving few. So long as the few do not control the regulatory process, private regulation might work as well or better than external regulation.

To illustrate the concept, imagine there are two types of brokers: "good" brokers and "bad" brokers. Furthermore, assume customers cannot readily distinguish between the two before choosing a broker. This supposition is reasonable inasmuch as brokers purvey an intangible service, making it difficult to distinguish good from bad through mere inspection. In the absence of an ability to discriminate, customers will discount the amount they will pay for brokerage services because of the possibility of choosing a bad broker and therefore the possibility of being cheated. If good brokers cannot credibly signal their quality, they will be unable to charge the full price for their services, and therefore good brokers will exit the market, reduce the quality of their service, or cheat. As such, the overall quality of brokers is inclined

[8] *Ernst & Ernst* v. *Hochfelder*, 425 US 185 (1976).
[9] "Study Regarding Financial Literacy among Investors," *SEC*, August, 2012, available at: www.sec.gov/news/studies/2012/917-financial-literacy-study-part1.pdf
[10] See www.usfinancialcapability.org/

to fall. This is the so-called "market for lemons" problem.[11] If purveyors of good products or services cannot signal their quality, only bad products or services (i.e., lemons) will remain in the market. Good brokers therefore have strong incentives to identify bad brokers and to remove them from the industry, since doing so would allow good brokers to charge more for their services. Industry private regulation is an organic part of a successful brokerage industry, and government is not obviously necessary to deliver it.

THE LIMITS OF PRIVATE REGULATION

The logic of private regulation does not apply in every regulatory situation. In some other industries, private regulation may not be very effective. The classic problem of externalities illustrates this story. Consider a loud music venue next door to a meditation studio. If no mechanism exists to force the music venue to pay for the damage to the interrupted meditators, the music venue will most likely emit more than the socially optimal level of noise, and the meditation studio may be forced to shut down and relocate. The meditation studio, its customers, or taxpayers will in turn pay for some of the benefits felt by the music venue's customers. Only when costs are internalized to the production function, and therefore priced by the market, are production and consumption likely to be optimized.

Brokerage is amenable to private regulation because the harm caused by bad brokers (i.e., ones taking too little care or engaging in too much harmful activity) is primarily borne by the individuals who are in a contractual relationship with the broker. When the broker cheats, the customer loses. In contrast, when the nightclub blares loud music, its customers *gain*. This reversed outcome occurs because the costs of the nightclub's products are lower than they would otherwise be, since some of those costs of production are borne by others. Noisy clubs therefore do not have strong incentives to police other noisy businesses, and thus private regulation may be less effective in contexts where externalities are high, such as zoning regulation.

FLAVORS OF PRIVATE REGULATION

Although, up to this point, the story of Wall Street regulation has been compared to that of modern-day taxi regulation – a private company (FINRA or Uber) supplies a mechanism for providing trust in competition with the government – a closer look reveals how the analogy breaks down in interesting ways. There are several reasons why they are different, but the essence of the point can be seen in the fact that FINRA is known as an SRO, while Uber is just a company offering a product, which happens to mostly be trust. The SRO model is one in which the individual members

---

[11] See George A. Akerlof, "The Market for 'Lemons': Quality Uncertainty and the Market Mechanism," 84 *Quarterly J. Econ.* 488 (1970).

of the industry (i.e., brokers of all shapes and sizes) create a regulatory body that is akin to government. While the securities laws permit there to be several different SROs, only one, FINRA, has been created and authorized to serve in this role. This monopoly power of FINRA makes the current SRO model one with a quasi-governmental feel. In contrast, Uber is just a business offering a service, along with other competitors. The SRO is a private version of government, while the digital tribe platform is a business that sells trust. The platform enables peer-to-peer regulation, a new type of regulation that taps into our oldest regulatory or community-based governance instincts.

The quasi-governmental nature of the SRO model of private regulation has some potentially significant downsides. Empowering "good" brokers to police "bad" brokers risks giving those good brokers the ability to reduce competition and to raise their own profits. For example, there is the possibility that relatively larger or more well-established firms might exert disproportionate influence on the self-regulator, and manipulate the organization into imposing costs on relatively smaller or less established firms. In such a way, private regulation might also give rise to anti-competitive behavior. Thus, the SRO approach has similar problems to government regulation, and has similar costs. After all, it is an intermediary that will have inevitable agency costs, be potentially captured by powerful and concentrated interests, and will be less responsive to demands than a pure market-based approach.

As an example, suppose that compliance with rules carries both a fixed and a variable cost. A simple way to appreciate this dynamic is to recall our example from Chapter 4 where the only cost of compliance for firms in a particular market is personnel in a compliance department. If we make the modest assumption that the number of compliance officers does not scale directly with the assets under a particular firm's management, then smaller firms will find themselves at a competitive disadvantage, all else being equal, owing to their greater compliance costs. Consider two firms: one with $100 in assets under management and one with $1,000 in assets under management. If each officer can oversee $250 in assets, but there is a minimum of at least one compliance officer, then the regulatory costs for the smaller firm are one, while those costs for the larger firm are four. On a per-asset basis, the regulatory costs are lower for the larger firm. Smaller firms in this kind of system must substantially outperform larger firms to maintain competitive parity. In this example, the smaller firm must outperform the larger by 60 basis points.

This handicap in scale is a significant problem only if larger firms dominate the regulatory process, through either the making or the enforcing of rules. Such discrepancies may, of course, be inevitable. Fees levied upon their members generally fund private regulators, and these fees are often disproportionately borne by larger firms. In addition, the US population of financial firms comprises relatively few large firms among thousands of smaller firms. Thus, the large firms enjoy low coordination costs and highly aligned interests. Moreover, the political influence of larger firms, be it with the SRO, the SRO's governmental overseer, or Congress, is likely to be much greater.

In some instances, efforts have been made to minimize this problem. For instance, after several scandals, the SEC required FINRA, the modern SRO for the securities industry, to include more members of the public on its board of directors. Similarly, the fourteen-member, quasi-judicial body that hears appeals from FINRA disciplinary and membership matters (known as the National Adjudicatory Council) also comprises an equal number of industry insiders and outsiders. Whether these governance mechanisms constrain large firms from dominating the rule-making process is unclear.

The official link between the government and the SRO has also warped the SRO in ways that make it more governmental. These forces have changed the nature of SROs for securities brokers since 1938. What were perceived as regulatory failures in each of the past five decades all led to SRO regulation taking on more of the character of government regulation. This has the potential to be the worst of all worlds: a world in which SROs act like the government, but have no restrictions that limit government action.

To demonstrate the point, consider the one-way ratchet that operates on SROs. The successes and failures of the self-regulatory process may add up over time in a way that biases the locus of regulatory authority toward government or government-like conduct. If SRO successes in preventing or reducing the costs of misconduct are relatively less politically salient than SRO failures, then the private regulator will face one-sided pressure to change its approach to regulation from government overseers. In other words, even if SROs are engaged in the optimal amount of regulation, they may face political pressure from inevitable regulatory failures to deviate in the direction of more (and socially suboptimal) levels of regulation.

The recent failure of commodities broker MF Global provides a possible example of the one-way regulatory ratchet. MF Global was a leading commodities and securities broker, regulated by, among others, the private regulator arm of the Chicago Mercantile Exchange (CME). MF Global made a disastrously incorrect $6.3 billion bet on European sovereign debt that drove the firm into a hasty bankruptcy. As the firm approached insolvency, about $1.6 billion in customer funds disappeared. When facts surfaced suggesting that this customer money, which CME is charged with ensuring is segregated from firm money, was used to try to shore up the firm's finances, the incident created a political firestorm. Congressional committees convened numerous hearing, the former head of the FBI was appointed trustee of MF Global, and countless ongoing lawsuits and investigations were launched.

This incident caused the Commodity Futures Trading Commission (CFTC), CME's government overseer, to conduct a wholesale review of the way in which futures brokers, such as MF Global, are regulated. Both Republican and Democrat commissioners of the CFTC made public statements suggesting that the private regulator model failed in the MF Global case. Bart Chilton, a Democrat commissioner, said: "I think we've gone too far in allowing the exchanges to be so self-regulatory that it's obfuscated the need for the cop to be on the beat all the time."[12] Similarly, Scott O'Malia, a Republican commissioner, said: "The MF Global collapse was a huge broken window in the [CFTC's] neighborhood ... [and] [t]o restore public confidence and deter future violations ... [the CFTC] needs to continue taking action."[13] These comments and the CFTC's response no doubt have been influenced by strong pressure from Capitol Hill. Leading congressional Republicans and Democrats have used the incident to call for greater oversight of regulated entities by the CFTC, as well as for enhanced procedures by private regulators to protect customer funds. For instance, Senator Pat Roberts, a Republican from Kansas, used the failure of MF Global to denounce the CFTC in congressional hearings, demanding an accounting on behalf of "folks in Kansas ... [who] have been severely damaged economically by the actions ... of MF Global."[14] In numerous hearings and in countless news and opinion pieces, the CFTC has been severely criticized for its failure to ensure MF Global's customers were not harmed.

CME, for its part, however, has argued that it did everything it could reasonably do to prevent the collapse of MF Global. In economic terms, CME's argument is that its regulation was efficient, even though it failed to detect this particular allegation of fraud. The optimal failure rate of nearly everything is not zero, and the existence of an ex post failure does not necessarily refute the regulatory choice.

According to CME, examiners from its SRO audited MF Global's accounts in the days before the firm's bet on European debt went bad, and found that the customer fund accounts were "overcollateralized" by $200 million. CME has defended the private regulator approach, arguing that MF Global duped regulators, and that no amount of reasonable oversight could have prevented those who wanted to break the rules from doing so. For instance, CME points to an email it sent the general counsel of MF Global the day before several hundred million dollars in customer funds were illegally moved out of a customer account and used to pay down a collateral call from a British unit of JP Morgan. The email commanded that "effectively immediately, any equity withdrawals must be approved in writing by CME."[15] But CME did not learn of the nearly $200 million moved offshore to JP Morgan until three days after the transfer.

[12] Christopher Doering, "MF Global Triggers Regulatory Rethink at CFTC," *Reuters*, February 1, 2012, available at: www.reuters.com/article/2012/02/01/us-mfglobal-cftc-policy-idUSTRE8102IV20120201/
[13] Ibid.
[14] Ronald D. Orol, "Senators Target CFTC over MF Global Failure," *Wall St. J. Market Watch*, December 1, 2011, available at: www.marketwatch.com/story/senators-target-cftc-over-mf-global-failure-2011-12-01
[15] Aaron Lucchetti & Julie Steinberg, "MF Response to CME Edict Probed," *Wall St. J.*, March 29, 2012, available at: http://online.wsj.com/article/SB10001424052702304177104577312073753226142.html

Whether the SRO model was to blame or not for the violation of segregation rules in the MF Global case seems to be a minor factor relative to the political pressure that the CFTC is facing to reform in the wake of the failure. If the CFTC is going to be blamed for the MF Global failure, it is more likely to try to reform the regulatory process to exert more direct control. Furthermore, if successes of the SROs are not celebrated in a manner proportional to the way in which failures are denounced, then the forces will inevitably lead to a more governmental form of regulation, even if that approach may not be the most efficient regulatory approach. The nature of regulations (of various types) is that they often grow from a crisis, and once they grow, they are difficult to shrink, even where the underlying regulated activity shrinks, subsides, or eliminates the crisis-causing condition through other means.

LESSONS LEARNED

The case of private regulation of Wall Street professionals offers an interesting set of similarities and differences in comparison with the regulatory disruption considered earlier. Both the stock exchange and Uber offer an alternative to government regulation by offering private mechanisms of trust creation. The nature of this trust creation in these cases is also somewhat similar. Both use customer feedback as an essential tool in filtering for good and trustworthy service providers, although Uber does so in a more direct and transparent manner. Even here, however, the two approaches are more similar than may appear – FINRA has deployed a new online system, called BrokerCheck, for aggregating customer complaints against brokers.

But there are some key differences. The exchange or SRO approach grew out of an absence of government regulation, while Uber and its ilk are challenging *existing* government regulation. FINRA is authorized by statute and has a monopoly position on the private regulation of brokers, while Uber is often operating in arguable violation of statutes and has no privileged position in the market. Thus, the key problems emerging in the SRO approach, especially in the case of FINRA, are not yet troubling in the case of the new digital tribe platform.

Perhaps most interestingly, however, is how both FINRA and Uber demonstrate ways in which private regulation, be it a mere platform or an SRO, offers ways in which there can be *more* regulation. As William O. Douglas argued to the Hartford Bond Club when defending the SRO model in the 1930s, private regulation offers ways of getting into the cracks of misbehavior that government cannot reach. Uber too can regulate customer transactions in ways that the taxi commission of a US city cannot. Uber tailors regulation, gets immediate feedback, and even rates customers, thus incentivizing good behavior on both sides. Can we imagine government rating citizens?!

These examples show how the debate about the amount of regulation in society is often misleadingly characterized as about the size of government. Instead, the right

questions to be asking are how much regulatory control is demanded by the market
and which supplier of that control is the most efficient at meeting this demand.

We can think of the transition from the FINRA model to the Uber model as the
evolution from self-regulation to peer-to-peer (PTP) regulation. The chief benefit of
the PTP approach is that there is no intermediary organization that can be corrupted. FINRA can be captured or distorted in ways that are not aligned with social
welfare. And there is no competitor to take its place or offer an alternative. FINRA
may be better than the SEC along certain dimensions, but it is a monopolist, just like
the SEC and other government regulators. Uber, eBay, and Amazon, on the other
hand, are merely mechanisms that enable PTP regulation. The content of the
regulation cannot be captured as easily, if at all, because of its diffuse nature. And
there are multiple competitors offering the mechanism, thus reducing the threat of
capture.

We explore the evolution from SRO to PTP regulation, from the New York Stock
Exchange and FINRA to Uber, in the next chapter.

8

Providing Trust in the Ridesharing Market

Regulation in all its various forms has been used over the past century and more to create the trust necessary to enable strangers to share rides. As we explore in this chapter, the initial regulation of the ridesharing market was provided by government, which limited entry, set rates, and prescribed service standards. But, as the history we briefly survey in this chapter suggests, this approach, while beneficial, was not sacred. It was, given the resources and information available at the time, the best approach possible. That is no longer true, which gives us deep insights into the very nature of regulation and government power. The regulation of taxi cabs is another example of the interaction between private and public provisions of trust. Government regulation of some activities has been viewed as the only solution possible, imperfect as it is, for certain problems. Taxi regulation fits this description. As we will see through an examination of its rise and perseverance, despite well-known and well-documented problems, the government-enforced taxi cartel lasted for nearly 100 years. But the rise of ridesharing platforms, such as Uber, calls all this into doubt.

Importantly, the story of taxi regulation defies the traditional overlays of too much or too little regulation. Instead, it perfectly illustrates that the optimal trust provider can evolve alongside the industry and technological progress, irrespective of the amount of government regulation.

HOW THE TAXI INDUSTRY CAME TO BE REGULATED

Although taxi cab regulation had ancient antecedents in England,[1] the first US regulations appeared in the 1920s.[2] As in other industries, regulation came in response to the taxi industry's demand for a way to prevent new competition, although it was justified as a way to ensure quality. During the Great Depression,

---

[1] Taxis were regulated as soon as they appeared on London streets. For instance, in 1635, a license was required for London hackneys to "restrain the multitude and promiscuous use of coaches." US Department of Transport, "Taxicab Regulation in US Cities," 5 (1983).

[2] Mark Frankena & Paul Pautler, "An Economic Analysis of Taxicab Regulation," 75 (1984), available at: www.ftc.gov/sites/default/files/documents/reports/economic-analysis-taxicab-regulation/233832.pdf

shocks to the supply and demand for cabs created dislocations that caused public outrage over the state of the industry. A newspaper editorial in 1933 summarized these views:

> Cut-throat competition in a business of this kind always produces chaos. Drivers are working as long as sixteen hours per day, in their desperate efforts to eke out a living. Cabs are allowed to go unrepaired … Together with the rise in the accident rate there has been a sharp decline in the financial responsibility of taxicab operators. Too frequently the victims of taxicab accidents must bear the loss because the operator has no resources of his own and no liability insurance. There is no excuse for a city exposing its people to such dangers.[3]

Depression-era economists provided another justification for government control: competition, especially from part-time entrants, was limiting supply efficiencies, which ultimately raised costs for a given level of quality.[4]

For several decades, taxi regulation was an accepted part of the US landscape. Defenders of the regulatory regime during the 1960s and 1970s offered many justifications for it. One was that the normal forces of supply and demand could not operate in the taxi market because of the lack of price competition in the taxi cruising market.[5] While consumers can shop around for the best deal on pickles or puffy winter jackets, this is much more costly when standing on the corner in the rain trying to hail a ride. The greater costs of finding a better alternative ride made the possibility of a non-functioning market higher, and thus required government regulation.

Another defense of government regulation was the alleged externalities imposed by "excessive entry" into the taxi business. One author noted that additional cabs above the artificial ceiling imposed by government-required licenses would "increase traffic congestion and raise the level of air pollution …" and concluded, "[t]he price of a ride in a system of free entry will cover only the private cost. The social cost per ride, which includes the externalities, will necessarily exceed the price."[6]

Finally, others argued that the must-carry requirements of a taxi license resulted in cross-subsidization from rich to poor areas – without regulation, the argument went, taxis would only pick up relatively rich people.[7] Ultimately, the consensus view was that the industry was simply not sustainable in the absence of regulation.[8]

---

[3]   "Taxicab Chaos," *Washington Post*, January 25, 1933.

[4]   Sandra Rosenbloom, "The Taxi in the Urban Transport System," In: *Urban Transit: The Private Challenge to Public Transportation*, Charles Lave (ed.) (1984).

[5]   Chanoch Shreiber, "The Economic Reasons for Price and Entry Regulation of Taxicabs," 9 *JTEP* 268, 270 (1975).

[6]   Ibid. at 274.

[7]   James Foerster & Gorman Gilbert, "Taxicab Deregulation: Economic Consequences and Regulatory Choices," 8 *Transportation* 371, 383 (1979).

[8]   Chanoch Shreiber, "The Economic Reasons for Price and Entry Regulation of Taxicabs," 9 *JTEP* 275–76 (1975). Commentators frequently described the taxi market as an "empty core." See John Shepard Wiley, Jr., "Antitrust and Core Theory," 54 *U. Chi. L. Rev.* 556, 560–61 (1987).

THE MOVEMENT TO DEREGULATE

However, during this time, there were serious efforts by economists to look more critically at regulation in general, and specifically at taxi regulation. In his 1962 textbook *Price Theory: A Provisional Text*, the economist Milton Friedman included seventeen problems in an appendix. The one on taxi regulation generated the most interest. In a subtle hypothetical, he asked students to comment on cabbies' concerns that an increase in licenses would lead to lower wages for drivers. Friedman was pointing to a new narrative: restrictions in the supply of taxis could be motivated by the self-interest of the industry. Other economists, who viewed the regulation as inefficient, shared this view.[9]

Within a decade, the anti-regulation story was gaining visibility. A famous 1971 article examined in amazing detail the cab market in Chicago. It took for granted the consensus view among academics that taxi regulation was a "clear case of unwise government policy."[10] Limiting supply resulted in fewer cabs than optimal, and at higher prices. In addition, regulation concentrated power over customer service issues and reduced innovation. So, in their article, Ed Kitch and colleagues therefore tried to answer a different question: "Why has a policy adverse to the interests of consumers been so frequent and so persistent in US cities?"

Through a detailed examination of the different types of services offered in all parts of the city, they determined that the city deliberately under-enforced the regulations in order to prevent public backlash and political pressure from the policy. In their words: "Tacit acceptance of illegal operations by the city has sidetracked and contained political forces which otherwise would have been directed against the ordinance itself."[11] For instance, in poor areas where taxis would not go, despite the legal requirement to do so, the city tolerated illegal jitney services. This policy relieved the political pressure that would have come from the poor communities, and satisfied the demands of cabbies who did not want to travel to these areas of the city.[12]

But the combination of legal taxis and illegal jitneys was inferior to a system in which legal providers served all customers. Being illegal suppresses both supply and demand. It means that jitneys were beyond the reach of some laws, just as loan sharks don't end up in court. Not everyone is willing to ride in illegal cabs, nor are some potential providers willing to risk the prospect of being charged with violating the law. In addition, not everyone is aware of the services being offered, since illegal services don't advertise in the newspaper or on television. One of the authors moved to the South Side of Chicago in the early 1990s, long before Uber existed and at a time when taxis did not regularly serve the overwhelmingly African-American

9 J.R. Meyer, J.F. Kain & W. Wohl, *The Urban Transportation Problem* (1965).
10 Edmund W. Kitch, Marc Isaacson & Daniel Kasper, "The Regulation of Taxicabs in Chicago," 14 *J. Law & Econ.* 285 (1971).
11 Ibid. at 286.
12 Ibid.

community. The only knowledge he had of jitneys was from the law review article and, over more than a decade of living there, he never rode in one. Uber now serves the South Side, providing work opportunities for many local residents. It has, in short, brought the illegal ridesharing market out into the open, making it more accessible to a broader segment of the population, improved the quality of service, and subjected it to tax authorities and safety regulations.

DEREGULATION AND RE-REGULATION

Despite the case marshaled by defenders of regulation, the deregulatory mood established by the end of the Carter administration and culminating in the Reagan–Thatcher revolution of 1980 swept over the taxi industry. From 1979 to 1984, over twenty US cities, mostly in the south and west (e.g. Atlanta, Charlotte, Jacksonville, Kansas City, Oakland, and Phoenix), deregulated their taxi industries in whole or in part. The deregulatory mood peaked with a 1984 report by the FTC, which concluded that there is "no persuasive economic rationale ... available for some of the most import regulations" of the taxi industry.[13] Contrary to the above-mentioned claims of defenders of regulation, the report concluded that, "[r]estrictions on the total number of firms and vehicles and on minimum fares waste resources and impose a disproportionate burden on low income people."[14]

But, notwithstanding the economic theory and the FTC's conclusion, the experiments with deregulation were largely failures. A 1993 report issued by Price Waterhouse (sponsored by the International Taxicab Foundation) concluded that, while deregulation had resulted in obvious benefits in other industries, these benefits were illusory in the taxi industry.[15] The Price Waterhouse report noted that seventeen of twenty-one cities that deregulated the taxi industry in the early 1980s had re-regulated by 1993 and that, overall, the results of deregulation were negative: prices rose while service quality declined. The report concluded that the taxi market had "imperfections that reduce or remove incentives for price and service quality competition," and that the effects of "taxi deregulation have ranged from benign to adverse."[16]

The solution may have been elusive but the facts on the ground were simple. The benefits of taxis were great, but the complexities of the market were tricky. The government's regulations were bad but the alternatives were worse.

There was a real trust problem here: someone needed to provide the trust that getting into a stranger's car on a city street would be a safe and fair transaction, and

---

[13] Mark W. Frankena & Paul A. Pautler, "An Economic Analysis of Taxicab Regulation," (1984), available at: www.ftc.gov/sites/default/files/documents/reports/economic-analysis-taxicab-regulation/233832.pdf

[14] Ibid.

[15] Price Waterhouse, "Analysis of Taxicab Deregulation and Reregulation," (1993).

[16] Ibid.

the nature of the market was such that brand or other non-government mechanisms were unavailable or, at least, ineffective. After all, a prospective rider doesn't have a lot of choice when hailing a cab, doesn't ride enough to form an attachment to a particular brand, and doesn't have enough at stake to sue if cheated. National brands might have solved some, but not all, of these problems, but at the time these were extremely costly to create. Instead, the requirement that cabs pick up all riders, charge a fixed cost per mile, and post a bond against cheating (in the form of a medallion) proved a workable, but imperfect, solution to this trust problem.

AN ECONOMIC DEFENSE OF REGULATION

The strongest argument for regulation was that two rules – must-carry and average-cost pricing – were designed to solve a particular economic problem presented by the taxi industry.[17] Specifically, in the taxi market, bargaining is impossible or, at least, prohibitively expensive and inefficient.[18] The problem is that buyers (riders) do not know the reasonable price for a ride at any particular time and location. There are several reasons for this, but the primary one is that the costs for the sellers (drivers) varies significantly based on information, such as distance, driving conditions, and whether or not there is likely to be a return fare, which are likely known by the driver but not the rider.

The informational asymmetry is two-sided, however, since sellers do not know how much buyers would be willing to pay for any particular ride. Negotiation and competition are standard solutions to this problem, but such solutions are impossible to imagine in the cab space, whether they are in a taxi stand at the airport or in the so-called cruising market. As proponents of regulation see it, government regulation of cabs is a second-best solution to this problem. By mandating a standard-form contract, the government regulator can provide the trust about price and service conditions that allows the market to clear and transactions to occur. The requirement that sellers take all possible riders and charge an average cost (i.e., the per-mile, metered rate) is good for both buyers and sellers, since it makes the price for a ride predictable. Riders therefore will not be surprised or cheated, and sellers know that less lucrative rides will be offset by more lucrative ones.

THE SHORTCOMINGS OF GOVERNMENT REGULATION

The same lack of customer information that caused deregulation to fail also causes problems in the regulated taxi market. Just as the average consumer doesn't know what a ride should cost, she also doesn't pay close attention to the regulators or rules

---

[17] Edward C. Gallick & David E. Sisk, "A Reconsideration of Taxi Regulation," 3 *J. L. Econ. & Org.* 117 (1987).
[18] Ibid.

of the local taxi industry. The only people who most likely do vote for public officials based on cab-related issues are taxi cab owners. While political backlash can affect government monopolies, causing real changes in policy – as the recent Black Lives Matter protests undoubtedly did on police policies – there are simply too many parts of government that are too obscure or too small to muster marches in the streets or turn votes at the ballot box.

If each of us suffers a small harm, and remedying that harm costs more than the harm itself, we are unlikely to see the problem fixed. When your driver drove like a maniac or lied about the credit card machine not working, you were annoyed. But not annoyed enough to fundraise for an advocacy organization that can hire lobbyists to fix the problem (or even to write to your congressman about it). When you add these small inconveniences up across a broad population, they can represent an enormous aggregate harm, but they persist because it doesn't make sense for any individual to do anything about them. Economists call this a "collective-action problem."

This point is made worse by the fact that regulation of cabs is indirect from representative government, thus raising the costs of obtaining information and acting against bad policy. The regulators on the taxi commission are unelected and thus are unaccountable to political scrutiny. They're usually appointed by an elected official who probably did not give great thought to this appointment. As such, the taxi commission most likely provides only the bare minimum in terms of matching regulation to customer demands. Regulators can't provide the optimal level of trust for the following familiar reasons: bureaucracy, influence peddling, and regulators being too cozy with the businesses they regulate. And without a feedback mechanism, regulators cannot know what consumers want, and voters can do little about it.

Imagine a city's mayor appoints members to the cab commission. Taxi companies donate heavily to a candidate's mayoral campaign and, when it comes time to select a cab regulator (a position that will generate very little public attention), it would not be surprising to see the mayor appoint someone friendly to the interests of the taxi companies. This familiar public-choice problem persists throughout the political system, but produces stark and easily observed downsides in the cab industry.

On the service side, anyone who has ridden in a taxi has experienced the low quality of vehicles and the poor customer service. Innovations, such as credit card payment machines, also come only via the regulators, which inhibits experimentation and imposes costs on riders without consideration of the benefits. The screens installed in cabs to show clips of news programs are a prominent example of a regulator-inspired "innovation" with little connection to market demand. One sees snacks, water, and magazines appearing in the back of some Uber vehicles today, but no video screens or glass shields. Whether customers demand these innovations remains to be seen, but the answer will come through market experimentation, not the guess of a cab commissioner.

But there are larger failures in the regulated taxi market. A prominent example is longhauling, where a cab runs up the fare by taking an unnecessarily long route. Longhauling is a common problem in Las Vegas, one the taxi commission tried repeatedly to solve through tactics such as roadblocks, posting giant signs at the airport with typical fares, giving passengers the opportunity to fill out complaint forms, shaming longhaulers by putting their names on a website, and so on.[19]

THE SOLUTION: DIGITAL RIDESHARING PLATFORMS

Unsurprisingly, none of these approaches worked. They were misguided attempts to do something that Uber and other digital ridesharing platforms can do at an extremely low cost: monitor drivers to ensure rides are efficient and provide an easy mechanism for dispute resolution. Because rides are tracked by GPS, if an Uber tries to longhaul a passenger in Las Vegas, the rider receives an instant rebate. These are also available when customers provide highly dissatisfactory reviews – in the form of a five-star rating system accessible on the rider's mobile device. This system takes into account the behavioral quirks of modern riders – the ubiquity of mobile devices, the familiarity and simplicity of the rating system, and the need to give instantaneous feedback – whereas the attempts of the Las Vegas taxi commission paid them no attention, relying instead on bureaucracy, overcomplicated legal documents, and delays.

For instance, one iteration of the cab commission's approach to solving the longhauling problem involved riders filling out, notarizing, and mailing in a "Long Route Voluntary Witness Statement," and then hoping that the bureaucracy would someday rule in their favor and send them the extra $5 they paid for a longhaul trip.[20] This was impractical for passengers and potentially unfair to drivers. Getting your $5 back is not worth suffering through this bureaucratic misadventure. And even if you did, there is no way for the regulator to verify that you were actually longhauled in the first place. So the longhauling continued. The same collective-action problems that prevent accountability of the taxi commission also enable Las Vegas taxis to make significant profits by skimming a bit from each longhauled passenger.

In short, both the Las Vegas taxi commission and Uber were trying to create a system of rules and behavior in which riders leaving from the airport and heading to the Strip could trust that they would be treated fairly. They competed to offer a legal framework in which voluntary exchanges could happen at the lowest possible cost. Seen in this way, Uber is a competitor of government, not of existing taxis. Neither Uber nor the taxi commission owns any taxis or employ any drivers. Instead,

---

[19] Blake Ross, "It's Time to Let the Government Drive," *Medium*, December 2, 2014, available at: https://medium.com/@blakeross/.uber-gov-29db5fdff372#.xmiax7x5z

[20] See http://taxi.nv.gov/uploadedFiles/taxinvgov/content/Complaints/complaint_form/LongRouteForm_Interactive.pdf

both provide a platform of tools and rules that enable buyers and sellers to contract for rides.

LESSONS LEARNED

What made the Uber innovation successful in breaking down the government's monopoly, while the deregulatory attempts of the 1980s failed? We see two primary differences between these two experiences that explain the failure of deregulation and the success of Uber and other ridesharing companies.

First, the deregulation of the 1980s was a political act. Ideologically motivated legislators pushed for deregulation based on a high-level view about the power of markets and the inefficiencies of government regulation. Whether or not you share these views, examining the economics of the taxi cab market demonstrates that it isn't a simple market that can thrive when unshackled from regulation.

Moreover, as an act of politics, deregulation had to be a matter of compromise among legislators who were subjected to the same political pressures and distortions discussed earlier. Breaking down the government's monopoly on regulation entailed overcoming these distortions to a certain extent, but the details of the deregulation were still left to negotiations among interested parties such as cab companies. Consumers were not represented in these decisions.

The other missing piece in the process were potential new market competitors (such as ridesharing companies), who did not yet know of the innovations in the market that they might bring. Regulations were thus an opening but only a partial opportunity for new possibilities of service. After all, as discussed earlier, Uber offers an entirely new alternative – which entails, in some ways, *more* regulation than the government alternative – that would not have been possible under even the deregulated cab markets of several jurisdictions. Deregulation is a product of the same sausage-making process as the regulation it is meant to eliminate, and thus is vulnerable to the same problems. Therefore, even where regulated markets function poorly, the process of deregulation may not be an improvement.

Second, the technology at the time was not sufficient to solve the economic problems presented by the cab market. The typical market-based solutions did not work for cabs because it was virtually impossible for passengers to know a fair price or differentiate between honest and dishonest cabs. The Las Vegas cab commission's notarized "Long Route Voluntary Witness Statements" were no technological revelation, and were far too cumbersome to prevent cab drivers from taking advantage of passengers. Where too much and too little regulation failed, the digital tribe succeeded.

These problems were finally solved by ridesharing companies: distributed, reputation-based regulatory systems that offer a passenger not only GPS ride maps, but also the information and curation of thousands of riders before. You may not know whether it is safe to get in Bob's car, but the 5,000 previous passengers who've ridden with Bob before can attest to him, and his five-star rating on Uber's platform instantly and inexpensively delivers you this information. It is information that has always existed, but Uber has made it accessible to the person who most needs it at precisely the moment they need it.[21] The answer wasn't an unaccountable expert or an unregulated market, it was the digital tribe.

The information problem facing regulators is resolved to a great extent when the regulator is a platform with real-time information flows from providers and consumers.[22] To solve trust problems, the right question is not *how much* regulation should there be, but rather *who* should do the regulating.

---

[21] Interestingly, some research suggests that former cab drivers tend to have lower ratings when driving for Uber than drivers who began their driving careers with Uber, perhaps because they were never rated before and thus didn't value passenger experience.

[22] The economist F.A. Hayek called this the "knowledge problem." See F.A. Hayek, "The Use of Knowledge in Society," 4 *Am. Econ. Rev.* 519 (1945). But perhaps the best description was from French statesman Anne Robert Jacques Turgot (1727–1781): "For, in order to direct trade and commerce it would be necessary [for the government] to be able to have knowledge of all of the variations of needs, interests, and human industry in such detail as is physically impossible to obtain even by the most able, active, and circumstantial government."

PART III

In Part I, we set out the problem of trust, a brief history of how it has been created, and an analytical framework for thinking about how trust is provided. We introduced the idea of a market for trust, with governments and businesses, among others, competing to offer trust that is demanded by individuals in society.

Part II then considered two examples of the private provision of trust as an alternative to regulation. The stock market started as an alternative to government regulation, driven by necessity after the government refused to enforce brokerage contracts. Self-regulation, which had ancient roots in the medieval cartels and the Law Merchant, blossomed as an alternative to government regulation. Even New Dealers, such as William O. Douglas, recognized the efficiency of private regulation, including it in the overarching federal securities regulation regime of the 1930s.

Ridesharing regulation is the next step in the evolution of trust. The SRO model, in both medieval Europe and in early stock-exchange regulation, arose because of the absence of regulatory power; the innovations of Uber and other internet-platform companies are instead a challenge to existing government regulation. Such innovations are promising to unring the bell.

In the next part, we examine this possibility in more detail. In Chapter 9, we consider how companies such as Uber have taken on established government monopolies on trust. Then, in Chapter 10, we sketch on a blank slate, imagining a future in which more and more types of trust, which we traditionally think of as provided by government, are provided by internet-enabled platforms such as Uber, eBay, and the like. Our tour covers some ground that may soon be ripe for challenge and other ground that lies far in the future. Our goal in this chapter is not to predict the future, but rather to open our minds to the possibilities of trust being provided in new and innovative ways. We are not entrepreneurs and so we cannot predict what technologies will develop or what the next Uber will look like. We only hope to inspire others to build alternatives to government in enabling social cooperation.

9

Hacking Trust

Although viewers of the USA Network series *Mr. Robot* may associate the term "hack" with unauthorized access to and disruption of computer services – the so-called 5/9 hack that brought down E-Corp. – in Silicon Valley parlance, a hack also has a much rosier meaning: a hack in the Bay Area is a solution to a problem. Techies routinely hold hackathons in which they put their computer programming skills to work to solve discrete problems. When we say that Uber has "hacked" trust, we mean it in this way. It has figured out a way, using software code, the internet, and human ingenuity, to solve the problem of trust in an elegant way. And Uber is only the beginning.

Uber and other platform companies are providing trust in new and exciting ways, as we have looked at in previous chapters and will discuss more in the pages that follow. But it is important to consider them in the chain that started with the family and moved through tribes and nations, and, most recently, through the use of brand. It is worth briefly revisiting the story so far in order to see the innovations that, as part of the trust hack, have been brought to the conversation by ridesharing companies and other trust-delivery platforms.

The first modern trust innovation was brand. The rise of brand was an early trust hack, although no one would have thought of it this way or used these terms. Instead, brand just a means of competitive advantage. Corporate brands, such as McDonalds, offered trust to consumers – one could trust that a Big Mac was a Big Mac, whether it was in Boston, Bucharest, or Bangalore – as a means of winning business. McDonalds was able to profit and grow, relative to mom-and-pop diners or the like, because of the brand it built.

As part of this expansion of its business, McDonalds created opportunities for more voluntary interactions among people – more social cooperation as we've described it – without the need for much additional government action. McDonalds and countless other brands built reputations that permitted trust at levels that, in the past, would have required government intervention. One could trust in a McDonalds experience across the United States in the 1960s, not because the government stood behind it, but because "McDonalds" did. The rise of brands, starting seriously in post-War USA, offered alternatives to government regulation at the margin of regulation, preventing the need for additional government regulation.

We can imagine how new government regulations – such as inspections, insurance requirements, certifications, tweaked tort rules, and so on – could have created the requisite levels of trust necessary for individuals to eat hamburgers from roadside restaurants anywhere in the nation or world. But McDonalds provided most of this trust instead, through the bond created by its advertising and through its own supply-chain regulation. (The government also plays an important supporting role here, providing courts, legal causes of action, some inspections, and so on, and these have expanded as the private provision of trust has expanded. The point is merely that they have expanded less than they would have without the private supply of trust.)

eBay and Amazon are like McDonalds. They have enabled massive scaling of trust through the use of a decentralized process – namely the five-star customer review process and associated customer feedback mechanism. As we described earlier, this has enabled voluntary transactions across the globe in ways that were unimaginable just a few years ago. If these platform companies had not developed these technologies, there were two possibilities: either the transactions would not have happened or governments would have had to build additional bureaucracies and mechanisms for supplying the necessary trust.

In both the case of brand (McDonalds) and the internet platform (eBay), trust innovation forestalled additional government regulation that would have been necessary for the same transactions (in scope, volume, frequency, size, and so forth) to happen in the absence of brand or the platform. The expansion of trust to permit additional voluntary transactions happened through non-governmental means. In the next section, we will look at how ridesharing companies and other platform companies are going a step further, not only providing new trust, but also challenging the government trust that is already being provided.

UNRINGING THE BELL

Uber and other ridesharing companies have done something different: they did not build additional trust mechanisms on top of the old ones, like McDonalds and eBay and Amazon did; instead, they reimagined trust mechanisms from the ground up, taking account of new technologies and cooperation methods. They have offered an alternative to existing regulations, instead of forestalling new ones. Where traditional brands supplied trust, it meant government had to create less new regulation. Uber has demonstrated the possibility that even *existing* regulation can be disrupted.

New trust providers are "hacking" old, monopolistic trust mechanisms to build a new kind of regulation, what we'll call "microregulation," which delivers better results at lower costs. As the world grows more complex, demand for trust will grow exponentially as more and increasingly complex cooperation becomes possible, and new digital institutions are rising to meet this demand. New businesses are being created that are selling primarily trust, and these businesses have the potential to supply trust even in areas that we've historically thought of as solely the responsibility of government.

Uber disrupted the old taxi regulatory model. In essence, when Uber launched, its major competitor was not existing businesses, in the way that Amazon was trying to take the business of brick-and-mortar retailers. Instead, Uber's competition was *government*. Uber wasn't building an alternative to any taxi company, it was building an alternative to the taxi *commission*; it was competing with the government in the market for trust.

Just like the Chicago taxi commission, Uber owns no cabs; instead, it offers a regulatory and supervisory system designed to ensure that independent drivers provide a good service.[1] Uber's value proposition was that they could be trusted more than the cab commission to ensure that drivers gave passengers what they actually wanted – a clean, safe ride at a reasonable cost.[2] Unlike traditional brands, which forestalled additional government regulation, Uber used technology to do what government could not and, in the process, rendered the existing regulations obsolete.

What Uber has done in both aspects of its business is to link the amount and type of regulation it offers more closely with the customer experience. Government regulators are funded through taxes, which are paid by all citizens, while Uber's regulatory model is funded only by customers. Therefore, payment for and delivery of trust are more closely linked in Uber's model. This should, all else being equal, result in better performance, since it enables a level of feedback and responsiveness that is unavailable when benefits are concentrated and costs are dispersed. Government regulators are beholden to all citizens or, perhaps more realistically, the ones who vote or otherwise buy influence; Uber, on the other hand, is beholden only to its customers. Government only acts (e.g. offering more, less, or different regulation) when there is enough political pressure to do so, and only within the boundaries of law.

Consider that all government regulation is a temporal snapshot. Government fixes the "safe" course of action in time based on the moment a law passes. Since political consensus is difficult to build, laws are passed and often forgotten by regulators unless enforced or revisited in another crisis (which usually signals an increase, but rarely a decrease, in the amount of regulation). As a result, creating laws or regulations that are hard to change effectively fixes a current state of the economy in time, despite the fact that the economy changes rapidly. On top of this,

---

[1] Uber, of course, can be viewed in many other lights. For example, as the ultimate enabler of microfirms, it enables a person to monetize their own assets and labor while handling all back-end aspects, from customer acquisition to payment. This empowers labor in much the same way that Amazon Web Services, Zenefits, and Stripe allow entrepreneurs to quickly mimic scale, and effectively lowers the barrier for becoming an entrepreneur to near-zero.

[2] It is worth noting that the simplicity of Uber's ratings system comes at the cost of granularity. It's impossible to tell whether a driver with a mediocre review is rated this way because she is rude, has a dirty car, or drives erratically, etc.

regulators' incentives largely align them with risk aversion and maintaining the status quo. A regulator doesn't receive credit for the value created by phenomenal new products available to people, but it does get complaint calls from angry constituents when some new technology threatens their established businesses. These factors together are a recipe for stagnation, forcing any new innovation to sidestep a minefield of complicated regulation that may no longer serve its original health or safety purpose, if indeed it had one to begin with.

Such regulations will also be far less consumer focused than private industry is. They may also be driven by the selfish interests of the cab owners or other stakeholders, as opposed to customers. Uber's model, on the other hand, is one of rapid response, tailoring, and customer accountability.

This means that Uber can do things – can *regulate* – in ways that government cannot. Not only are there constitutional limitations,[3] but our natural distrust of government power will put limits on the kinds of things that governments can do. For instance, Uber and other ridesharing companies allow consumers to rate drivers, but also allow drivers to rate consumers. This affects consumers' ability to obtain rides, and therefore incentivizes good behavior on their part as well. This is something that is uniquely in the province of businesses, at least in the United States.

One response to this is that government should just adopt these tools itself. In her book *Smarter Citizens, Smarter State*, Beth Noveck argues essentially that government should become a provider of digital trust services.[4] While it might be sensible to enhance existing government services by using the trust technologies created by private businesses, we have strong concerns about government meandering into this area without a clear justification. Government operates based on a monopoly on violence and, given the innumerable and vital areas of government activity, letting the political branches collect this kind of data would be risky. One could imagine citizens being rated not based on factors germane to the government decision, but rather by political party, membership in a particular constituency, or another illicit ground. Not to put too fine a point on it, but would you want to empower the politicians we actually elect to deploy these technologies?

It is this concern that raises alarm bells about China's experimental social credit system. China is deploying an Uber-style rating system that assigns a score to citizens based on a range of factors from spending habits to turnstile violations.[5] China plans to condition certain social services and rights (such as the ability to travel) on a citizen's score. A world where government controls essential goods such as food

---

[3] Government, for good reason, cannot cater to only certain portions of the population or favor some citizens over others. By contrast, businesses can, meaning that different market needs are customized.

[4] See Beth Noveck, *Smarter Citizens, Smarter State* (2015).

[5] See Josh Chin & Gillian Wong, "China's New Tool for Social Control: A Credit Rating for Everything," *The Wall Street Journal*, November 28, 2016, available at: www.wsj.com/articles/chinas-new-tool-for-social-control-a-credit-rating-for-everything-1480351590

and healthcare and has the ability to ration based on citizen obedience is a scary one indeed.[6]

And yet, millions of consumers willingly tolerate this conduct by the Ubers of the world. Perhaps because it is less creepy when a private business, subject to market competition, does it and perhaps because consumers see the real benefits of the policy in action, instead of imagining the pros and cons in a theoretical political debate.

The platform of regulation provided by the New York Stock Exchange (and now FINRA, the successor organization to the New York Stock Exchange's regulatory authority) is another example of the value of regulators unmoored by constitutional constraints. As noted earlier, when FINRA conducts an investigation, brokers cannot assert their constitutional rights to avoid warrantless searches or self-incrimination. In addition, the burdens of proof and legal intensity of proceedings implemented by FINRA are much lower, increasing the efficiency of regulation. FINRA can do things government cannot, and this additional regulatory capacity enabled by its private character is a significant benefit to the overall regulatory scheme.

The pace of private trust providers is an asset not only for reducing regulation that no longer makes sense, but also for increasing regulation where more is called for. FINRA can act much more quickly when a market distortion appears or before a crisis takes place, in contrast with dragging the behemoth of Congress to a crash site and hoping to salvage what is possible from the ruins. We have more trust in brokers than we would in a world of solely government regulation.

FOR-PROFIT REGULATORS

The fact that Uber is motivated by profit surely complicates its ability to supply trust. This fact can enhance the creation of trust, just as the investments in global brands during the past fifty years have. McDonalds' selfish motive for profit was the fire that forged its trust innovations. But the profit motive may also lead to problems or concerns that are worthy of further examination. Profit seeking generally encourages trust creation, but not in all scenarios. For instance, profit-making businesses necessarily try to reduce cross-subsidies that are not efficient for the business.[7] As discussed earlier, proponents of government regulation of taxis argued that

---

[6] It could be argued that this is already starting to happen in the UK, with public outcry at the result. Consider the rationing of healthcare based on body mass index (a measure of obesity). See Henry Bodkin, "Obese patients and smokers banned from routine surgery in 'most severe ever' rationing in the NHS," *The Telegraph*, September 2, 2016, available at: www.telegraph.co.uk/news/2016/09/02/obese-patients-and-smokers-banned-from-all-routine-operations-by/

[7] Cross subsidies – where one group pays for another group – are a common feature of government policy and feature in many areas of law. For instance, if products liability law makes compensation very easy to recover from the maker of an appliance, this will raise the cost of the appliance because the maker will factor the cost of lawsuits into the overhead costs of the appliance. Importantly, in this case, careless users who are likely to harm themselves with the appliance will pay the same price to buy it as careful users who would be unlikely to harm themselves. The careful users pay more than they should

deregulation would harm poor city dwellers, since must-carry rules and average-cost pricing effectively resulted in subsidies from rich to poor. There are problems with this account, both in economic terms and in terms of real-world behavior – as the study by Ed Kitch noted, cabs routinely flouted must-carry rules, leaving parts of US cities such as Chicago unserved by regulated cabs. But, insofar as taxi regulation achieves these redistributional cross-subsidies, then "unregulated" cabs might engage in the kind of cream skimming (i.e., serving only wealthy passengers) that defenders of regulation in the 1960s and 1970s praised. In reality, taxi regulation not only failed to achieve such redistributional goals, but actually failed to provide access for lower-income citizens. If anything, the anecdotal evidence suggests that ridesharing services provide much greater access to rides in low-income neighborhoods, through lower fares, an increase in available drivers, and the use of drivers from low-income neighborhoods that do not see driving in them as risky.

Moreover, the new models provide a profit-based incentive to undo perverse redistribution. If the poor were really subsidizing the rich having access to cabs in the old model (as we think is a more accurate assessment of the facts), then ridesharing companies have every incentive to avoid this by ensuring that their customers maximize what they receive in return for what they pay.

Not all for-profit trust providers are created equal, and there is certainly a risk of certain types of digital trust systems being gamed by outside entities or manipulated internally by a trust provider.[8] A particular platform provider might provide an algorithm that does an imperfect or even a bad job of sorting and weighting different reviews, for example.[9] Consider the familiar five-star rating system employed by TripAdvisor, Yelp, and others. There's an estimated 5 to 9 percent revenue bump for independent restaurants associated with adding a Yelp star, for example, which could raise the incentive for a restaurant to try to artificially raise its rating.[10] But no corresponding benefit exists for Yelp. In fact, Yelp's goal is to ensure accurate ratings because, the more that consumer experience diverges from the expected rating, the less consumers will value its platform. Accordingly, the platform has an incentive to combat fraud. It won't be perfect, of course. No regulatory system is. We

(to compensate for the lawsuits of the careless) and the careless users pay less than they should (because they increase the overhead). In this way, the careful can be said to be subsidizing the careless. If there were no products liability laws, profit-driven businesses would tailor their products to the overhead costs of particular customers. One familiar and efficient example of this is the insurance space, where insurers charge higher premiums for those whose risk profile indicates that they will be more costly to insure.

8 Brad Tuttle, "5 Outrageous Ways People Try to Game Online Reviews," *Money*, August 6, 2014, available at: http://time.com/money/3083615/yelp-tripadvisor-trust-user-review-sites/

9 See Michael Luca & Georgios Zervas, "Fake It Till You Make It: Reputation, Competition, and Yelp Review Fraud," *SSRN* (May 1, 2015), Harvard Business School NOM Unit Working Paper No 14-006, available at: https://ssrn.com/abstract=2293164 or http://dx.doi.org/10.2139/ssrn.2293164

10 Michael Luca, "Reviews, Reputation, and Review: The Case of Yelp.com," *SSRN* (September 16, 2011), Harvard Business School Working Paper No 12-016, available at: https://papers.ssrn.com/sol3/papers.cfm?abstract_id=1928601

are not here to compare it or other systems with perfection; instead, we make a comparison with the next best alternative. Economists call the failure to do so the Nirvana Fallacy.

This is slightly different from examples such as Uber and Airbnb, where the relationship between the rating and the company's services are closer. If an Uber driver receives consistently low ratings, they'll be removed from the platform because, unlike Yelp, Uber as a matchmaker bears some degree of responsibility for the service received. Consider, for example, the risk that Uber, during a shortage of drivers, artificially inflates driver ratings to provide service in a given locality. This is of course a concern, but one that is mitigated by the ease with which consumers can switch to a competitor such as Lyft.

It is also worth mentioning that ratings systems are limited by the ability of the rater to provide valuable information, which is strained where an informational asymmetry exists that may not be easily remediable. Think of rating not drivers but heart surgeons. When a person has surgery, they may be under the impression that the surgeon did a poor job because she had a poor bedside manner, but that is mostly irrelevant to the value of the underlying service (the surgery). Similarly, one might believe a surgeon did a good job because the patient survived, but it may be that she had a high probability of surviving and the surgeon did a sub-par job. The point is that, in these situations, the patient would not have a reason to know much about the value of the service received, but may *think* she does. The information provided might then be of limited (or even negative) value to someone relying on the information.

This raises some broader questions about what can be rated and the what the underlying motivations for ratings are (maybe some Yelp reviewers are more concerned with a restaurant's atmosphere, or service, or food presentation, or taste, for example). Our point here is not that incentives are perfect, but that they are a marked improvement over old-economy trust providers such as government, which are subject to public-choice problems, move slowly to remedy problems (where, for example, Yelp is quick to kick abusers off its platform), and offer no competition. We also note that ratings are only one of many digital trust suppliers, and others, such as blockchain or prediction markets, are not vulnerable to the same information problems or incentive concerns, although they may have their own limitations, as we'll discuss later.

Consider a recent example experienced by one of the authors, who published a legal/political thriller, *Mental State*, in 2018. In an attempt to build interest in the book, the author asked some friends to read it and post reviews on Amazon. Many tried, but only a few were successful at getting their reviews up. When they contacted Amazon about the problem, they were told that Amazon screens all reviews to ensure that the system is not corrupted. Although the algorithm and criteria Amazon uses are unknown to the author, there were some factors that seemed relevant – individuals that lived on the same block, that worked in the same job, and that had close social media ties with the author were far less likely to have their reviews accepted or remain up on the website. This was bad news for the author, who wanted as many reviews as possible, especially from friendly voices, but it is reassuring as regards the five-star rating systems we are increasingly relying upon. Amazon's substantial investments in integrity are evidence that the system is robust and provides valuable information, not just noise or biased/manipulated data.

MONOPOLY

There are also monopoly concerns. Our colleague Eric Posner worries that ridesharing companies will put the taxi commission out of business and then, using a monopoly position, raise rates and reduce supply to maximize profits.[11] He argues that all regulators are the same and that once Uber has a monopoly position – as the taxi commission had before the advent of Uber – it will abuse this position. This may be true and warrants scrutiny by anti-trust officials regarding businesses as regulators, just as businesses offering other goods and services are scrutinized. There are reasons to believe, however, that the ability of any ridesharing company to become a monopoly regulator is limited.

Although Posner rightly describes Uber as a "platform" company and notes how other such companies, such as eBay and Amazon, have become extremely sticky, the current experience with ridesharing companies is notably different. There are competing ridesharing companies in every jurisdiction, and many drivers work for multiple companies at the same time. Moreover, since drivers supply all the capital required, the only switching costs are on the customer end, and these amount to nothing more than awareness and a free downloadable app. For example, Google's popular Maps app provides price comparisons between Uber and Lyft (see Figure 20), and perhaps eventually other competitors, facilitating competition. This should be no surprise: it is just another example of platform disciplining brand (brands that, in this case, happen to also be platforms themselves). This dynamic will continue to reverberate throughout the economy, slicing trust (along with other parts of the value chain) into ever-thinner slices, creating ever-greater efficiency and social value. If Google Maps didn't have this feature, another app would've popped up showing the price for Uber and its competitors, such as a miniature Kayak for cab rides.

In a real sense, Uber provides a platform to make each driver a one-man enterprise, handling back-office, payments, insurance, and the other back-end aspects of a company and allowing the owner of a capital asset (the driver's car) to apply labor to it and make a microenterprise. Accordingly, where there is misbehavior toward the driver, Uber risks losing drivers to competing platforms. Consider the recent example of Uber adding a tip feature meant to appeal to drivers, with Lyft having long included this

[11] Eric Posner, "Why Uber Will—and Should—Be Regulated," *Slate*, January 5, 2015, available at: www.law.uchicago.edu/news/eric-posner-why-uber-will-and-should-be-regulated

FIGURE 20: Screenshot of Google Maps comparison of Lyft and Uber prices

feature. These platforms set the terms of transactions between drivers and riders, which puts them at the whim of both supply forces and demand forces. In some ways, this makes it even more difficult to stake out a monopoly position.

The monopoly concern around two-sided markets in this context largely means that the drivers will want to be on the platforms with the passengers – that is, that they will follow the money. This is also a two-way street: as these companies drive toward fully autonomous ridesharing, autonomous vehicles will be able to price in these factors and switch rapidly where there are more advantageous conditions on another platform, forcing the platforms to compete on price.

And digital platform companies are vulnerable in real time to democratic objection to their decisions, as displayed by a reported 200,000 customers deleting their Uber accounts in response to disagreement with Uber's willingness to provide rides from airports where taxis were striking as part of a political protest.[12] As easily as Uber's users can become advocates for its right to operate, they can nimbly turn against it if it abuses that right.[13]

[12] See Nick Statt, "#DeleteUber reportedly led 200,000 people to delete their accounts," *The Verge*, February 2, 2017, available at: www.theverge.com/2017/2/2/14493760/delete-uber-protest-donald-trump-accounts-deleted

[13] We note the possibility of informational asymmetry here too: consumers can only criticize problems they can see, and tweaks to Uber's algorithm are as hard for a customer to discern as the appropriate

The recent experience in Austin, Texas, is also illustrative. When Lyft and Uber left the market over what they viewed as excessively burdensome regulation – finger printing of drivers, for example – new ridesharing platforms entered to fill the void.[14] Where it is clear that a model works, the costs of replicating the technology are trivial compared with the potential profits. This is not to say that the monopoly problem is not real, but rather the monopoly problem is not a reason to doubt the value of these companies, which are, in the first instance, challenging an existing (government) monopoly.

EXTERNALITIES

Another concern is apparent from the fact that platform microregulators are driven by customer demands. If the costs of a particular activity fall on individuals outside the contracting process, then external regulation might be justified as a means of reducing these external costs. Taxi cab regulation was in part based on concerns about traffic and pollution. If this is a concern, then Uber and its ilk will not be good regulators on this dimension. They do not directly bear the costs of the additional traffic and pollution they create. While this concern is real, it is not clear that limiting the number of cabs to those determined by a monopoly regulator is the most efficient solution to the problem. A Pigouvian tax[15] on miles driven would be a more efficient mechanism, since it would treat all drivers the same, leaving to the market the best way to allocate rides. We suspect that these arguments are thus merely an attempt to justify regulation of ride sharing generally, which, as we've shown, is not optimal in any sense, except for incumbent owners of government-granted monopoly rights (i.e., medallions) and government regulators themselves.

MOBILIZING THE CONSUMER CITIZEN

It is true that Uber fought (and won) numerous fights with local governments in order to operate,[16] but Uber isn't just a technological end-run around regulation. It offered a practical mechanism through which its users could act to change the

---

price for a ride used to be. But competition is a powerful tool for solving problems such as this one, particularly with low switching costs and observable outcomes.

[14] Note that, as Uber and Lyft reentered Austin, the new upstarts waned. This may be because of leftover market power, even after the platforms had left the market, but it more likely shows that Uber and Lyft are the market leaders because of the quality of their services. See Harriet Taylor, "What happened in Austin after Uber and Lyft got up and left," *CNBC*, August 18, 2016, available at: www.cnbc.com/2016/08/18/what-happened-in-austin-after-uber-and-lyft-got-up-and-left.html

[15] A tax levied on any market activity that produces negative externalities, such as a carbon tax on companies that create pollution.

[16] See John Byrne, "Aldermen OK weaker Uber rules after Emanuel threatens to adjourn chaotic meeting," *Chicago Tribune*, June 22, 2016.

existing regulatory model. The Uber story is probably the first time that customers have organized to fight for the right of a new business to operate.

As noted earlier in our discussion of the market for trust, the government is not just Uber's competitor in providing trust, but also Uber's regulator. As seen in cities across the world, government has used its regulatory power to limit Uber's ability to compete. In response, Uber has not only fought back in traditional ways (such as by hiring lobbyists and lawyers), but also devised a novel technological solution to enlist customers as champions for its cause.

In effect, each ride in an Uber results in a small payment to the regulator (i.e., Uber the company), which then uses it in part to assert its position in battles over attempts to regulate it out of existence. In effect, Uber has tried to solve the rational apathy of taxi passengers when it comes to political action by spreading the costs of lobbying across all users and embedding it in the price of the service. Uber also uses technology to build a democratic weapon in these political battles. Uber users are asked to fill out petitions, with the push of a button, which are then used to express to government the value its citizens place on Uber.[17] Just as Uber's technology platform lowered the cost of information about cab safety and honesty, it also lowered the cost for consumers of engaging in the political process to the mere push of a button.

Going directly to the people with a regulatory product has another interesting benefit. When deregulation happened in the taxi industry in the 1980s, it happened through the existing political process. This meant that various interest groups had an outsized say in the scope and form of the deregulation. Taxi commissioners had a say, and so did powerful medallion owners, people willing to show up at city council meetings, and politicians, who were predicting what their constituents would want. Accordingly, states and localities deregulated in various ways – some lifted medallion caps, others allowed rates to be set independently, while some merely increased the number of medallions.

Uber's innovation, however, was not to try to shape the law or change the law; instead its innovation was to offer an alternative to the law, which individual consumers could accept or reject as they saw fit by choosing whether or not to use the service. This meant that deregulation (or, as argued later, simply better trust provision) proceeded in a more tailored and democratized way. It also allowed the alternative law to evolve over time as the needs of its customers changed.

SHOW, DON'T TELL

Uber used an innovative approach to resolving the collective-action problems of regulation in another sense as well. Uber chose not to mobilize citizens with

---

[17] As mentioned earlier, when you don't like something about a cab experience, you're unlikely to start a non-profit to remedy the problem: it's too much trouble for too little benefit. However, you might press the one button that Uber sends you in an email that alerts the relevant regulator of your displeasure.

a hypothetical and instead delivered a service whose legal status was still dubious in the hopes that the experience of using it would persuade user-citizens to lobby (through usage of the service and directly contacting regulators) for legal change.

The mantra of this new trust provider was "show, don't tell." Uber didn't approach politicians or regulators and say, "just let people get in cars with strangers if they have our app, it'll be fine!" This would most likely not have worked. It is difficult to imagine the wonders of Uber or any market process in an abstract sense. To someone whose bread has always been provided by the state, it would be difficult to imagine that if the state got out of the bread business, bread would appear in bulk on store shelves. Claims that it would would sound like magic. Just go to North Korea and see what the people say when you tell them that, if government got smaller and less powerful in North Korea, there would be more abundance.

Instead, Uber went to politicians, regulators, and the people with concrete, demonstrable evidence of what it was proposing to offer as an alternative to government regulation. It needed to invest significantly in building a trust platform that would work and then it needed to prove it would work to customers.

After all, if one tried to explain the power of the division of labor, namely that it would increase the wealth of people who had always produced their own shelter, food, and clothes, the benefits might have been impossible to imagine and the risk of transition thought to be too high. It would be a hard decision to stop growing food and focus on making clothes for your whole village when you can't be sure you'll be able to buy dinner with the proceeds.

But, when people experience the superior alternative, their willingness to support a new model increases. This approach is potentially powerful, although there are increased risks for innovators that flout the law and such a strategy adds lawlessness to the list of arguments of defenders of the status quo.

BEYOND RIDE SHARING

This solution can be a substitute for law in a range of different ways. After all, when two parties to a contract leave ambiguities in an agreement or do not provide answers to questions that might arise, they are, in effect, outsourcing the resolution of such questions to a legal body, such as a court or a jury. One could just as easily imagine having an algorithm that serves this purpose – artificial intelligence that is designed to optimize the legal rule by ruling in a particular case. What Uber has done is slightly different, in that it is going beyond interpretation of the standard-form contract; in a sense, it is letting the digital tribe construct the terms of the various contracts that Uber uses. If Uber is, in corporate law speak, a nexus of contracts, then the community of users is, through Uber's algorithm, helping to create and recreate these contracts.

While not a panacea, these new regulatory tools are revealing a shortcoming of modern debates about the optimal level of regulation. These debates are stuck in a false dichotomy. The question is not whether there should be more or less regulation (how should any politician, academic, or other person know such a thing?), but what is the best method for delivering trust.

Although some would characterize Uber as providing an unregulated service, in fact, Uber provides *more* regulation for the typical cab ride than the government. It offers a different type of law. Uber tracks all rides by GPS and can know when a passenger has been longhauled or given a sub-standard ride. Uber uses ratings not only to kick badly behaving drivers off the system, but also to process instant rebates for bad experiences. Uber provides riders (on their phone) with the name, photo, phone number, and license plate number of drivers. Drivers and riders are tracked in real time, making an Uber an unwise place to commit a crime.

Uber and other ridesharing companies offer far more accountability than government rules, which require that drivers' licenses be kept in the cab, although often behind thick glass and obscured by stickers or grime. Uber also rates passengers, which is something government could not possibly do efficiently (or get away with if it could). These are additional "regulations" of drivers and riders, but they are provided by non-governmental actors. That Uber provides them suggests the demand for regulation in the cab business is actually greater than the current level provided by government. The problem is that taxi commissions are sub-optimal suppliers of trust in a world where multiple digital platforms can compete to provide trust to consumers. It is easy to imagine all kinds of other areas in which the digital tribe might provide a better experience than a traditional trust supplier, but they can do so only if they are able to solve the political problems necessary to operate.

It is to these new possibilities, lying at varying distances on the future horizon, that we turn to in the next chapter. If the market for trust is unencumbered, we suspect that new trust technologies will appear that have the potential to disrupt much of what government provides today in the trust business. We don't think government spending will go down – the military and insurance aspects of government (the overwhelming majority of the budget) are not what we are talking about. But we do think that many of the trust services that government provides today will be disrupted. This should not scare us, because, as we've seen, the history of trust is about innovation and change, and we are advocating that, only where private trust can be provided at an overall lower cost for the same or better results, should government get out of the trust business. This would be a win for everyone. After all, the money and effort saved when government stops acting inefficiently can be redirected into other things that government is more efficient at doing. Social insurance, writ large, is a good example of a service that could be provided in greater amounts by a government that would no longer be needed to provide second-best trust solutions to the market.

10

Sketching on a Blank Slate

In the first nine chapters, we made our affirmative case for trust as a central feature of human development, for trust being delivered by social technologies of various types, for many different providers of trust, and for the central question of society regarding who is the most efficient supplier of trust. In this chapter, we imagine how the history and theory of trust that we've set out in earlier chapters may play out in various areas. Our views here are half-formed, at best, and are mere speculation. Many forces operate to influence the nature of trust, including social values, technological advancements, and political power. We may be wrong about how this all plays out, but we suspect that, if we are, it will be because those interested in the status quo constrain free operation of the market for trust. We can be certain, however, that trust will evolve, as it always has.

* * *

While government in all its forms has long been the dominant (and, in many cases, arguably the most efficient) provider of trust, the present portends a future in which trust is decentralized and brought back to the people. In the ever-evolving stack of different trust mechanisms upon which the present rests and the future will rest, digital platforms will, as brand did before, forestall and complement government trust.[1] But while government and brand will continue to play an important role in delivering trust,[2] digital platforms are poised to radically expand their share of the trust market.

These new forms of trust creation not only alleviate the need for government action or brand certification, but also seek to rethink the optimal way to supply trust

---

The companies used in this book are meant for illustrative purposes only. We have worked with some of them through a clinic at the University of Chicago Law School and Trust Ventures may be invested in or considering investments in some of them as well.

[1] The many different trust providers also interact. Consider, for example, the way platforms are beginning to replace consumer relationships with brands. Where you might've gone to United Airlines to book a flight, now you start with Priceline, which shows you flights from every airline and allows you to choose based on price. The difference between this and competing with a government trust provider is that United Airlines cannot shut Priceline down.

[2] Consider that even these new platforms use branding to their advantage. Even the platform aggregator of brands is itself branded. Amazon's white-label, or "un-branded," items are seeing tremendous growth, not because people do not demand brand of any kind, but rather because they see these items as Amazon-branded.

from the ground up. Brand built incremental solutions on top of the obsolete foundations of existing regulations. New technologies, on the other hand, open up the possibility of not only creating additional trust, but also replacing existing trust-delivery mechanisms. Uber, for one, has built an alternative to one government service, replacing the taxi commission with a platform and ratings system that arguably deliver better regulation than government.

Uber's tremendous success is likely to spawn other companies seeking to take a similar ground-up approach to providing trust in traditionally monopolized industries. The fact that Uber took on a government monopolist provides not just inspiration, but also an insight into how to win these battles. But cities have wised up since Uber and now are requiring prior discussions with city officials before the rollout of new Uber-like services. Uber also had the benefit of leveraging the assets of private citizens, whereas most startups may face their critical infrastructure being impounded or access to city services being terminated if city officials oppose them. It is also rare to combat a monopolist that is as deeply unpopular as taxis in the popular arena. Uber has certainly inspired startups, but there is no one playbook that can be easily replicated.

The government and established interests will not roll over without a fight, as there is much to be lost if they lose their grip on pieces of the trust market. Government workers will lose their jobs, hurting both them (in the short run, at least) and the unions that represent them (in both the short and the long run). Those who have purchased or otherwise obtained influence with regulators will also suffer, since these "assets" will be devalued. Anytime the rules of the game change, the people who have earned profits by knowing the rules suffer. Transitions are costly. But the net effects for society are usually incredibly positive.

Taxis and Uber again offer a good illustration of this. Prior to the arrival of Uber and other ridesharing services, businesses offering rides to strangers required a license from the government, known as a "medallion." Because the government limited the number of taxis operating in the market – about 7,000 medallions were issued in Chicago – the price of a taxi medallion exceeded the marginal value of a taxi. Prices of Chicago taxi medallions rose from about $70,000 in 2007 to more than $357,000 in 2013.[3] For obvious reasons, individuals who paid $357,000 for a medallion were strongly opposed to new entrants, such as Uber, offering rival services that did not have to pay for a piece of the existing monopoly. In effect, these medallion holders had purchased a monopoly right from the government, and at great cost. The fact that medallion prices fell by 25 percent in a year after Uber and other ridesharing services entered the market demonstrates the interests of incumbent monopolists in restricting innovation.

The losses to medallion owners are potentially large: at their peak, they were valued at about $2.5 billion in Chicago alone! For an even starker example, the price

---

[3] Aamer Madhani, "Once a sure bet, taxi medallions becoming unsellable," *USA Today*, May 18, 2015, available at: www.usatoday.com/story/news/2015/05/17/taxi-medallion-values-decline-uber-rideshare /27314735/

of a New York City taxi medallion dropped from $1.3 million in 2014 to a mere $250,000 just two years later.[4] There were other losses too, as noted earlier. Taxi commissioners lost some of their power and the influence peddlers that had invested in understanding the taxi game in Chicago were worse off too. All of these losses were real and we should not poo-poo them.

Some have argued that the medallion holders should be compensated for the diminution in value that their medallions experienced as a result of government not preventing ride sharing. After all, these medallions were purchased on the assumption that they restricted competition to holders of the medallions. One could imagine a tax on new entrants that would compensate the medallion holders. However, our view is that the economic harm endured by the medallion holders will shake the faith of any would-be buyer of monopoly powers from government in the future, and this is a good thing. Ultimately, it forces subsequent buyers of monopoly interests (such as medallions) to consider the possibility of democratic pressures from citizens rising up and eventually breaking the monopoly.

This is just what happened in the case of Uber, and it worked because the social gains from its service are enormous. Although we have not yet heard the final word on these gains, there is evidence of the value of ridesharing services to citizen-consumers. Most obviously, Lyft and Uber, the biggest two public ridesharing companies, are valued at nearly $80 billion (a valuation earned in under a decade of operation).

In addition, some early evidence suggests significant positive non-monetary gains from ride sharing as well. Mothers Against Drunk Driving released a study providing some evidence of a drop in the number of accidents and fatalities related to drunk driving in cities where ride sharing was permitted. This is bolstered by some early economic analysis. In "Ridesharing, Fatal Crashes, and Crime," two economists find that "Uber's entry lowers the rate of DUIs [driving under the influence] and fatal accidents."[5] Anecdotal evidence from various cities support this claim. For instance, in Austin, Texas, the introduction of Uber and Lyft to compete with the government taxi monopoly was associated with decreases in the rate of drunk driving.

In 2014, before ride sharing came to Austin, the city averaged about 525 drunk-driving arrests per month; two years later, there were only 358, a decrease of over 30 percent. Within months after Uber withdrew from the market (because of onerous new regulations), the monthly average rose, returning to nearly 500. While correlation is not causation, this evidence, which corroborates the above-mentioned research paper findings, raises, at least, the distinct possibility that there are significant social gains from breaking the taxi monopoly.

4 Elena Holodny, "Uber and Lyft are demolishing New York City taxi drivers," *Business Insider*, October 12, 2016, available at: www.businessinsider.com/nyc-yellow-cab-medallion-prices-falling-further-2016-10

5 Angela K. Dills & Sean E. Mulholland, "Ridesharing, Fatal Crashes, and Crime," *SSRN*, February 13, 2017, available at: https://ssrn.com/abstract=2783797

More casually, anyone who has ridden in an Uber has experienced the convenience and service that has generated its popularity and value. Moreover, Uber has brought service to underserved areas. We speak from personal experience. In our neighborhood on the South Side of Chicago, taxis were not readily available until the city permitted ridesharing services. Cabs could not be hailed. This was, in part, because of the density of people on the street, but also surely because of racial bias. As noted earlier in the discussion of taxi cab regulation, the west and south parts of Chicago (the parts with a greater percentage of African Americans) have historically been served by illegal jitney services, not licensed cabs. Ridesharing services have empowered citizens in these neighborhoods to become drivers and caused drivers to pick up riders without knowing their race, thus addressing this problem to a great extent. Rides with strangers are now freely available throughout the city.

Ride sharing has another benefit. Removing the artificial limit on the number of cabs, as well as the bureaucratic licensing process and the burdensome signaling required by law (the color, graphics on the side, and light on top of the vehicle), has enabled individuals to deploy capital assets (their automobiles) in more efficient ways. Permitting individuals to utilize idle assets to create value is a potential mechanism for addressing concerns about income inequality. In his book on the subject, *Capital in the Twenty-First Century*, the economist Thomas Piketty blamed rising inequality, in part, on the greater returns available to owners of capital than to wage workers.[6] Insofar as trust hacks can enable average US citizens to mobilize idle assets, this potential problem can be addressed to some extent.

Importantly, we do not believe that the Uber story was a one-off historical correction in which badly needed changes were finally made. Instead, many of the social benefits of Uber can be replicated across the economy with new technologies that are currently in development or are just on the horizon. Uber was a beachhead, not an aberration.

We've discussed the limitations in some of these new systems and the characteristics that might result in digital trust systems being sub-optimal regulators in certain circumstances, but the more interesting question is: where else will they be optimal? What other microregulators might soon change our everyday lives in the same way as Uber?

Of course, we do not have a crystal ball and, in a rapidly changing economy, it's hard to predict day-to-day changes. However, we'll offer a preliminary sketch of some of the important themes and spaces in which we expect to see the seeds of these new trust providers germinating. We will trace two broad themes that power the new trust economy: (1) the rise of peer-to-peer market mechanisms, where new techniques for verification – without a bank, brand, or government – guarantee easy, trusted exchange between peers; and (2) the shift from atoms to bits, whereby the confluence of the "internet of things," virtual reality and augmented reality, and

---

[6] Thomas Piketty, *Capital in the Twenty-First Century* (2013).

artificial intelligence will increasingly exert influence on the physical world. What follows is neither mutually exclusive nor collectively exhaustive, but instead is a speculative attempt to bring to life the idea of trust providers in the new economy, and it will hopefully help develop the idea of trust as a valuable framework for evaluating new technologies.

PUBLIC SECTOR

A natural starting point here is the provision of trust by government itself. This may, at first blush, look like an expansion of government trust (in the vein of Beth Noveck's argument in *Smarter Citizens, Smarter State*[7] or the Chinese digital social credit experiment), but what we are actually examining here is a hollowing out of inefficiencies in government trust and supplementation with privately supplied digital trust. This could occur either by government procurement or through the Uber model, where alternatives are developed outside government and functionally replace certain operations within government. We think that the optimal approach is for government to remain cautiously optimistic about new technologies that may serve a regulatory function, allowing innovators to experiment and grow without endangering its constituency.

Critically, the current government procurement regime leaves much to be desired and is especially vulnerable to the sorts of public-choice dilemmas that we have explored in this book. Consider that the US military has more procurement officers than Marines and, as the botched rollout of Healthcare.gov displayed, for all these procurement "experts," our government often does not make intelligent decisions about what to buy. The government's procurement process led to the selection of a vendor to build bespoke software for the critically important healthcare online portal that was meant to simplify the process of shopping for coverage under the Affordable Care Act (often referred to as Obamacare). The portal and its rollout were a disaster and only after a group of prominent technologists led by Marc Benioff (founder of Salesforce) stepped in was it improved.

Even the actual products that government purchases are often subject to deep public-choice problems. Consider the development of the F-35 fighter jet, which is manufactured in forty-seven states with a production process designed to include 127,000 jobs.[8] This is almost certainly not the optimal way to produce a fighter plane, but it is a very good way for members of Congress to claim that they have created

---

[7]   Beth S. Noveck, Smarter Citizens, Smarter State (2015). In this book, Noveck argues that the state could be more effective if it deployed technology to "create more open and collaborative institutions" with an eye on increasing the vibrancy of participatory democracy. In effect, she is advocating for government to maintain its virtual monopoly on many aspects of trust creation but to do a better job by taking lessons from technologies deployed by the private sector.

[8]   Trae Stephens, "Innovation Deficit: Why DC Is Losing Silicon Valley," *Medium*, March 1, 2016, available at: https://medium.com/@traestephens/innovationdeficit-why-dc-is-losing-silicon-valley-bbd oa5744c4f

jobs, even when those jobs come at the cost of security and ballooning the federal budget by paying for overpriced weapons.

The technology industry is largely aware of these problems, but is powerless to fix them because government speaks a completely different language and operates under its own set of rules. The military defense of the United States is, first and foremost, the responsibility of government, so it is not surprising that government has a monopoly in this domain. But, as in the examples we discussed earlier, monopoly power comes with substantial downsides and costs. While we do not expect Amazon or Uber to disrupt this monopoly anytime soon,[9] the nature of the procurement problem and other similar problems in the operation of government shows the potential of the trust hack.

While the challenges in implementing better technology within current government are significant, the opportunities are tremendous. Everything from the court system to land records is likely to benefit from the application of new technologies. Our point here is not that the government should privatize the military.[10] Rather, we seek to illustrate that government is often not a great builder or buyer of technology, so it is not an ideal place for this sort of new innovation to spring from. The FBI infamously spent several hundred million dollars to build a virtual case management system, but, after nearly a decade, the project was abandoned.[11] No computers, software, or usable technology were ever delivered, despite the enormous costs to taxpayers. Accordingly, where new technology can offer trust in the same way as government safely and efficiently, government should avoid trying to "outcompete" these new trust providers.

Our picture of the past is one in which government rushed to fill a trust vacuum with imperfect solutions that were difficult to clear away once they'd outlived their usefulness. Our hope for the future is that the optimal providers of trust will supply it in the areas in which they can supply it best and, in many cases, where government does operate, such trust can be more efficiently supplied by private trust providers. Accordingly, we'll look both at the ways that government can increase efficiencies in its core competencies and at the places where outside trust providers are likely to obviate government trust supply. This does not mean that government must unilaterally disarm or pre-emptively withdraw from different areas. Rather, government should welcome these trust hacks and allow them to operate alongside itself. Put another way, let Uber operate alongside the taxi commission. If some people

---

[9] This is not to be confused with an oligopoly among defense contractors, which can and very well may be disrupted. An analogue is the space industry, where a few powerful suppliers of space equipment were eventually massively undercut by a nimble Silicon Valley startup, SpaceX, which dramatically lowered the cost of launches. See Clay Dillow, "Engineering Exec Departs ULA After SpaceX Comments," *Fortune*, March 17, 2016, available at: http://fortune.com/2016/03/17/ula-exec-admits-company-cant-compete/

[10] There are, however, analogues of core government services working alongside private analogues.

[11] Dan Eggen & Griff Witte, "The FBI's Upgrade That Wasn't," *Washington Post*, August 18, 2006, available at: www.washingtonpost.com/wp-dyn/content/article/2006/08/17/AR2006081701485.html

continue to prefer taxis, great. If others prefer Uber, great. The trust economy of the future is based on choice and competition and, where government can safely allow choice, it should.

Importantly, permitting some individuals to opt out of government-provided trust does not mean that those continuing to use those services will be worse off. For one, as noted earlier, when government monopolies are broken down and governments are forced to compete – as taxi cabs have recently – there is usually an increase in the efficiency and quality of government services. An example is the emergence of apps through which riders can hail a yellow cab, mimicking Uber's efficient system.

Perhaps more importantly, the rise of microregulators need not make the system worse off for those who want to continue to use government regulators. The savings from the more efficient delivery of trust for one group can be used to provide better services for the other group. Those who opt for a private microregulator for a particular activity will no longer need to pay for the government to provide those services, thus saving the government some money. This money can then be reallocated to subsidize the production of trust for the group choosing to remain with the government regulator. For instance, imagine that there is a community, let's call it Hyde Park, where there is a private police force that patrols the streets. This police force is paid for by the University of Chicago, not the citizens of Chicago or Illinois. Because of the existence of this police force, the public police force needs to expend fewer resources in this area than it otherwise would. This is true even though citizens in Hyde Park pay the same taxes for public services. The public services saved can be used in other areas, giving people in those areas more services than they would otherwise get. The gain can be mutually beneficial for all parties, since the citizens of Hyde Park get better policing tailored to their preferences, while the other citizens of Chicago get more policing than they would have if the private services had not been provided.

Alternatively, consider the work by our colleague John Rappaport at the University of Chicago,[12] which examines the private provision of justice by retail merchants. Retailers not only deploy private security guards that can deter shoplifters or detain them until the police arrive, but also engage in the administration of justice, such as levying fines on customers in lieu of calling the police. Although not perfect, there is a significant benefit of this type of justice – the costs of it are paid for only by the merchant, instead of by the public at large. This means that those with a stake in the business – be they workers, owners, or customers – bear the costs of protecting the business from theft. So, depending on the elasticities of these various markets, it is possible that the costs of justice are paid for by customers through higher prices. Thus, merchants that do a better job of deterring theft and administering justice will succeed in the market, since they will be able to offer lower prices for the same products, all else being equal. There is competition for efficient justice. In addition, those who are not harmed by the illegal conduct do not have to pay,

---

[12]   John Rappaport, "Criminal Justice, Inc.," 118 *Colum. L. Rev.* 2251 (2018).

meaning the police can focus on other matters that may affect them, such as gun violence, home invasions, or bank robberies.

There are other areas in which gains in the public sector can be achieved. In the government's core competencies (the courts, the military, etc.), improvements can certainly be made in purchasing decisions. At the most basic level, government record-keeping is due for an upgrade. Companies such as OpenGov have created platforms that save time and eliminate waste while making it easy for governments to increase transparency and share information with their constituents. Esper deploys technology that allows governments to efficiently quantify the costs of a particular regulatory pronouncement, allowing them to better perform cost-benefit analyses. Another startup, Avisare, has developed a platform that simplifies data aggregation and reduces duplicate bids for businesses seeking to participate in government procurement. And age-old systems such as property records or educational records could benefit from the use of blockchain verification technology (more on this later).

Occupational Licensing

One area in which government supplies trust that seems to be the target of bipartisan condemnation is occupational licensing. Occupational licenses are certifications that are required by government to practice a given trade. Occupational licenses usually create some sort of an obligation (such as training, payments to the government, or requirements to keep insurance) that a worker must satisfy and, in exchange, confer the ability (in the form of a government-granted license) to offer a certain type of service to the public. In these areas, government forbids anyone without such a license to pursue such a vocation.

Most people are familiar with licenses, such as those needed to practice law or medicine, but similar types of licenses now cover things such as flower arranging and cosmetology. The Institute for Justice, a libertarian law firm, found that, in 1950, only one of every twenty US workers needed an occupational license to do their work; by 2012, that number had ballooned to one in three.[13]

The ostensible reason for a requiring a license is consumer protection. The common example is that we don't want unlicensed doctors performing operations.[14]

---

[13] Dick M. Carpenter II, Lisa Knepper & John Ross, "License to Work: First Edition – Executive Summary," *Institute for Justice*, April 2012, available at: http://ij.org/report/license-to-work/executive-summary/

[14] We believe that getting rid of medical licenses might be a sensible strategy, in that the clumsy government system of certification would be replaced with a more market-driven assessment of doctor quality. Today, patients rely on the state and various monopoly providers of medical licenses to certify doctors, and the failings are legion. We suspect that a market for doctors – with rankings provided by intermediaries based on data – would be better, perhaps dramatically so. However, we realize that this is not a widely shared view. Nevertheless, we picked this example because it is the case in which licensing probably makes the most sense. Even if one believes that doctors should be licensed, one can still believe that licensing is out of control. Do we need licenses for hair braiders or tour guides or dog walkers? We trust the market. We trust Yelp and other aggregators to deliver the requisite trust.

Most licenses cover areas with few or no real risks to the public, such as flower arranging or being a tour guide. One might wonder why, when such inequities exist, those who grant licenses don't eventually seek to change the rules. Much like those who complain of the drinking age of 21, once they reach this age, few feel compelled to fight this perceived burden because they no longer bear it. The license holders are like cab drivers with medallions. In the latter case, the last thing they want is for Uber to come along and break the monopoly. Similarly, in the case of license holders, there's a strong incentive for those who have scaled the wall to receive a license to ensure that the wall stays up behind them.

Why? The answer is money. Licenses create an artificial barrier shielding license holders from competition, thus increasing monopoly rents for those who have traversed the barrier. In practical terms, this means that a licensed flower arranger knows she will be paid more if DIYers cannot compete and every bridal shower must seek a licensed flower arranger. It is hard to imagine the danger to the public of a poorly arranged bouquet, but it is easy to see the harm this could cause to a low-income person who cannot afford a license but could otherwise earn an honest living selling flower arrangements.

Many such licenses have ludicrous requirements that bear no relation to the service the licensee will eventually offer. Consider a cosmetology license that requires over 1,000 hours of training in how to cut and style hair, including learning specific and outdated hairstyles (think "the beehive"). Now imagine you are an immigrant entrepreneur with a talent for hair braiding, just like Taalib-Din Uqdah.[15] He opened a business that only braided hair (never cut it) and was threatened with heavy fines and jail time by the government of Washington, DC. The training involved in acquiring such a license teaches many things that are irrelevant to Uqdah's craft and nothing that is relevant – getting good at 1950's women's hairstyles won't help you start a business braiding cornrows. Furthermore, the high cost of cosmetology licensing may prevent those like Taalib-Din from being able to afford the services of new companies such as CosmoSafe, which provides more pragmatic, cost-effective training that is aligned with the realities of a business.

And, as with many types of regulation, the costs are often not quantified or balanced against the benefits. Occupational licenses create real costs in the economy, as some potential new competitors don't end up entering the market, keeping prices high and limiting economic opportunities (in particular for those grasping for the first rung of the economic ladder). The Institute for Justice has long fought for the economic liberties of low-income people who wish to practice a particular vocation, but this is not just a libertarian issue. Recently, the Obama administration agreed, releasing a report advocating for the rolling back of occupational licenses.[16] With such bipartisan support,

---

[15] Valerie Bayham, "A Dream Deferred," *Institute for Justice*, December 2005, available at: www.ij.org
      /report/a-dream-deferred/
[16] "Occupational Licensing: A Framework for Policymakers," *The White House*, July 2015, available at:
      https://obamawhitehouse.archives.gov/sites/default/files/docs/licensing_report_final_nonembargo.pdf

one would expect these costly licenses to be eliminated from the economy. But they persist, demonstrating the power of entrenched interests in resisting what seem like obvious welfare gains.

With occupational licenses, the government is seeking to solve an information deficit: you don't know if a particular service provider is safe or reliable. If this story sounds familiar, that's because taxi medallions serve the same sort of role. They also have a similar economic consequence: a monopoly right that the government sells to particular operators. Just as Uber improved the medallion problem by harnessing information, digital platforms have the power to transform our occupational licensing regime.

In the following, we give examples of a few popular companies that serve some of the functions of occupational licensing. Consider the licensure of restaurants and how consumers choose where to eat: are you more likely to consult restaurant inspection ratings or Yelp to decide where to eat dinner? Data show many problems with the way restaurant inspectors perform their jobs, from subjectivity and being too friendly with the businesses they inspect to plain old laziness.[17] Yelp, on the other hand, aggregates the reviews of real people and scores restaurants accordingly. Of course, tastes vary, ratings platforms are imperfect (as discussed in Chapter 9), and just because consumers enjoy a food experience doesn't mean the kitchen is sanitary. However, as with all new trust providers, we cannot compare them with a perfect state of the world; instead, we can only compare them with the real alternative that exists today.

Yelp solves some, but not all, of the concerns associated with licensing. It speeds up the process of information being shared about unknown restaurants. If a few consumers have bad experiences, this will be shared quickly and it will put the restaurant out of business, because new customers won't want to try it. Conversely, if the restaurant makes early Yelp reviewers happy, more customers will want to try it. Yelp allows you to pick between a five-star and a three-star burger joint, while restaurant licenses indicate only that you're probably not going to get food poisoning.

In a sense, these pieces of information are complementary. Even the best burger on earth (probably) isn't worth getting food poisoning for, so it stands to reason that Yelp's information is valuable only with the underlying information about safety. But what if Yelp could help supply this information as well? There are nascent examples of similar platforms approaching this problem.

Consider EatWith, Mytable, Feastly, and similar peer-to-peer platforms for home-cooked meals, where food is prepared in a chef's home rather than in a licensed commercial kitchen, where the preparer lacks a restaurant license (so called "eat with strangers" apps).[18] EatWith, for example, is a chef-driven platform for sharing unique

[17] Ginger Zhe Jin & Jungmin Lee, "The Imperfection of Human Inspectors: Lessons from Florida Restaurant Inspections," March 30, 2011, available at: http://economics.mit.edu/files/6642

[18] Airbnb's new "Experiences" feature contemplated the possibility of home-cooked meals, and offers reference to Chicago's extreme restrictions on selling home-cooked food: www.airbnb.com/help/article/1946/experiences-involving-food-in-chicago

food experiences. While laws on food preparation vary by jurisdiction, regulations typically do not allow the sale of food unless it has been prepared in a commercial kitchen and served by a licensed restaurant or food vendor. These laws are often quite vague, making it difficult to discern the line between a sale and an unregulated dinner party: you can go to a friend's cookout, but if you pay them, it's possible you've violated food safety laws. And there are exceptions, as localities have exemptions for food prepared in a traditional bed-and-breakfast, for example.

The regulatory status of eat-with-strangers apps is unsettled. Like Yelp, many of these apps offer information about the quality of consumer experiences. Like Uber and Airbnb, many perform an internal permitting function, such as performing background checks, conducting kitchen-quality reviews, or requiring insurance. Critically, these platforms could replace wholesale the entire restaurant-permitting process. EatWith or its ilk could perform basic inspections (perhaps using real-time video footage), handle consumer complaints, and kick bad actors off the platform, creating the same virtuous cycle that has driven so much value in ride sharing and the market for short-term housing.

Like these analogues, eat-with-strangers apps have many foes. Just as taxis fought Uber and hotels fought Airbnb, the restaurant lobby and the inspectors at government agencies will fight to protect their advantage. If these apps are allowed, the market will contain many new food options that established restaurants view as competition. Restaurants have organized in similar contexts to fight against new market entrants before, successfully passing restrictive laws on food trucks in recent years.[19]

There is obvious concern about eating in a stranger's home, as there is with staying in a stranger's home (Airbnb) or riding in a stranger's car (Uber). But, as with these examples, these are things that we trust our friends to do with us, and digital platforms are often great ways to aggregate the information necessary to supply this sort of trust. It is unclear whether eat-with-strangers apps will succeed or fail, for regulatory reasons or otherwise. But the potential benefits are great. Imagine you're a great chef who now stays at home with children. Instead of your talents being reserved just for close friends, you can share your gift with a broader foodie audience and make extra money on the side. Or, perhaps you're a diner who longs to try authentic Szechuan cuisine and learn more about the cultural aspects of your meal. With something as foundational as food, the potential is great.

Eat-with-strangers apps have the potential to be a model microregulator. They have good incentives to ensure quality food experiences on their platform, or else they'll lose consumers. They regulate the particular chefs that provide food on their

[19]   Mark Albert, "Restaurants say food trucks are eating up their profits," *CBS News*, August 16, 2014, available at: www.cbsnews.com/news/restaurants-say-food-trucks-are-eating-up-their-profits/. For research on food truck permitting and suggestions for jurisdictions on how to be friendly to street food, see Robert Frommer & Bert Gall, "Food Truck Freedom," *Institute for Justice*, November 2012, available at: http://ij.org/wp-content/uploads/2015/03/foodtruckfreedom.pdf

platforms, not food consumption generally, so people can shop between platforms, creating competition. And they can respond to consumer concerns in real time.

One need not be convinced to *try* one of these apps in order to believe they should exist. There are always early adopters who are more adventurous, taking risks for the chance to try the next big thing before it goes mainstream. Very few people are afraid to get in an Uber today, although the idea probably seemed scary to most consumers a few years ago.

However, government has treated these businesses unfairly, driving many out of business. Josephine was a California-based startup that paired home cooks with spare capacity with hungry neighbors without the skills, facilities, or time to make their own meals. The business model, which was praised in the popular startup manual *Regulatory Hacking: A Playbook for Startups* by Evan Burfield and J.D. Harrison, was for dinner what Uber is for rides.[20] Josephine had early success. It raised over $3 million in funding soon after its launch in 2015 and it saw nearly 100 home cooks providing meals for members of their community.

It seemed like a massive efficiency and welfare gain, but government killed it. The health inspectors came first. Whether out of a belief that only government inspections can ensure safe services, to protect their turf, or at the behest of restaurants (with whom they have personal relationships and from whom they take money) to take out the competition, the regulators shut Josephine down. Its well-meaning managers tried to appease the government. The first step was to rent a commercial kitchen where home cooks could meet the sanitary and working-condition requirements of the law. But even this massive concession wasn't enough. It then lobbied for new legislation, but that too faltered. Eventually, Josephine died. In a blog post, its founder wrote the epitaph: "[O]ur team has simply run out of the resources to continue to drive the legislative change, business innovation, and broader cultural shift needed to build Josephine."[21]

There are other novel technological approaches to unlocking the societal value that is obscured by occupational licenses. Consider Thumbtack, a digital platform for getting all sorts of tasks completed, from hanging a TV to getting a personal trainer. On Thumbtack, consumers can post a job they need done and service providers will send the consumer offers. Consumers then sift through the service providers, read up on their reviews, and choose the right person for the job at the right price. Before Thumbtack, if you wanted to hang a TV on your wall, you could do it yourself (and maybe damage your wall or TV), call Best Buy (and overpay), or google "TV wall hanger" to try to find a licensed handyman. With Thumbtack, you can find someone who has hung 100 of the same make and model TV on a similar wall type, for less money than a licensed handyman, and book them in minutes. When this is done, you're unlikely to know or care whether this person had any particular license. You spent the minimum necessary time and money safely

[20] Evan Burfield & J.D. Harrison, *Regulatory Hacking: A Playbook for Startups* (2018).
[21] Ainsley Harris, "Food-sharing startup Josephine is shutting down," *Fast Company*, February 2, 2018, available at: www.fastcompany.com/40525947/food-sharing-startup-josephine-is-shutting-down

mounting your TV, and the person who did it made a little extra cash to help make ends meet on their own schedule.

Another example is the eyeglasses business. Many states require an eye examination every two years, meaning that you can't buy a new pair of glasses without another eye exam. This hassle is often unnecessary, as the harm from an old eyeglass prescription is low – after all, if it were dangerous, then using your old glasses would be dangerous too. Visibly, a new competitor aiming to make this process easier, offers online eye exams. Rather than going into your local eyeglasses shop for an eye exam performed on a hundred-year-old machine, you can cheaply perform an equivalent exam on your computer in your living room or maybe in the lobby of a retail pharmacy. Their process is overseen by eye doctors and you can use that prescription to buy glasses anywhere. Unsurprisingly, the American Optometric Association is not thrilled about the possibility that a computer can offer a similar service and it has lobbied to ban Visibly in a number of states.[22] The arguments leveled against Visibly smack of bootleggers and Baptists – customers won't be screened for eye cancer!; the test won't be reliable!; the poor won't have access! Of course, the real argument – this will reduce our profits! – will never be made. And these arguments are unavailing. While eye health is important, most people are not screened for eye cancer, since people with good vision never go to an optometrist. Moreover, nothing about using Visibly precludes individuals from seeing an ophthalmologist on occasion – it merely reduces the costs of regular vision screening for corrective lenses. As regards its effectiveness, whether one's vision is improved or not by the eyeglasses received from the prescription given is something that is immediately apparent to the customer. Unlike determining the effectiveness of cardiac surgery, determining whether one's glasses are effective is within the capacity of every individual. If Visibly offers an inferior service, consumers will turn elsewhere. And, of course, the point of the alternative is precisely to lower the cost, especially for areas not served by optometrists. Consider that 2.5 billion people worldwide lack access to eye exams today, including about 25 percent of US counties. Optimetrists cannot address these issues, but technology can, with massive benefits to society. But only if we let it.

Even risk-averse consumers should cheer the efforts of new trust providers to create easier, better, and cheaper ways to get the products and services we want. But, even if one is convinced of the safety risk posed by a product, banning it is not the only approach. Instead, we believe in applying creative ideas that address public health and safety concerns while leaving room for innovators to build the future. In the occupational licensing context, this might mean a new "badge, not wall" structure, where the local government could perhaps create a list of companies that have satisfied certain criteria, which people could refer to. Unlike a traditional license, this wouldn't prevent other competition or other upstarts.

[22] Meg Graham, "Opternative fighting states that try to ban its online eye exams," *Chicago Tribune*, April 5, 2016, available at: www.chicagotribune.com/bluesky/originals/ct-opternative-legislation-online-exams-bsi-20160405-story.html

Alternatively, why not create a system that allows certain types of consumers to take greater risks if they understand them? Imagine that a jurisdiction stopped licensing businesses and started licensing consumers, a sort of early adopter license. This reverse license structure would allow consumers to opt in to trying exciting new products and services, absolving the regulators of safety concerns. This is not unprecedented: consider the Accredited Investor concept in the regulation of securities under the SEC. This rule allows investors who meet certain criteria (knowledge, wealth, or income) to invest in riskier asset types than the broader population. Such a structure could provide a testing ground that ensures safety, with the early adopters having a heightened awareness of risks, similar to a beta release of software.

The point is not to argue in favor of this particular outcome, but rather to encourage creative thinking that seeks to promote innovation where there are real safety concerns, instead of indulging the impulse to ban innovations outright because of a safety concern. Almost all world-changing innovations have attendant dangers, and the increased danger of the automobile is poor justification for a ban in favor of the horse and buggy.

To be clear, it is often preferable that the regulator recognize when a better alternative has been offered, and back off in response. This, too, has precedents beyond the Uber example.

Consider the regulation of the reselling of event tickets, commonly called "ticket scalping." The banning of scalping in many jurisdictions followed the familiar pattern of a socially valuable activity with dangers being banned to avoid these dangers. Imagine you have purchased $1,000 tickets to the Super Bowl in the hope that your team will make it to the big game, but unfortunately your team disappoints in the early rounds of the playoffs (a sensation better understood by Churi, a Cincinnati Bengals fan, than Henderson, a Pittsburgh Steelers fan).

Now these tickets still have some value to you, as you'd still enjoy seeing the Super Bowl (let's say that would be worth $200 to you), but not nearly as much as another lucky fan who has a chance to see her team compete for the championship. Accordingly, you'd seek to sell the tickets to such a fan for $1,000 or more. But if that is illegal, you'd be forced to either skip the game altogether (a total loss, as the full $1,000 you spent would yield no value at all) or go and see the other teams play (a loss of $800, namely the $1,000 cost minus the $200 worth of value you got from being at the big game). Clearly, the ability to scalp the tickets has social value, as you can sell your ticket and break even or make a profit, and another fan will get greater enjoyment out of the use of the tickets.

Two major reasons explain why scalping was banned in the first place: first, as a way to keep first-sale ticket prices high by eliminating cheaper substitutes on the secondary market and, second, because of fraud among scalpers who could print fake tickets and pass them off as authentic, fooling jilted buyers who will be frustrated at the gates to find they can't get in to the event. Few people would argue that government should ban scalping just to increase the price of tickets and enrich Ticketmaster or the Yankees. However, everyone can agree that we'd like government to prevent fraudsters from ripping us off.

Much like the cab monopoly example we've explored, this is a situation in which genuine concern about the dangers of scalpers, coupled with an inability of existing technology to remedy such a situation, resulted in a ban that prevented the danger at the cost of social value and to the benefit of a third party in the market. Before the internet, there was simply no mechanism to create a secondary market in tickets where buyers and sellers could trust each other. In this case and many others we explore, the internet has provided a new type of social infrastructure, a digital layer that will eventually suffuse the economy with trust and allow previously impossible or intermediated transactions.

One of the reasons scalpers were able to get away with fraud is that they were decentralized, making it difficult to drag them into courts to punish them for scamming you. Once you've purchased tickets from a scalper outside a venue, you'll most likely not see that person again, meaning that you take them at their word that the tickets are authentic. Without a way to verify this, it's easy for the scalper to sell you fakes with impunity, creating an incentive to sell fakes. Of course, if the scalper can make a fake for $1 and sell it for $60, they'll make more per transaction than if they have to buy an authentic ticket at $45 and sell it for $60.

Enter Stubhub, a great example of a technological solution that prevents fraud in the ticket resale market. Because Stubhub is centralized, everyone purchases from the same organization, and they're easy to find and drag into court if they wrong you. Furthermore, Stubhub employs trust technologies such as guaranties to ensure the authenticity of tickets. For a small fee of $50, Stubhub might allow you to sell your Super Bowl Tickets for $2,000 and another fan who values them at $3,000 to buy them. The fan got tickets worth more to him than what he paid for them, Stubhub got its fee, and you made a profit on the tickets instead of them going to waste or you going to a game that was worth less to you than what you paid for the tickets. This is a win for all parties.

We won't address the question of whether this is best for the particular NFL teams in question, which might still prefer that this option not exist. As this technology popped up, it created a new activity that was previously illegal, opening up a new avenue of value creation. And the government took notice of this, lifting the ban in many places, dramatically increasing social welfare.

Yet this withdrawal was of a different character from that in the case of taxis. Rather than setting out an elaborate licensing scheme that yielded the government profit from medallions, scalping bans merely prohibited a type of activity that was valuable but dangerous, and the bans were lifted when that risk was eliminated. Just as the New York Stock Exchange arose out of the ashes of a brokerage business killed by a New York statute in the late 1700s, so too did companies such as Stubhub arise to fill a demand created by a legal system attempting to protect consumers from fraud.

The Legal System

There is also potential for trust technologies to improve the functioning of the legal system. Exciting but uncertain developments are afoot in core areas of law, such as judging and legal interpretation. In a variety of areas, silicon-based intelligence has the possibility of providing trust to participants in our legal system far more efficiently than human judges. Although we are just at the cusp of this possibility, it is worth considering some examples.

When viewed through the prism of occupational licensing, as discussed earlier, state bar associations control the licensure of lawyers and attempting to practice law without a license is illegal. This results in extremely high costs to hire a lawyer, which makes the justice system less accessible to the economically disadvantaged. But many legal functions could easily be made less expensive and more efficient (and better) through automation. For example, J.P. Morgan applied an artificial intelligence algorithm to the task of parsing loan agreements and the algorithm completed 300,000 hours of attorney work in seconds.[23] In another case, startup EasyExpunctions has created automated document-generation tools that drastically cut the cost of expunging an arrest from a criminal record. Where EasyExpunctions charges customers a $400 flat fee, criminal attorneys usually charge upwards of $1,400 for the same services.[24] We will discuss more such efficiencies later, but critical questions exist going forward about what elements of a lawyer's role may be automated or changed without being treated as unauthorized practice of law. Despite many of these solutions being demonstrably more efficient and accurate than traditional lawyering, getting the bar associations to agree will be a major barrier.

Already, courts are using computer algorithms as *inputs* into the judging process. The case of Eric Loomis, a Wisconsin man found guilty of involvement in a drive-by shooting, is illustrative. Loomis's sentence was based in part on input to the judge from COMPAS, an algorithm developed by Equivant, a private company. Although Loomis's sentence, which was affirmed by the Wisconsin Supreme Court, has generated significant controversy,[25] the use of a simple tool designed to inform "decisions at every step" is relatively benign.[26] After all, the judge retained the authority to issue the sentence, and the technology was in this way no different from any other aid available to the judge, such as a database of prior sentences, a pre-sentence report comparing this case with others, or any number of other inputs.

[23] Hugh Son, "JPMorgan Software Does in Seconds What Took Lawyers 360,000 Hours," *Bloomberg*, February 28, 2017, available at: www.bloomberg.com/news/articles/2017-02-28/jpmorgan-marshals-an-army-of-developers-to-automate-high-finance

[24] Kristen Mosbrucker, "Tech startup that cleans criminal records moves from Austin to San Antonio," *Austin Business Journal*, August 7, 2016, available at: www.bizjournals.com/austin/news/2016/08/07/tech-startup-that-cleans-criminal-records-moves.html

[25] Jason Tashea, "Courts Are Using AI to Sentence Criminals. That Must Stop Now," *WIRED*, April 17, 2017, available at: www.wired.com/2017/04/courts-using-ai-sentence-criminals-must-stop-now/

[26] See www.equivant.com

It is not difficult to imagine a more automated version of COMPAS, which sentences criminals without any judicial involvement. Human judges could be replaced at the sentencing phase with algorithms that take account of all the inputs that human judges would get – the criminal history, the family circumstances, the damages caused, the nature of the crime, victim impact statements, sentences in similar cases, the sentencing guidelines of the legislature, etc. – and then set the optimal sentence. While this would undoubtedly generate widespread opposition (not least from human judges!), it is likely that, in the long run, this would generate *more* trust in the criminal justice system.

A recent paper from the National Bureau of Economic Research (NBER) makes just such a claim. The NBER researchers, from various fields, developed a machine-learning tool that simulated bail decisions made by judges.[27] Bail decisions – whether the defendant in a criminal case should await trial at home or in jail – are "the judge's prediction of what the defendant would do if released."[28] Because this prediction happens entirely inside the mind of the judge, it is subject to biases of various sorts and therefore may deviate from the efficient outcome – that is, reducing the total social costs of detainment. If these biases are based on illicit factors, such as the race or other immutable characteristic of a defendant, the decisions may erode public trust in the criminal justice system.

The variation in sentences between different judges for similar crimes suggests the potential for bias. The problem was so acute that, in 1984, Congress passed the Sentencing Reform Act, which established a commission to promulgate sentencing guidelines that would constrain judicial discretion. We couldn't trust our human judges, so we gave them a clumsy algorithm that more or less determined the sentence based on a variety of factors.

Nevertheless, the legal literature is replete with examples of the bias of human judges. In a recent study of criminal sentences in Cook County, Illinois (Chicago), David Abrams and his co-authors compared the sentences of white and black defendants.[29] They used a novel empirical approach to address the problem of comparing one case with another, since many factors, including the details of the crime or the quality of the lawyers, might influence the sentence. The researchers compared sentences across judges, since cases are randomly assigned and therefore the specific case details should average out in a large sample of cases. They found a race gap in sentences and found that this gap varied widely across judges – the gap in incarceration rates between white and black defendants varied by nearly twenty percentage points across judges. Race matters in sentences, even though it is not legally supposed to matter.

---

[27]   Jon Kleinberg, et al., "Human Decisions and Machine Predictions," NBER Working Paper No 23180 (February 2017).

[28]   Ibid.

[29]   David S. Abrams, Marianne Bertrand & Sendhil Mullainathan, "Do Judges Vary in Their Treatment of Race?," 41 *J. Legal Stud.* 347 (2012).

There is some evidence of bias going the other way too. In another recent empirical study by the NBER, Briggs Depew, Ozkan Eren, and Naci Mocan found that judges were actually harsher against members of their own race. Looking at juvenile sentences in Louisiana, the researchers observed own-race sentences (a white judge and a white defendant or a black judge and a black defendant) were 14 percent longer, and 5 percent more likely to require jail time instead of probation, compared with cross-race sentences.[30]

These biases are difficult to eradicate because they live in the minds of judges, and the sentence in any individual case is difficult to explain by racial bias, since it cannot be readily compared with a case that is exactly the same that got a different sentence. In other words, the hidden variables or unique circumstances of each case that confound researchers, which also require huge datasets for identifying the problem, make fixing the problem nearly impossible. Research by Jeffrey Rachlinski and co-authors supports this point. They administered implicit bias tests to a large sample of judges and found that they, just like average citizens, exhibit a subconscious preference for their own race.[31]

Any racial bias in sentencing, as well as potential biases based on wealth, ethnicity, religion, gender, sexual orientation, or the like, is both illegal and immoral. Bias also undoubtedly undermines the public trust in the criminal justice system. In ancient Rome, there was initially no public enforcement of crimes – violence was treated as a "tort," or civil wrong, and punishment came in the form of retribution from the aggrieved party. If someone killed the slave of another person, the law permitted the victim to kill the slave of the perpetrator. There was no public prosecution. For obvious reasons, this system was not tenable – minor cases became blood feuds – and eventually the idea of "crime" was invented. The Romans established the role of the government as a neutral and formal arbiter of social violence. In our trust frame, the state became the more efficient mechanism for delivering the trust necessary for the society to flourish. Citizens could not trust other citizens to mete out justice or to provide the deterrence necessary to control crime. The government was a trust-based innovation in criminal law.

While the government has been a reasonable provider of trust in criminal law over the millennia, we are on the verge of an exciting trust hack in this area. Machine learning has already shown the potential to do better. Returning to the above-mentioned bail study, in their policy simulation, the authors showed that replacing a human judge with a machine, which was fed all of the same information that the judge would have had, made better bail decisions. The authors concluded that crime could be reduced by about 25 percent without any change in jailing rates pre-trial, or instead that jail populations could be reduced over 40 percent without any

---

[30] Briggs Depew, Ozkan Eren & Naci Mocan, "Judges, Juveniles, and In-group Bias," NBER Working Paper No 22003 (2016).

[31] Jeffrey J. Rachlinski, et al., "Does Unconscious Racial Bias Affect Trial Judges," 84 *Notre Dame L. Rev.* 1195 (2008–2009).

increase in crime rates.[32] These are startling figures. If they could be replicated in real-world settings, the benefits to society in real terms, and in terms of trusting the judicial system, could be enormous.

Although judges are doing more than "selling" trust to the public in such settings, they play a central role in the overall trust level in society. Trust in the judiciary – the rule of law – is an essential element of human wealth creation and human flourishing. More specifically, trust in the criminal justice system – trust that it will be fair and that it will result in efficient deterrence of crimes – is foundational for a well-functioning society. If machines can do a better job at reducing the biases of human judges, we would be able to improve individual outcomes, reduce social costs, and increase levels of overall societal trust.

Contract Law

The potential for machine intelligence in law goes far beyond criminal sentencing. Can you trust that the contract you enter into will be efficiently and effectively interpreted and enforced? We rely on human judges and juries to do this today, but, as Anthony Casey and Anthony Niblett point out in a recent paper, this is about to change:

> Predictive capabilities created by big data and artificial intelligence increasingly allow parties to draft contracts that fill their own gaps and interpret their own standards without adjudication. With these self-driving contracts, parties can agree to broad objectives and let automated analytics fill in the specifics based on real-time contingencies. Just as a self-driving car fills in the driving details to get its passenger to a designated end point, the self-driving contract fills in the contract details to achieve the parties' designated outcome.[33]

They imagine "contracts being interpreted by their own internal software," instead of interpretation by costly judicial processes. Trust may be able to be delivered without these costs and government involvement.

The potential social welfare gains from this possibility are significant. Law is expensive and proceeds slowly. The uncertainty of legal processes also opens up the possibility of individuals trying to game the system by investing in strategies to exploit the other party based on a better understanding or prediction of the law. Corporations and individuals spend billions of dollars in advice from lawyers and other professionals on structuring deals and fighting about contractual meaning in court after the fact, all because we do not have an efficient mechanism for making these determinations.

---

[32] Jon Kleinberg, et al., "Human Decisions and Machine Predictions," NBER Working Paper No 23180 (February 2017).

[33] Anthony J. Casey & Anthony Niblett, "Self-Driving Contracts," *SSRN* (2017), available at: https://papers.ssrn.com/sol3/papers.cfm?abstract_id=2927459

The world Casey and Niblett imagine is one in which the basics of contract interpretation are made by a truly neutral and hyper-efficient machine intelligence that would reduce these costs. With lower costs and less uncertainty, there will be less need to invest in potential exploitation (on one side) and less need to insure against potential exploitation (on the other side). Today, not only are these costs – what economists call "dead-weight costs" – wasted, it is most likely the case that many contracts are not formed that would be if trust could be provided at lower cost. These deals that don't get done are potential human cooperation that is left unrealized solely because of the transaction costs of providing trust through our current, human-flawed legal system. And having machine intelligence with virtually limitless capacity for entering into agreements means that we can enter into value-increasing contracts that human businesses may never have known of. Such a system could create central digital value-maximizers, speeding up the efficiency and capacity of businesses, lowering costs, and allowing dramatic gains in productivity and cooperation.

Another point here is a distributional one. Law being expensive not only operates as a tax on all transactions, but also affects rich and poor differently. Wealthy individuals and companies have an advantage in the current system because they have access to more expensive advice and can spread the costs of transaction planning and litigation across a greater asset base. If we can reduce the costs of providing trust (both before and after problems have arisen), the playing field can be leveled somewhat, opening up opportunities for more cooperation across the spectrum of individuals and businesses.

Corporate Regulation

There are intriguing possibilities to go even further. Consider corporate law. When investors get together to create a business, they pick a CEO to run the company. They cannot trust the CEO completely, so they hire a board of directors to oversee the CEO. The law then creates a costly system of corporate governance and a judiciary and legal system to enforce the promises that have been made. Economists call the deviations from optimal conduct here "agency costs," because our agents do not have the same incentives that we do. While no one has estimated the size of agency costs, most of what we term "business law" is a response to them. And the costs are not just borne by shareholders. The public is harmed when CEOs act in ways that maximize their wellbeing and not social welfare.

What if we can replace the trust infrastructure of corporate law and much of business regulation with machine algorithms that will maximize corporate objectives more efficiently? The following is what Anthony Casey and Todd Henderson have in mind in a forthcoming paper. Today, shareholders pick a human CEO and tell her to maximize shareholder value (or firm value or whatever); the government observes the choices and outcomes, and then decides whether or not the company did something "wrong." The government can then, if proved correct, punish the CEO or the firm. If the CEO cheats – say by arguably exaggerating a cancer drug's prospects or taking an overly aggressive risk – the shareholders can sue and the government can too. The point is to provide compensation to those harmed by the lie or the wrongdoing, and to deter other CEOs from doing the same thing to others.

Businesses cannot be punished easily, since we cannot jail an entity or punish shareholders beyond taking all the money they invested in the business. So instead we rely on punishing the CEO, perhaps by tarnishing her reputation or by jailing her in extreme cases. But this punishment will be imperfect, because of both proof problems and concerns about taking away the CEO's freedom based on what might have been arguably reasonable business risk taking. This means that there will be less trust in CEOs on the part of shareholders, and less trust in businesses among society generally.

Imagine instead a computer CEO replaces the human CEO and shareholders program the computer CEO to maximize according to a certain algorithm, be it shareholder value, firm value, or social value. The computer CEO may be able to maximize value better than a human CEO, but this is uncertain at this point. What is certain is that it is very easy to punish a machine CEO that "misbehaves" as determined by a government regulator. So long as the algorithm the machine CEO is maximizing includes the ability of the government to impose negative utility on the computer if the regulator determines it engaged in socially destructive behavior (determined after harm has occurred), then regulation will be much easier and much more effective.

To picture this, imagine the CEO is asked to maximize firm value. There are two project choices: Project A has a 50 percent chance of returning $1 million and a 50 percent chance of returning zero; Project B has a 50 percent chance of returning $10 million and a 50 percent chance of returning –$10 million. The expected value of Project A is $500,000; the expected value of Project B is $0. However, shareholders and the CEO will strictly prefer Project B, since, if the project is a failure, they will not have to bear the $10 million loss, as limited liability means losses are capped at zero. Thus, Project B now has an expected value of $5 million.

Now, further imagine that the CEO picks Project B and it is a failure. Society eats a $10 million loss. Seeing this, the government wants to punish the firm for making this choice, perhaps because of a view that the choice was somehow impermissible under current law or perhaps as a signal to other CEOs to not choose projects that have the potential to externalize losses onto society.

The government can try to punish the CEO, perhaps by bringing charges against her based on a novel theory of law or based on technical violations of this rule or that rule. Perhaps the government may even go after the CEO on unrelated charges that might not have been brought otherwise. This may cause the law to be distorted and demeaned and, for the CEO, it may mean large fines or the loss of their liberty. The process will definitely involve a costly trial and it may not achieve the desired outcome.

Now, imagine the same case with a machine in the C-Suite. Under these facts, assuming limited liability, the machine will also pick Project B. But, when the government decides that this was not a good choice, it will be very simple to "punish" the machine. A regulator will not have to engage in a costly trial against a CEO and, if victorious, require society to pay to incarcerate the CEO to achieve deterrence against this and other companies. Instead, the computer CEO will be debited the social cost of its decisions – here, 10 million units – and this computer CEO and other computer CEOs will update their optimization decisions based on this regulatory choice. The machine CEOs will learn that, in cases such as this, the decision was a bad one and that the expected value of Project B was $0, not $5 million.

US shareholders, workers, and consumers spend billions of dollars each year to support a corporate law and corporate governance system that is, at its core, about helping to ensure trust in the operation of business enterprises. Millions of hours are spent by executives, lawyers, government regulators, and others to establish the conditions necessary for investors to invest, workers to work, customers to purchase, and citizens to feel that business is advancing social interests. If we can hack this system, with computerized CEOs or other techniques beyond our imagination, then these hours and monies can be saved and put to better use, whether that be feeding the poor, educating the ignorant, or curing the sick.

There is a very real and significant problem lurking in this example. President Harry Truman summed it up neatly when he noted, "When you have an efficient government, you have a dictatorship." The possibility of government being able to instantaneously and perfectly dial in punishment to decision-makers brings about the possibility that this power could be abused. In Truman's view, and ours, the delay and cost and uncertainty of law is a feature, not a bug. The story is a familiar one to those with even a rudimentary understanding of civics. The Founding Fathers of the United States built into the constitutional structure a system of checks and balances designed to limit the power of the government to operate efficiently. And this concern about government power and monopoly on violence is an animating element of our brief here for disrupting the current system of creating trust.

So, where does this leave us? We have no answer at present and see no easy solution. The possibility of machine CEOs being able to better optimize social risk taking is a real one with exciting possibilities and potential. But, it raises a potential large cost. If we can better design government regulators to be less susceptible to this problem, then we may be able to unleash a new mechanism for creating trust among corporate stakeholders and society.

The Financial System

We take it for granted that the government issues money. The words "The United States of America" are right there on the front of our currency, as well as pictures of government leaders, government iconography (e.g. the eagle), and government buildings. Importantly, so are the words, "In God We Trust." Money itself is designed to inspire trust. The imagery is all designed to create confidence in the money and its purpose as "legal tender for all debts public or private."

This confidence provides the basis for exchange in the economy and dramatically lowers the costs of transactions. We trust that when someone gives us $5 in return for a product or service that we will be able to turn around and give the $5 to someone else in return for the equivalent amount of goods or services. The invention of money, which moved us away from a barter economy, was one of the greatest trust innovations of all time. It dramatically increased the amount of trust in economic transactions.

But the government providing the trust in the financial system is not obviously necessary. Bitcoin is a modern example of a non-governmental currency. Bitcoin is a currency that is currently accepted by over 100,000 merchants across the world and is "issued" without a government or other central authority involved. The bitcoins are "created" by miners who use computing power to solve extremely difficult math problems. The difficulty of solving these problems limits supply in a perfectly predictable amount – only 21 million bitcoins will ever be created, and the rate at which they can be mined is predictable. Then, once available, the bitcoins can be exchanged in the economy, just like dollars or gold. What is needed to make the system work is simply trust. Individual buyers and sellers will use bitcoins if they can trust that the bitcoins they have will be accepted at their value. This is the same thing that makes the US dollar have value, since it has no inherent value except for the promise or trust that stands behind it. Although more people currently trust in the US government to stand behind the value of the dollar, there are millions of people using Bitcoin around the world today because they have sufficient trust in the system.[34]

The potential for efficiency gains from private money is extremely large. One source of costs of the government money system is the regulation necessary to ensure that users of money trust the financial system. Consider banking regulation. While the government issues money, private banks are responsible for managing the financial system. Because the government might not trust private banks to do so in the public interest, there is widespread and extremely costly regulation of private banks. Throughout history, this system has failed repeatedly.[35] The recent financial crisis (2008) is just one of countless examples.

---

[34] Garrick Hileman & Michel Rauchs, "Global Cryptocurrency Benchmarking Study," SSRN (2017).

[35] Carmen M. Reinhart & Kenneth S. Rogoff, This Time Is Different: Eight Centuries of Financial Folly (2011).

The central issue in most crises is liquidity. Banking is a fractional reserve business, meaning banks do not keep all deposits on hand, but rather lend them out to others to create economic growth. We know that our banks keep only about $5 in the vault for every $100 we deposit, but we are OK with this because we trust that they will not squander the money and that not everyone will demand their money at the same time. Everyone who has seen *It's a Wonderful Life* knows what happens when everyone does demand their money at once – bank runs, which are caused by a lack of trust, can bring down even financially healthy banks.

Today, we trust banks not because of the reputation of the bank, but because the government explicitly guarantees that it will stand behind the deposits even if they are squandered. The system of insurance, managed by the FDIC, a division of the US government, provides the trust that makes the system work.

But this is expensive trust, because knowing that the government guarantees the deposits means that banks will take more risk than they otherwise would – this is the so-called "moral hazard" problem, and it was a central feature in the banking crises of the 1930s, 1980s, and 2000s in the United States. The social costs of this risk taking have been enormous, as are the costs of the regulations put in place in the aftermath of each crisis to prevent another.

Bitcoin offers a potential trust hack that might be more efficient. But one doesn't have to be a believer in cryptocurrencies to see the point or the potential. If you've used PayPal or a similar system, you'll understand the potential for non-governmental currencies to function. While it is true that there are greenbacks standing behind our PayPal balances, this need not be the case. After all, what stands behind the greenbacks? It used to be gold, of course, but this too was just a promise of trust. If we believe that PayPal or Bitcoin or some other artificial indication of value is going to be accepted and trusted, that is enough to enable transactions to happen.[36]

Consider prison. Federal inmates are not permitted to hold US currency, but they want to engage in voluntary exchange. The prisoners' trust hack? Mackerel. According to a story in *The Wall Street Journal*, prisoners replaced cigarettes (banned in 2004) with the small fish because it was readily available, portable, and something that nobody consumed.[37] Based on the supply available in the prison, each mackerel turned out to be worth about $1, making the system easy to understand. In addition, the supply of mackerel coming into the prison was set by outsiders (the Bureau of Prisons) and therefore was inherently inflationary at a predictable level. It was a stable currency. If mackerel can work, then surely Bitcoin or other rival currencies can also be used for exchange, so long as people trust in the system.

[36] Consider the use of shells or wampum as currency among early societies. See Nick Szabo, "Shelling Out: The Origins of Money," *Satoshi Nakamoto Institute* (2002), available at: http://nakamotoinstitute.org/shelling-out/

[37] See Justin Scheck, "Mackerel Economics in Prison Leads to Appreciation for Oily Fillets," *The Wall Street Journal*, October 2, 2008, available at: www.wsj.com/articles/SB122290720439096481

There is another cost of government money – the errors made by the government agents who set the value of the currency. Although, in the US system, a private entity – the Federal Reserve – determines the supply of US currency in circulation, the approach is governmental. The Federal Reserve is comprised of human agents who meet, analyze data, and then determine by fiat the prevailing interest rate for banks to borrow from the supply of money printed by the government. This is a command-and-control solution that has failed repeatedly, both because of what F.A. Hayek called the knowledge problem – no human minds can possibly analyze the vast amount of information necessary to determine the optimal level of money – and because of political or social factors. As to the latter point, former Federal Reserve Chair Alan Greenspan said that the job of the Federal Reserve Open Market Committee, which sets rates, is to take the punch bowl away from the guests just when the party has really gotten going. In other words, he viewed the Federal Reserve as being responsible for juicing the economy, but not giving it so much juice that it goes crazy. Although aware of this, Greenspan himself was guilty of not taking the bowl away in the 2000s, in part because doing so is, as it is with party guests, very unpopular. It is for this reason that Milton Friedman famously dreamed of hacking the trust system underlying the Federal Reserve: "I've always been in favor of abolishing the Federal Reserve, and substituting a machine program that would keep the quantity of money going up at a steady rate."

Bitcoin and other rival currencies may be a potential solution, although, as with government pushback against Uber and Airbnb and other trust hacks described earlier, the government is unlikely to give up its monopoly on money easily. Just recently, the SEC refused an offering for a Bitcoin exchange-traded fund because it was not deemed reliable enough. We should expect more of this, under the guise of protecting consumers, but perhaps motivated by serving to simply protect the government's monopoly on trust supply in the money business.

But the government did not always have this monopoly. Periods of so-called "free banking," where private banks issued their own currencies whose values depended on the level of trust individuals had in those banks, existed throughout the world in the past. Most famously and successfully, Scotland had a thriving period of free banking from 1716 to 1845, during which three banks issued different currencies that traded openly and freely. According to the economists and others who have studied the system, it resulted in a highly stable and competitive banking system that operated at relatively low cost.

While the United States had periods of free banking, we moved to a system of government money in part because government was by far a more efficient trust supplier given the technology of the time. In the nineteenth century, information was costly to obtain, especially at great distances, and the costs for buyers and sellers of comparing currencies issued by different banks and deciding where they could be used was prohibitive. It might work in a small area where information was easy to transmit and everyone knew everyone else, but establishing a national economy with nineteenth-century free banking, given the information technology of the day, would have probably been impossible. We needed government to stand behind a national currency as a way of increasing trust, lowering transaction costs, and increasing liquidity in the economy.

But today, it is easy to see why government is no longer essential here. If banks or other large institutions, such as Amazon or eBay or Walmart or Apple, issued their own currencies, they could be readily stored on portable devices that would be able to compare values, decide which currency was accepted at different locations, and so forth. As noted earlier, some people already do this, using PayPal accounts or Bitcoin. We predict there will be many more options in the future; we also predict that the government will stand in the way in an attempt to preserve its monopoly on the trust underlying our medium of exchange.

Lending, another area of finance implicitly conditioned upon the conditions of trust, is also ripe for a trust revolution. Historically, trust has been handled in this industry by a range of actors, from banking dynasties such as the Medici and Rothschild families to modern banking apparatus. But the phenomenon of peer-to-peer lending, namely digital platforms through which individuals make and receive loans such as Lending Club and Cashcall, recalls a much older system of personal credit updated with the tools of the twenty-first century. In some cases, new fintech entrants (startups using technology in the finance industry) have built entirely new financial instruments with higher degrees of personalization – think of the income share agreements marketed by Align and Lambda School. Other companies, such as Celsius Network and Unchained Capital, are providing new means for cryptocurrency holders to generate liquidity and earn interest. And companies such as Avant Credit are hard at work using algorithms to build a superior formula for creditworthiness that aim to make credit scores, known in the US as "FICO" scores, and the like obsolete, creating better predictability through more and better information.

Perhaps the subset of the financial world most directly poised to benefit from the increased information of digital connectivity is insurance. Insurance is fundamentally an exercise in quantifying risk, and the better information one has, the better one can price risk. Insurers have typically thought of "cyber risk" as a self-contained category of risk dealing with hacking and other data vulnerabilities. And in an economy where hardware and software are largely disconnected, that made sense.

But, with the rise of the internet of things, all sorts of hardware from thermostats to refrigerators to automobiles are now connected to software and feeding data into software platforms that can make better-informed decisions. Telematics instruments in cars can measure driving and incentivize safety, and a smart thermostat can alert the fire department upon sensing a temperature high enough to indicate a fire. Recently, a connected pacemaker device's records were brought in as evidence in an arson trial, ultimately contributing to the conviction of the accused.

Innovative insurers are also adapting to new business models and states of the world. Companies such as Metromile and Slice Labs are building new sharing economy-focused insurance policies that charge by the mile and allow drivers to switch from a personal driver policy to a commercial policy when driving for Uber. Lemonade is using a "peer-to-peer" insurance model that groups people in an insurance pool by philanthropic interest to prevent fraud and lower costs. And savvy insurance companies are working proactively to build in the trust infrastructure necessary to enable these new activities. American International Group (AIG), for example, recently established a new sharing economy group to help its customers find insurance solutions for emerging business models.

These new innovations present the opportunity for democratizing insurance in ways previously thought impossible. Take the case of self-funded health insurance. In a self-funded insurance plan, an employer assumes the financial risk for its employees' healthcare costs by paying individuals' claims out of pocket. At first blush, this type of plan sounds both risky and complex and, historically, it was both of those things. The level of risk associated with self-funded pools spooked businesses and regulators into rejecting these plans. Only the largest companies, with their own built-in trust infrastructure, were allowed to take on these risky plans. Flash forward to the present day and startups, such as Sana Benefits, have used technological integration to make self-funded insurance both safer and more cost-effective for small businesses. While over 90 percent of large companies self insure, almost no small ones do. With level-funded solutions like those offered by Sana, small businesses can save 30 to 40 percent on a per employee basis for healthcare. This means more employees covered at lower costs. By better integrating and automating the exchange of information, Sana has become a new segmented trust provider that can level the playing field for companies that could not afford to manage these technical plans on their own.

In a world where trust is proliferating rapidly and the trust value chain is becoming more and more segmented, insurance is the mesh underlying many other trust providers, pricing risk and providing a safety net. It has served this role historically, and there are encouraging signs that the industry will continue to fulfill this role in the future.

Education

Many of these innovations span the public and private spheres, as there is great crossover where government regulates a given activity (consider healthcare or education). Some activities, such as education, are provided by the public sector but may be disrupted by trust hacks to supply trust privately. Some innovations, such as AltSchool, a technology-enabled private school, work in the current system and may never conflict directly with public schools. However, as technology becomes a larger part of education, the argument for all or some K-12 education to be purchased privately with public funds may grow more salient.

While a future of fully digital educational content seems remote, the possibility of Hollywood-sized budgets for virtual-reality educational content spread across students nationwide could create great opportunities.[38] Unlike traditional teachers who eventually must retire, these software platforms would improve accretively over time and, given that software scales costlessly, the inexpensive model available to lower-income people would probably be very close to the newest version. This point is shown by comparing the difference between an entry-level and an expensive piece of software versus the difference between great private schools and public schools in lower-income areas. The difference between a struggling inner-city school and Exeter is far greater than the difference between Google and any of its competitors in search. In these areas, trust hacks will be necessary to circumvent stumbling blocks and entrenched interests such as teachers' unions.

Other, more current, examples, such as General Assembly, a coding boot camp built to help people enter the technology space, would not directly supplant a government-run service, but they have run into regulatory problems with credentialing and licensing. Given the importance of credentialing in education, the ability of these startups to offer educational services and attendant credentials will in part determine the degree to which they'll be accepted by the market. This has wide-ranging consequences for the economy, and a host of other digital educational companies such as Khan Academy, Udacity, and Coursera are also focusing on digitizing the educational experience.

Affordable Housing

Finally, some innovations can help mitigate the costs associated with public trust networks, even if private providers cannot replace those networks. Take a look at the US housing crisis. The core challenge for policymakers looking to promote affordable housing is simple: how can you reduce housing prices? Ironically, the costs of public trust providers actually worsens this problem. Wherever the government regulates home standards, it generates costs that drive up the overall minimum price of housing. Zoning, permitting, housing administration, and taxes all combine to create an artificial floor on home prices.

While it may be difficult to disrupt zoning laws and neighborhood plans, innovations in affordable housing technologies are reducing the costs of these public trust networks. Returning to Austin, a startup called ICON recently unveiled the first permitted 3D-printed home in the United States. The company estimates that their construction technology will reduce the price of a building a home to less than

---

[38] "Marc Andreessen on the Potential Promises of EdTech Investments," *Fast Company*, December 2, 2011, available at: www.fastcompany.com/1678918/marc-andreessen-on-the-potential-promises-of-edtech-investments

$10,000 per unit.[39] By drastically reducing the price of housing, companies such as ICON can minimize the impact that less efficient, but difficult to replace, trust services impose.

We'll now turn to primarily private sector-operated industries and examine the trust dynamics.

PRIVATE SECTOR

Across many industries in the private sector, the opportunity to build trust systems represents one of the greatest potentials for growth in a world where technology has already been applied to solve many of the obvious problems. In many ways, digital trust systems will restructure our economy for a new type of firm. Rather than investing heavily in brand and relying on that as the primary indicator of quality, information shared by markets will drive this new type of business ecosystem.

The opportunities that lie behind regulatory barriers are myriad and varied. Some entail steep uphill climbs, as in the healthcare sector, but promise huge potential. One revolutionary example is Counsyl, a direct-to-consumer genomics-testing startup.[40] For a nominal fee, you can learn of any genetic correlations you have that may indicate heightened risks of certain medical conditions by taking a simple saliva at-home screening test. Such companies have faced (and so far successfully navigated) serious pushback from the FDA.

But, as the science around genetics pushes forward, we can expect many more potential clashes. While such tests are today used to screen for breast cancer, they could also be used in the *in vitro* fertilization process to find zygotes with genes that correlate with higher IQ or other desirable traits. While this holds great potential to improve lives, there is sure to be pushback.

Food also portends potential clashes. Consider Memphis Meats, which is creating beef from stem cells harvested from cows and chickens.[41] Animal-free meats or "clean" meats hold tremendous promise as cruelty-free, environmentally friendly alternatives to the same traditional meat-packing industry that inspired Upton Sinclair to write *The Jungle*, which is widely thought to have sparked the outcry that led to the creation of the FDA.[42] If companies such as Finless Foods, which is developing cell-cultured tuna, are successful, their technology may even save highly over-consumed species

---

[39] Vanessa Bates Ramirez, "This 3D Printed House Goes Up in a Day for Under $10,000," *Singularity Hub*, March 18, 2018, available at: https://singularityhub.com/2018/03/18/this-3d-printed-house-goes-up-in-a-day-for-under-10000/

[40] Stephanie M. Lee, "Counsyl gets funding for new genetic tests," *SFGATE*, May 8, 2014, available at: www.sfgate.com/technology/article/Counsyl-gets-funding-for-new-genetic-tests-5462605.php

[41] Marta Zaraska, "Lab-grown meat is in your future, and it may be healthier than the real stuff," *The Washington Post*, May 2, 2016, available at: www.washingtonpost.com/national/health-science/lab-grown-meat-is-in-your-future-and-it-may-be-healthier-than-the-real-stuff/2016/05/02/aa893f34-e630-11e5-a6f3-21ccdbc5f74e_story.html?utm_term=.ab861f9da6b2

[42] Upton Sinclair, *The Jungle* (1906).

from extinction. But, ironically, these companies will face considerable pushback from the United States Department of Agriculture (USDA) and perhaps the FDA, as they push into uncharted territory.[43] And, unlike Uber, which took on disperse city councils where public pressure was an obvious motivator, the FDA, as a federal agency staffed by expert administrators, is less vulnerable to these democratic pressures. Are trust hacks still possible in such cases?

At least in some cases, it may be possible for new trust providers to avoid old regulatory schemes by circumventing the business development used by established competitors. For example, the Federal Aviation Administration (FAA) imposes strict rules on the certification and testing of new aircrafts. However, Kitty Hawk, a company building a vertical takeoff and landing (VTOL) aircraft that may one day act as a form of air taxi, has avoided the FAA's radar by qualifying as an "ultralight aircraft." As a result, Kitty Hawk can have individuals test its aircraft without a pilot's license or physical exam.[44] While the FAA did not build the looser ultralight aircraft regulations for the VTOL market,[45] these new competitors are using the rules to rack up flight time and demonstrate the safety of their design.

Another company in the aviation space may offer an alternative answer. Zipline,[46] a startup that uses drones to deliver medical supplies, has not been allowed to operate in the United States because the FAA allows drone deliveries only within the line of sight of the deliverer.[47] So Zipline partnered with the Rwandan government to demonstrate the safety and effectiveness of its longer-range delivery service in a market where it was urgently needed. With Zipline, a medical professional in a far-flung town can text an order for rare medical supplies to a distribution center, where the supplies are packed onto an autopiloted drone that parachutes them down to the health worker within fifteen minutes. In Rwanda, where infrastructure can make deliveries to such places difficult, this service is a godsend.

But it could also have great value in the United States. By proving the effectiveness and safety of the service elsewhere, the argument is stronger for adoption in the United States. This regulatory arbitrage strategy is a novel way of approaching calcified regulations in a given jurisdiction, creating a sort of competition among nation-states that would allow innovation to flourish everywhere. Prolific venture capitalist and technology thought-leader Marc Andreessen (whose fund has invested in Zipline) has captured this concept in his idea that there should be many Silicon

[43] Elizabeth Devitt, "Artificial chicken grown from cells gets a taste test—but who will regulate it?," *Science*, March 15, 2017, available at: www.sciencemag.org/news/2017/03/artificial-chicken-grown-cells-gets-taste-test-who-will-regulate-it
[44] Dan Neil, "The First Flying-Car Review," *The Wall Street Journal*, September 12, 2018, available at: www.wsj.com/articles/the-first-flying-car-review-1536753601
[45] Indeed, the relevant regulations restrict the use of lightweight aircraft to "sport and recreation" use.
[46] See http://flyzipline.com
[47] Jake Bright, "Backed by White House, Zipline to test U.S. medical drone delivery," *TechCrunch*, 2016, available at: https://techcrunch.com/2016/08/12/1368312/

Valleys,[48] jurisdictions that are open to experimentation in a particular area. Once these experiments yield fruit, they'll be copied worldwide.

There is reason to believe that demonstrating success in real-world applications will convince some regulators. The FAA, for instance, was initially resistant to move quickly on approvals for new unmanned autonomous drone systems. However, as the benefits of these technologies has begun to bear fruit elsewhere, political pressure from the Department of Transportation has pushed the FAA to innovate faster and allow more flights over people and at night.[49] Critically, these politicians have supported innovation because they do not wish to be fall behind other places in the world where we are seeing the benefits of these transportation advances.

Another example comes from new competitors that utilize technologies from the United States' national labs, where innovations are tested and proven as part of the research process. One example is the wave of startups tackling Gen-IV nuclear reactors. These new reactor designs have the capacity to revolutionize the way we think about nuclear energy. One such company, Oklo, is developing a small-scale reactor that runs on recycled nuclear waste, produces zero emissions, and integrates passive safety features that are not susceptible to meltdowns.

While receiving approval for a nuclear reactor design is a daunting task, these startups have a leg up on other high-risk, technically complex technology companies because the underlying science has been proven to work in other contexts. Going back to Oklo, its nuclear reactor design relies on technology previously used at a federal nuclear reactor operated by Argonne National Labs for thirty years.[50]

A related idea is that Silicon Valley itself is built on precisely this spirit of ground-up rethinking and willingness to disrupt old ways of doing things. This is best exemplified by Balaji Srinivasan, a serial startup entrepreneur and investor, who applied Albert Hirschman's political science thinking to modern-day technology.[51] Hirschman, a political scientist, laid out a model of change in which a person within a given system could advocate for change within that system (voice) or leave the system to build or join another (exit).[52] In a speech at famed technology accelerator Y Combinator, Srinivasan applied this concept to our calcified regulatory system, arguing that rather than using voice to try to change our regulatory system, Silicon Valley should consider an exit approach, creating a new physical space for experimentation that is free from the regulatory and other impediments of the United States.

48   Marc Andreessen, "What It Will Take to Create the Next Great Silicon Valleys, Plural," *Andreessen Horowitz*, June 20, 2014, available at: https://a16z.com/2014/06/20/what-it-will-take-to-create-the-next-great-silicon-valleys-plural/

49   Natasha Bach, "Drone Deliveries May Arrive Sooner than Expected Thanks to New FAA Plan," *Fortune*, January 15, 2019, available at: http://fortune.com/2019/01/15/drone-regulations-proposal-faa/

50   Rebecca Kern, "Start-Ups Gain Helping Hand in Advanced Nuclear Energy Program," *Bloomberg*, March 15, 2017, available at: www.bna.com/startups-gain-helping-n57982085228/

51   See www.youtube.com/watch?v=cOubCHLXT6A

52   Albert O. Hisrchman, *Exit, Voice, and Loyalty* (1970).

Many famous Silicon Valley personalities have made similar calls, from Larry Page to Peter Thiel to Tim Draper. And, indeed, with the growth of virtual and augmented reality and other remote technologies, increasingly the concept of community is based more on shared ideas or groups (what we call digital tribes) than on a given geographic area. And this makes sense. In agrarian or industrial societies, the stores of economic value were centralized on farms or factories and so these were the relevant unit size for taxation, on which governments rely for their operation. However, in a knowledge economy, factories matter less and intellectual property matters more. The most valuable companies being built today just need a laptop and an internet connection, and those are available worldwide. As is the case in the economy, when communities change, governance and regulation may change in response. Regulation, previously tied directly to place (each nation-state or regulator has a jurisdiction beyond which its power does not extend), will increasingly splinter and become as placeless as community.

Consider Uber, the microregulator: its jurisdiction extends to its entire customer base worldwide and is limited by time and customer preference rather than place. This makes sense, because all of Uber's customers, whether you're a Chicago baker or a Hong Kong businessman, demand the same type of trust. And, as the world globalizes, it's increasingly convenient to bring your trust provider with you when you travel. Critically, one person's needs vary quite a lot from people fifty miles away from them: rural Illinoisans have different transportation needs and may demand different types of trust. In this sense, demand for trust is driven by customer need rather than regulatory scope.

While everyone is a customer of some regulator, we tend not to think of it that way because switching nations is hard. This is Hirschman's "loyalty" problem: you don't want to leave your family just to get a better taxi law. But, if you could import the trust supplier you choose for a given problem to wherever you happened to be, you'd make switching costs low, increasing competition between trust providers.

This conception envisions microregulators as being like apps on a phone. Each smartphone has an operating system (the nation-state), which sets the rules for the software that will operate on the phone, and the apps themselves must be accepted for use by the operating system. But, beyond that, the owner of the phone has a tremendous ability to customize their experience by filling their home screen with the apps they value and use most. One can imagine a future in which traditional regulators function like operating systems and ensure that the trust providers competing on their platform meet certain standards, but, beyond that, the individual selects the individual trust providers she wishes to use, lowering the switching costs and internalizing the benefits and costs of a given provider.

This idea of regulatory competition is not just techno-utopianism, and in fact has deep roots in US constitutional law. Around the time of the New Deal, we were answering similar questions about new technology, experimentation, and regulation. In the 1932 case of *New State Ice Co.* v. *Liebmann*, Justice Oliver Wendell Holmes penned a dissent which stated:

> There must be power in the States and the Nation to remould, through experimentation, our economic practices and institutions to meet changing social and economic needs. I cannot believe that the framers of the 14th Amendment, or the States which ratified it, intended to deprive us of the power to correct the evils of technological unemployment and excess productive capacity which have attended progress in the useful arts.
>
> To stay experimentation in things social and economic is a grave responsibility. Denial of the right to experiment may be fraught with serious consequences to the Nation. It is one of the happy incidents of the federal system that a single courageous State may, if its citizens choose, serve as a laboratory; and try novel social and economic experiments without risk to the rest of the country. This Court has the power to prevent an experiment. We may strike down the statute which embodies it on the ground that, in our opinion, the measure is arbitrary, capricious or unreasonable. We have the power to do this, because the due process clause has been held by the Court applicable to matters of substantive law as well as to matters of procedure. But in the exercise of this high power, we must be ever on our guard, lest we erect our prejudices into legal principles. If we would guide by the light of reason, we must let our minds be bold.[53]

This famous passage lays out a view of the fifty states being empirical laboratories that can be used to test different policy ideas. States are already doing these things to a degree. There are regulatory sandbox programs. Arizona has generated startup interest through its fintech sandbox. Nevada has attracted a multitude of crypto startups by enacting favorable laws. A crypto millionaire is even building a city in the desert to fully enable living on the blockchain (for better or worse). Nevada is using the same approach for autonomous vehicles, hence why Lyft is test-driving its vehicles in Las Vegas.

The examples here leverage cities, states, and nations in similar ways, with digital startups in search of fertile soil for experimentation and innovation. The trust in question will not always be of precisely the same character: Uber's five-star ratings system is not the same as a track record of safe drone deliveries. What they have in common is the characteristic of discovering creative, democratic approaches to finding fertile soil for innovation. But we believe that there will be an explosion of new methods of trust.

Platforms have helped create trust as a currency, but, in other ways, real assets are being shifted into digital ones, allowing trust to be provided in new ways. The paradigmatic example here springs from the world of cryptography, where blockchain technology is allowing the large, democratic network of computers to serve as a "trustless" way to clear transactions and verify information without the need for a traditional intermediary such as a bank or an insurance company.[54] Blockchain is

---

53   *New State Ice Co.* v. *Liebmann*, 285 US 262 (1932).
54   Gabriel Nicholas, "Ethereum Is Coding's New Wild West," *WIRED*, August 11, 2017, available at: www.wired.com/story/ethereum-is-codings-new-wild-west

known primarily for its role as the technological underpinning of cryptocurrencies such as Bitcoin, but its potential applications are broad and deep.

A key example of the power of blockchain is in the Ethereum blockchain, where units of "ether" are used as a currency to power decentralized actions and transactions in a system called the Ethereum Virtual Machine. This distributed computing platform allows all sorts of actions to be performed by a worldwide network of decentralized computers in exchange for ether, whose value has risen dramatically. One fascinating application is in the computing space. Around the world, many computers (and their computing power) sit idle at any given time. The Golem Project, powered by Ethereum, allows the owner of a computer to rent out their computing power when not using the computer, allowing someone on the other side of the world to use their computer to perform complex tasks such as rendering CGI images.

These transactions take place not on a centralized, branded application platform, but rather through "smart contracts" built on Ethereum's blockchain. These contracts function much like escrows, guaranteeing payment immediately upon the occurrence of a mutually agreed event. The possibilities for such smart contracts are myriad, including betting and prediction markets.

While Ethereum enthusiasts call it trustlessness, it is in actuality a new digital trust technology that removes the necessity for the intermediary. In many ways, the Golem Project is like Uber, but without a centralized brand that can be sued or regulated. Instead, it facilitates the terms of exchange between users, who must be specific about their desired outcomes. There is likely to be room for brands as intermediaries and simplifiers of the complexity inherent in using such cryptographic systems, but the key point is that trust is provided without a corporate headquarters to seize if taxes have not been paid, or a CEO to commit insider trading. And the users on both sides of a given transaction can remain anonymous.

A related concept is the decentralized autonomous organization, or DAO, also built on the Ethereum Virtual Machine. These are leaderless organizations built on complex rule-based systems.[55] A possible example of a future application is a driverless car that takes fares on Uber, uses the cash to recharge its batteries, and then heads back out on the road to take more fares. It would be programmed only once and its investors would program it to take the highest-paying fare off a slew of ridesharing platforms, recharge when it reached a certain level, and call for and pay for a service if an issue arises.

We are far from this being a reality, but the applications of Ethereum are growing quickly. As a signal of the growing interest in Ethereum, in the first six months of 2017, ether's value grew by 5,000 percent to a market capitalization of $36 billion.[56]

---

[55] Alyssa Hertig, "What Is DAO?," coindesk, available at: www.coindesk.com/information/what-is-a-dao-ethereum/

[56] Arjun Kharpal, "Ethereum hits another record high after bitcoin and is now up over 5,000% since the start of the year," *CNBC*, June 12, 2017, available at: www.cnbc.com/2017/06/12/ethereum-price-hits-record-high-after-bitcoin.html

What's more, Bitcoin, the original virtual currency, has continued its growth, with the price of one Bitcoin hovering around the value of US $4,000 at the time of writing. And these are just the two largest cryptocurrencies. Every day, new coins are created, some with increasingly specialized features and purposes.

An example of a new use case creating more coins is the Initial Coin Offering (ICO).[57] An ICO is a fundraising tool through which a given project raises money via a blockchain distributed ledger in exchange for digital coupons entitling the buyer to some sort of value resulting from the project. This coupon value is completely customizable by the ICO project founder, and could range from something resembling a traditional equity stake (such as that contained by stocks) to something more like frequent flyer miles (if the project were to build an airline).[58] Similar to traditional crowdfunding platforms such as Kickstarter, the money raised in the ICO can then be used to finance the project.

The SEC recently offered guidance on how to treat ICOs, signaling that it is closely following this fundraising avenue, although it kept its guidance vague.[59] It applied the *Howey* test, a legal framework for determining what constitutes a security, signaling that the SEC sees the potential that some of the coins sold in ICOs are actually securities (and subject to a very large body of SEC regulations).[60]

Last year, the SEC approved using blockchain cryptographic technology to facilitate the sale of securities of Overstock.com. Blockchain is pitched as a completely secure method of storing information about ownership in a series of numbers located in the virtual cloud. If perfected, it could revolutionize contracting and financial regulation of all kinds. The enormous social resources devoted to processing sales (e.g. securities clearing, land-title recording, banking settlement) could all be decentralized and moved into the cloud, with massive social efficiencies.

Consider the local property registry office at City Hall: when real property changes hands, lawyers are engaged to conduct a title search at a local government office, which keeps the title to particular blocks of land in paper or digital form. The process brings enormous trust to individual transactions, but, as the existence of title insurance suggests, is not without its errors. In any event, a large amount of scarce resources are devoted to maintaining this system. But, with the use of blockchain or an equivalent, we can imagine an entirely new type of land recording system. For about $2,500 in today's real money, Bitcoin miners will solve math problems that embed transaction outcomes – for example, Henderson transfers a house to Churi –

[57] Alex Wilhelm, "WTF Is an ICO?," *TechCrunch*, 2017, available at: https://techcrunch.com/2017/05/23/wtf-is-an-ico/

[58] Marco Santori, "Appcoin Law: ICOs the Right Way," coindesk, November 9, 2016, available at: www.coindesk.com/appcoin-law-part-1-icos-the-right-way/

[59] SEC, "Investor Bulletin: Initial Coin Offerings," July 25, 2017, available at: www.sec.gov/oiea/investor-alerts-and-bulletins/ib_coinofferings

[60] Marco Santori, "Appcoin Law: ICOs the Right Way," coindesk, November 9, 2016, available at: www.coindesk.com/appcoin-law-part-1-icos-the-right-way/

in a chain of numbers that is not breakable or alterable without commandeering more than 50 percent of the world's computing power.

This kind of system could hack the property recording system, Uber style, but it will be more difficult. The amount at stake in a typical real-estate transaction dwarfs that in a taxi ride, meaning parties are likely to be much more risk averse. In addition, the startup costs are likely to be much higher than in the taxi case. It is perhaps for these reasons that attempted hacks of financial regulation have yet to really take off. Instead of supplanting incumbents, existing banks or other financial entities have been buying the technologies, such as blockchain tools for securities settlements, broker accounts, and the like, in the hope of incorporating their efficiencies into their existing networks. Even here, the SEC, CFTC, and other alphabet agencies, as well as the exchanges, all stand between the entrepreneurs (whether they stand alone or under the umbrella of incumbents) and regulatory disruption.

Unlike the case of Uber, where the alternative law was offered against the will of the regulators, and adoption was fast because the stakes of trial and error were low,[61] in the case of financial regulatory disruption, it is likely that the SEC will be involved, not displaced. It would be better if a regulatory hack of the SEC itself, or FINRA, were possible, but the likelihood of this happening is extremely low in the near term. In other areas of financial regulation, such as insurance, the battle is different. Since it is illegal to even offer insurance or insurance-like products unless one is licensed to do so in the particular state, insurance-focused startups, known as "insurtech" companies, must fight fifty (perhaps more winnable) battles rather than one federal battle.

And yet, entrepreneurs, backed by tens of billions in capital, are actively pursuing regulatory hacks in all of these areas. In insurance alone, the venture capital industry is on track to invest more than $2.5 billion in startups in 2019, a twenty-fold increase in the past five years. If these investments here and elsewhere bear fruit, the change will come not just to incumbent businesses, but also to government monopolies on trust. And, if they do bring the change investors expect, the resources devoted to government regulation, as well as those of many private businesses built on the old contracting models, could be redeployed to more efficient functions. Regulation can then be tailored to harness the preferences of the emerging digital tribe.

Whether this takes the form of a platform company, a prediction market, or the Ethereum Virtual Machine, the lines are blurring between the firm and the consumer. The role of brand as a blunt intermediary is declining and in its place is arising a new breed of hyper-focused companies harnessing information to segment the economy into ever-more focused slices. It's tempting to say that this analysis

---

[61] There are many unique facets of Uber's situation that may make it difficult to replicate, such as a dramatically superior and cheaper product, wide adoption and frequent interaction with users, an obvious villain in the cab monopolies, the fact that its primary challenges came from city councils rather than well-funded and powerful federal agencies, etc.

misses the staggering scale of these digital platforms, but the point is that they are capturing ever-larger percentages of ever-narrower fields. We believe this is just the latest phenomenon in the thinking of our late colleague Ronald Coase.

Coase believed the firm would shrink as small as was efficient to optimize outcomes. If you were an office worker and needed a copy made, you could put out a broad request for proposals, asking far and wide who would be willing to Xerox a document for you, then sift through the potential workers and pick the right combination of price and quality. But the amount of work (what Coase called transaction costs) it would take to get the right person for this job is disproportionate to the amount of value you would have received for the task. So, if you needed a copy made, you either did it yourself or hired an assistant to complete that and many similar tasks.

But transaction costs have shrunk dramatically in the modern economy. If we return to the example of taxis, ten years ago it would be hard to put out a request for proposal (RFP) to all available drivers willing to give you a ride, so you had to write down the number of a taxi company. But this is precisely what Uber did: it produced a platform for mini-RFPs that allows you to select the right person for the job on a per-ride basis.

Of course, Uber did build a valuable brand in doing this, but in many ways Uber functions like a temp agency, matching drivers with riders, supply with demand. And, in many ways, Uber facilitates the shrinking of the firm to one, allowing any person with a car to become a business. Signing up for Uber, you can start a small business giving rides without worrying about becoming an expert in payments, HR, advertising, or software. In much the same way that Amazon Web Services and cloud computing made the previously expensive and complex IT infrastructure aspect of starting a company simple and scalable, digital platforms are shrinking the complexity of other aspects of starting a company. The trust flows not from rider to Uber, but rather from rider to driver, facilitated by Uber.[62]

These new microenterprises no longer require extensive investment to get off the ground (i.e. learning about payments, HR, advertising, etc.) and thus can be created spontaneously and disappear just as fast. The new enterprise exists as long as the founder wishes. Uber and its ilk are a shrink ray in the economy, reducing what was previously enormous complexity into a simple sign-up process and making entrepreneurship a realistic possibility for swathes of people who'd never have otherwise started companies. Rather than becoming a jack of all trades, these platforms free new entrepreneurs to focus on driving (Uber), hosting (Airbnb), shopping (Instacart), fixing (Thumbtack), or whatever other task they have a knack for, without worrying about the other aspects of running a business.

---

[62] Jason Tanz, "How Airbnb and Lyft Finally got Americans to Trust Each Other," *WIRED*, April 23, 2014, available at: www.wired.com/2014/04/trust-in-the-share-economy/

Now, of course, this new configuration has serious consequences for other aspects of the economy that are outside the scope of this book. For example, such companies have sparked debate about what labor classification is appropriate for such new microentrepreneurs: should they be viewed as employees, subjecting their employer to stringent and expensive employee benefits and reporting requirements, or independent contractors, a lighter touch framework built for less comprehensive worker relationships. These distinctions are based on a labor law framework that was built to protect workers against the dangers inherent in an industrial revolution-era manufacturing economy. In stark contrast with an Uber driver who is primarily a guitarist but does a few rides when convenient for supplemental income, these rules were created with a factory worker in mind.

The labor economy is reconfiguring based on the effect of digital technology on the physical world: the digitization of physical assets has created new capacity that simply did not exist before. A car that previously sat empty 95 percent of the time can now be used over 50 percent of the time. Uber took the first step in this direction, and Tesla founder Elon Musk has suggested a solution that would go a step further: a self-driving car that you can put on a platform so that it rents itself out whenever you choose to offer it.[63] In the same way you can rent out your home when you are out of town with Airbnb, now your car begins to blur the lines between an asset and a robotic employee.

This is emblematic of the fact that digital assets, which reside in the cloud, can be "outsourced" to one of Facebook's data servers near the Arctic Circle.[64] At a time when your company had paper records, the endless stacks of documents took up a linearly increasing amount of cabinet space, meaning most businesses required a file room. Just as Amazon Web Services made computing power scalable, Dropbox and Box made digital storage scalable.

The resulting digitization of the physical world has accordingly changed needs in the physical world. WeWork, for example, has made office space scalable.[65] For a monthly membership fee, you get access to a large shared workspace housing many entrepreneurs. As you grow into the need for office space, you can easily rent more space until it becomes necessary to move out and rent a dedicated office. The innovations that enable the running of a startup from a laptop have allowed a scalable solution for office space as well. Consider that even the co-working model is vulnerable to additional slicing: companies such as DeskPass offer the

---

[63] Cadie Thompson, "Elon Musk wants to let Tesla owners make money off their cars when they're not using them," *Business Insider*, July 21, 2016, available at: www.businessinsider.com/elon-musk-reveals-tesla-shared-fleet-2016-7

[64] James Vincent, "Mark Zuckerberg shares pictures from Facebook's cold, cold data center," *The Verge*, September 29, 2016, available at: www.theverge.com/2016/9/29/13103982/facebook-arctic-data-center-sweden-photos

[65] Omri Barzilay, "The Shared Office Is Hotter Than Ever, With 1.2 Million Co-Working," *Forbes*, May 30, 2017, available at: www.forbes.com/sites/omribarzilay/2017/05/30/the-shared-office-is-hotter-than-ever-with-1-2-million-co-working/#4a2691e21ba0

ability to use multiple co-working spaces at even lower cost, further utilizing slack capacity.[66] Change toward efficiency and the diminishing importance of place is rapid, but it is not merely the drumbeat of capitalism that drives it. The number of teens who get together with friends daily, for example, dropped more than 40 percent from 2000 to 2015, as they increasingly stayed in, communicating digitally.[67]

Ultimately, we are advocating that government acknowledges the reality and desirability of these changes and adjust its response accordingly. Practically, this means considering the benefits of a given technology alongside the costs. As we have explored in this book, because regulators bear all the risks of the downsides of a new technology (in the form of angry constituents) and none of the benefits, there is an irrational bias toward inaction and the status quo. These upsides are sprouting up rapidly throughout the economy and, accordingly, regulators should internalize the benefits of new innovations in addition to the costs (and increasingly they are).

There are two types of costs: public safety and private competition. The first is the legitimate province of government, ensuring people are safe from harm and fraud in their everyday lives. The second, we have argued, is illegitimate, as regulators should not protect established businesses from competition. Public-choice problems, such as established businesses lobbying for regulatory barriers to entry, have muddied the waters. We believe trust hacks are an antidote.

Many of these new efficiencies are largely costless to the consumer. In the case of WeWork, there is not much danger to society in people choosing open-air shared offices instead of traditional configurations. In some cases, there is real risk, as in the case of Uber. These costs are difficult to quantify before the trust provider is operating. In the case of Uber, the risk turned out to be insignificant (i.e. it was at least as safe as the yellow-cab system and possibly much safer).[68] And costs can be mitigated without outright bans or extensive regulations. Where the costs are quantifiable, requiring insurance (as discussed earlier) can provide the basic level of trust necessary for a company to operate and demonstrate its idea.

The costs to private competition are a persistent fact of business and innovation. Austrian economist Joseph Schumpeter viewed creative destruction as the engine of a capitalist economy, arguing that the death of old ideas and the birth and ascendency of new ideas was a natural state in the evolution of the economy.[69] Much like the Luddites, namely English textile workers who sought to destroy the machines

[66] See www.deskpass.com/benefits
[67] Jean M. Twenge, "Have Smartphones Destroyed a Generation?," *The Atlantic*, September 2017, available at: www.theatlantic.com/magazine/archive/2017/09/has-the-smartphone-destroyed-a-generation/534198
[68] See Sarah Buhr, "Regulators Should Favor Lyft and Uber, Not Taxis for Safety Reasons," *TechCrunch*, 2016, available at: https://techcrunch.com/2016/01/16/regulators-should-favor-lyft-and-uber-not-taxis-for-safety-reasons/; and James Cook, "Despite the Scary Rape Headlines, Uber Is Probably Still the Safest Way to Order a Taxi," *Business Insider*, December 8, 2014, available at: www.businessinsider.com/despite-its-problems-uber-is-still-the-safest-way-to-order-a-taxi-2014-12
[69] Joseph A. Schumpeter, *Capitalism, Socialism, and Democracy* (1942, republished 1994).

that they believed threatened their jobs, or horse and buggy owners who fought the rise of the automobile, progress tends eventually to overcome entrenched interests when the value of the new innovation is clear. Trust hacks show this value to the public and speed up the process of acceptance and creative destruction.

Uber threatens taxis and the taxi commission, Airbnb threatens hotels, and autonomous vehicles threaten large automakers, but these are the costs of change. And we argue that this cost must be borne by competitors in business, not consumers. While this has always been true, trust hacks have enabled consumers to push back, helping present regulators to develop a better approximation of the true cost–benefit analysis that society faces with the development of new technologies.

11

Concluding Thoughts

We cannot predict the future, but if what's past is prologue, we are confident that humans will demand increasing amounts of trust. There are billions of humans on the sidelines of the modern economy and bringing them into modernity will require that we trust them and that they trust us. This trust could be supplied by governments, by corporations, by NGOs, by microregulators, or by any number of other technologies or institutions. In all likelihood, it will be provided by a mix of these, operating in what we call the "market for trust."

But, for the market for trust to function well, that is, for it to supply given levels of trust at the lowest possible cost, the government, which regulates the market, must not favor itself over other providers of trust. To be sure, the government regulator of the trust market should make decisions about the potential externalities from trust providers, and should try to protect citizens from fraud. But it is illegitimate for the government to favor itself as a trust provider when there is no reasonable basis for it to do so.

We have made an additional linkage in this book: we have connected trust and regulation. We are talking here not about regulating the market for trust, but rather about regulating the underlying transaction or activity. Being in the trust business means being a regulator. Uber regulates. Uber rates drivers and riders, and it disciplines them when they misbehave. This is regulation. Walmart does this too, when it protects its brand by policing its supply chain.

The demand for regulation (when regulation is defined in this way), be it from microregulators, brands, or government, will continue to rise as the world becomes increasingly complex. We then have a choice: will government or private actors satisfy this demand for trust-inducing regulation? Our bottom line is simple: where government can provide trust most efficiently, it should do so. And where it cannot, it should not. If we can all agree on this, we can not only unlock the potential for addressing the world's rising trust gap, but also circumvent the political gridlock that prevents us from solving many of society's enduring problems.

What does this mean for government? Whether you're a progressive, a conservative, or really anyone other than a bureaucrat or an interest group, you should believe that regulatory disruption is a good thing. For the sake of argument, imagine that government expenditure were to remain unchanged. If this were true, then when government exited the taxi regulation business in whole or in part – or the securities settlement business or the property records business – then the money saved from this inefficient supply of regulation could be used to provide other public goods in areas in which the government retains a comparative advantage over non-government actors. The government could spend more on social welfare programs, on basic science research or the arts, on paying down the national debt, on issuing a dividend to taxpayers, or whatever the public wants. What it should not spend money on, we think we all should agree, is providing trust that can be provided better by someone else.

As discussed above, we can easily imagine machine learning evolving to the point where it can do the business of judging better than judges. "Better" here means reaching decisions that are as good or better than those that judges reach, and at lower overall costs. If this were achievable, then there would be no defensible reason for employing higher-cost and lower-performance humans to do the same work – the money saved could be put to more productive uses. It is a good thing that humans no longer ride behind beasts of burden to plow the fields of Kansas. The machines that do this work have lowered the costs of food and freed humans to be things such as singers and cancer researchers. The same kinds of efficiencies are possible in the trust business too.

Over the past several millennia, humans have invented many things that make the modern world possible – not only technologies and medicines and business methods, but also ways of expanding the tribe to include more and more of humanity. We all start out as a family unit and then expand our trust to more and more people. This is true for individuals and for humans in general. The human family was once quite small, but it is now reaching further and connecting more and more of the people on Earth. This has been made possible first by the inventions of language, writing, and law, but then through innovations such the corporation and criminal law. As we entered the modern era, government became the main provider or mechanism of collective action. The growth of government in providing trust made the modern world what it is today.

But the burst of technology that we have seen over the past few decades, first in information sharing and the internet, and now in machine learning, has brought us to a point in human history where the story of the future is less about government and more about the people it is meant to serve. Government acts slowly, is subject to capture by moneyed interests, and cannot tailor its services to local conditions and preferences as easily as non-governmental entities. In the past, however, it was difficult for these non-governmental entities to provide trust as efficiently as the government. In a wide range of areas, this is no longer necessarily the case.

US citizens pay many billions of dollars to the government and the other participants in the legal and regulatory system (including lawyers, accountants, consultants, and so forth) to supply the trust we all need in order to cooperate. We pay restaurant inspectors, judges, central bankers, clerks in the property office, taxi commissioners, and countless other bureaucrats to provide us with trust. If we see the possibility of trust being provided by businesses or other entities, and if the government is willing to relinquish its monopoly on trust (enforced at the point of a gun), then we can free up the money spent inefficiently creating trust, which could then be spent to deliver human flourishing in other ways. It is time that we start getting government out of the trust business, where it may no longer be needed, and put that money to better use.

The individuals who work for government and have specialized in using government to their advantage will not go gently into that good night. Citizens will resist too, not just because they are manipulated by those with an economic interest in the status quo. Another reason is that it is hard to imagine the future and how things can be radically different. Murray Rothbard described this problem famously:

> People tend to fall into habits and into unquestioned ruts, especially in the field of government. On the market, in society in general, we expect and accommodate rapidly to change, to the unending marvels and improvements of our civilization. New products, new life styles, new ideas are often embraced eagerly. But in the area of government we follow blindly in the path of centuries, content to believe that what-ever has been must be right. In particular, government, in the United States and elsewhere, for centuries and seemingly from time immemorial has been supplying us with certain essential and necessary services, services which nearly every-one concedes are important: defense (including army, police, judicial, and legal), firefighting, streets and roads, water, sewage and garbage disposal, postal service, etc. So identified has the State become in the public mind with the provision of these services that an attack on State financing appears to many people as an attack on the service itself. Thus if one maintains that the State should not supply court services, and that private enterprise on the market could supply such service more efficiently as well as more morally, people tend to think of this as denying the importance of courts themselves.
>
> The libertarian who wants to replace government by private enterprises in the above areas is thus treated in the same way as he would be if the government had, for various reasons, been supplying shoes as a tax-financed monopoly from time immemorial. If the government and only the government had had a monopoly of the shoe manufacturing and retailing business, how would most of the public treat the libertarian who now came along to advocate that the government get out of the shoe business and throw it open to private enterprise? He would undoubtedly be treated as follows: people would cry, "How could you? You are opposed to the public, and to poor people, wearing shoes! And who would supply shoes to the public if the government got out of the business? Tell us that! Be constructive! It's easy to be negative and smart-alecky about government; but tell us who would supply shoes? Which people? How many shoe stores would be available in each city and town? How would the shoe firms be capitalized? How many brands would there be? What material would they use? What lasts? What would be the pricing

arrangements for shoes? Wouldn't regulation of the shoe industry be needed to see to it that the product is sound? And who would supply the poor with shoes? Suppose a poor person didn't have the money to buy a pair?"[1]

The parable of shoes that Rothbard tells could equally apply to trust. The government has long been the most efficient provider of trust writ large and, for many people, any other possibility seems fanciful. Having made it this far, we hope we have convinced you, however, that government has never been alone in the trust business, and that the provision of trust is more diverse and flexible than our modern minds might imagine. In addition, we hope you can see a glimpse of the future that we envisage, where collective action – the reason we have government in the first place – can be achieved by much better and more efficient means. The return of interpersonal trust offers the best hope for the future of humanity.

---

[1]   Murray N. Rothbard, *For a New Liberty: The Libertarian Manifesto* 241–42 (1973), available at: https://mises.org/library/new-liberty-libertarian-manifesto

Index

accreditation, 76
Accredited Investor, 177
Adam Smith, 22, 23
Affordable Care Act, 4, 168
agency costs, 33, 34, 98, 119, 120, 121, 123, 134, 183
agricultural era, 7
agricultural period, 51, 84, 94
agriculture, 56, 57, 58, 59, 83, 84, 121
Airbnb, 19, 20, 127, 157, 173, 174, 188, 200, 201, 203
Albert O. Hisrchman, 194
Alex Tabarrok, 48
alphabet agency, 20
AltSchool, 190
Amazon, 5, 20, 34, 35, 88, 95, 97, 120, 122, 123, 138, 152, 153, 158, 164, 169, 189, 200, 201
American Jobs Creation Act of 2004, 41
American Law Institute, 80
American Optometric Association, 176
American Revolution, 4, 5
Angus Maddison, 91, 106
Anthony J. Casey, 182, 183
Anthony Niblett, 182
anti-competitive behavior, 37, 134
Anup Malani, 3, 116
app(s), 19, 111, 158, 162, 170, 173, 174, 175, 195
Apple, 3, 23, 36, 101, 118, 120, 189
Arthur N. Holcombe, 116
artificial intelligence, 83, 162, 168, 182
ATM machine, 26
augmented reality, 167, 195
autonomous vehicles, 159, 203
Avant Credit, 189

Balaji Srinivasan, 194
Barry Goldwater, 42

bees, 23
Beethoven, 23
Belton v. *Hatch*, 130
Bergen, 66, 67, 68
Bernie Madoff, 37, 64
Bernie Sanders, 12
Beth Noveck, 154, 168
Better Business Bureau, 109
Bitcoin, 186, 187, 188, 189, 197, 198
blockchain(s), 19, 58, 64, 157, 171, 196, 197, 198, 199
boards, 79, 80, 81
bootleggers, 39, 115
bootleggers & Baptists, 39
brand(s), 5, 7, 9, 15, 19, 23, 30, 36, 45, 51, 65, 76, 87, 88, 89, 90, 91, 92, 93, 94, 97, 101, 110, 111, 118, 122, 125, 143, 151, 152, 153, 155, 158, 164, 167, 192, 197, 199, 200, 204, 206
Bretton Woods Agreement, 101
broker, 76, 129, 130, 131, 132, 133, 135, 199
BrokerCheck, 137
Bruges, 68, 69, 70, 71, 72, 73, 74, 75, 77
Bryan Caplan, 13
Bureau of Justice Statistics, 60
bureaucracies, 20, 32, 34, 98, 152
bureaucracy, 19, 34, 93, 96, 113, 120, 123, 123, 144, 145
bureaucrats, 11, 120, 130, 206
business, 1, 3, 5, 7, 12, 22, 23, 28, 29, 30, 35–48, 64, 67, 68, 69, 79, 80, 84, 86, 91, 94–103, 109, 110, 111, 112, 113, 118–125, 129, 130, 132, 134, 140, 151, 153, 154, 155, 158, 161, 162, 163, 172–178, 183, 184, 185, 187, 188, 190, 192, 200, 202–207
business trust, 7, 29, 30, 35, 36, 37, 41, 44, 48, 112, 121, 122
Buttonwood Agreement, 128
buyers and sellers, 5, 20, 72, 143, 146, 178, 186, 188

canals, 85, 95, 101
capitalism, 68, 106, 202